JOHN MASSEY
WITH DAN CARRIER

LOCKS, BOLTS AND BARS

A LIFE INSIDE

JOHN MASSEY
WITH DAN CARRIER

LOCKS, BOLTS AND BARS

A LIFE INSIDE

The History Press

First published 2023

The History Press
97 St George's Place, Cheltenham,
Gloucestershire, GL50 3QB
www.thehistorypress.co.uk

British Library Cataloguing in Publication Data.
A catalogue record for this book is available from the British Library.

ISBN 978 1 80399 103 0

Typesetting and origination by The History Press
Printed and bound in Great Britain by TJ Books Limited, Padstow, Cornwall.

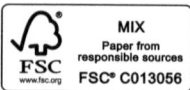

MIX
Paper from
responsible sources
FSC
www.fsc.org
FSC® C013056

Trees for LYfe

ONE

I don't like heights. I fucking hate them. Most of us do. It is a sensible phobia, vertigo. I'm not scared of much, but heights – well, it's one of those things.

I've been in some tight spots in my time, done stuff that would make the toughest man flinch. I've lived a life of crime, a life that suits few. Armed robbery, bank raids, car chases. I've done them a good few times. When the adrenaline is boiling and everything is happening at 100 miles per hour, you have to be able to hold your nerve. You have to be able to think clearly. You have to be able to make the right decisions. I had never once lost my bottle during a job. You can't be scared, you can't carry fear, because if you do, it's not going to work out.

And that day, vertigo or no vertigo, I had a very important job to complete. It was going to be a doddle. I wasn't going to lose my bottle now.

◆ ◆ ◆

There I was, standing on the roof of Pentonville prison, on the Cally Road, north London. It was about 6.30 p.m. on a June evening and there were darkening skies above me. It had been a wet summer so far, and it looked like we were in for another shower.

I had just climbed out of a skylight, completing a vital stage of my escape. I'd spent weeks carefully removing the mortar that sealed the skylight shut – like most panes of glass in prisons, it wasn't designed to be opened – and creating my own exit. So far my plan had worked.

Now I had to get to the edge of the roof, climb onto the stone topping of the perimeter wall and throw myself about 35ft down. If the makeshift 'rope' didn't hold, I was fucked – I'd land in a heap and at best it would be back inside for an extended stay.

I tried not to think about it, but my heart was racing and my legs were shaking. I might not like heights, but I liked prison even less. Months of planning had gone into this moment and I knew the risks I was taking were outweighed by the potential reward.

Yes – I knew the risks, but I didn't want to think about them. I locked away the long list of what could possibly go wrong. I had only one thing on my mind.

My old mum. She was ill, and I knew I was running out of time to see her. They knew she was dying, but I'd still been refused a home visit. 'Security risk,' they'd said dismissively when I'd applied for permission. She had a brain tumour and didn't have long left. I knew the bastards would use the same excuse when she died and I put in a request to attend my own mother's funeral. 'Sorry – security risk,' they would say.

Even the Krays were allowed out for their mum's funeral. 'So what?' I thought. 'I'm meant to be worse than the Krays? More of a danger?' It was bullshit, and no power-crazy prison bureaucrat was going to deny me a basic human right. It angered me. That was all the indignation I needed to do what had to be done. I stepped up to the edge, grasped the rope and wrapped it around my hands and wrists. I didn't look down. I just ran out across the roof and, without a pause, I jumped.

◆ ◆ ◆

The rope held well, supporting me for most of the 35ft of sky as I tumbled down and away from captivity. I was 64 years old, but fit as a fiddle – and I knew I needed to be.

The second my feet hit the pavement, the clock started. Boom! I landed, ready for the race.

Wednesday, 27 June 2012. My very own Independence Day. My legs were shaking. I had the sweats and the chills, and a vision of 1,000 angry, fat, red-faced coppers running behind me, waving their truncheons and tooting on whistles.

I tried to regulate my breathing, get myself sorted, relax, relax, but the emotion was rushing through me. You'd have to have been fucking Buddha to control it. I wanted to laugh out loud, smile like a Cheshire Cat, shout 'Fuck you!' at the prison walls.

I didn't, of course. I couldn't bring any attention to myself. I had to keep my head.

Every prisoner dreams of escape. Anyone who says they don't is lying. It's built into our DNA. Men are not born to be caged. Put a man in a cage and he will look for the lock before he looks for the food. I had spent decades listening to men talk about escape: what they were gonna do, how they were gonna do it and when. Despite all the talk, few ever did. It takes a lot of balls. It also takes a lot of planning, ingenuity and daring.

You start by creating a mental map of the prison, the layout of it, what leads where and what joins what. You're constantly scanning, looking for a way out, a weak spot. It becomes an obsession. You find yourself dreaming about it. It fills your minutes up, creating an architectural model in your mind's eye.

From the cell to the shower, the canteen to the gym, the landing to the exercise yard – you're scanning every door, every wall, every window, and even the ceilings. You're always, always looking for a way out.

I had taken risks all my life, and this was my third escape, so I had a bit of experience when it came to what to do and what to expect. I had to get out of north London as quickly as possible. The Old Bill knew it was my manor and home to most of my family and friends. And I couldn't go straight round to see Mum, although that was the first thing on my mind. That was off the cards. I had to get to my safe house and then find a way to get out of the UK, cross the Channel and escape for good.

◆ ◆ ◆

As I got a bit of distance between me and the prison walls, my sense of relief and excitement changed to anger. Anger that I had been forced into doing this. I shouldn't have been inside by now anyway. Why did they have the right to force me to take my liberty this way? I'd been released back in June 2007. I was on a life licence and under strict parole conditions.

But they had set me up to fail. For starters, after I'd been inside for over thirty years, the first thing they did was stick me in a filthy shithole of a hostel miles away from my family, ignoring the fact my sister Jane had offered to let me live with her and help me back into the outside world after all that incarceration. Instead, the Parole Board shoved me all the way down in south London.

The parole system did nothing to facilitate my release or help me make the transition to an ordinary life. If anything, they seemed hell bent on making it as difficult as they could. I resented having to clock in and clock out each day. I was on a time curfew, halfway across the capital from my family, and the bail hostel had more rules than the open prison I'd just been released from. But I swallowed it, because my dad was gravely ill and it gave me time with him.

When we all knew the end was near, I applied for an extension to my curfew. I told my parole officer I needed to stay at Dad's bedside. The hospital told us it was only a matter of days and two doctors were willing to verify this to support my request to be allowed to stay with him.

The Parole Board couldn't give two fucks. They showed no mercy whatsoever. What did it matter to them if I slept the night in their hostel or next to the bed of my dying father in hospital? I wasn't a security risk. But no – they refused.

I wasn't having it, so I decided to stay with Dad for one more night – it was his last few hours on earth.

The following day, I thought I'd best not wait for the Old Bill to come looking for me, so I handed myself in. I was taken straight back to prison. I got a lot of sympathy from other prisoners, and even the odd screw who understood my position. I was back behind bars nonetheless. Despite having served well over twenty years for my crime, I was banged up again, and all because I stayed by my father's side as he passed away. But I was with him when he died and the bastards could never take that away from me.

◆ ◆ ◆

Fast forward five years, almost to the month, and I was still languishing inside. I had no release date. There were no more prison courses to complete to show my all-round fitness for the outside world and I couldn't provide anything further to the authorities to expedite my release. I had excellent character references from the screws and staff who mattered, spotless prison reports and again – most importantly – I had served my time. But I was just a ghost, floating around the system, with no glimmer of light at the end of the tunnel. Lost within the prison walls, I was condemned to haunt prisons for the rest of my days.

My only hope was that the Parole Board would show me some mercy. But if their mercy matched the understanding I'd been shown when I requested time with my dad, I was fucked. Try, if you can, to imagine the utter futility of this situation and how it ate away at me. It tortured me every day. I had seen prisoners getting out, some on early release, some people who had done unspeakable things. Rape, ABH, GBH, assault and battery, multiple murders.

Yes – I had taken a life. I shot a man in 1975, and he died. But was I more of a danger now to the public than a rapist, or someone who kills for the thrill of it?

It was thirty-three years earlier when a fight in a nightclub had escalated beyond my imagination. Drinks had been flowing, the place had been heaving and a ruck had broken out. As my friends and I tried to make our way out, I heard a scream and realised my pal was missing. I fought my way back inside and found him. He was in a bad way. He had been glassed in the face and his eye was hanging out of its socket, dribbling down on his cheek like a pickled onion.

We left – and then came back with two handguns and two shotguns, tools of our trade. I banged on the door and the bouncer answered. I pressed a shotgun to his chest and ordered him inside. But for some reason, the guy didn't back away. He pushed towards me, and BANG – the gun went off. I didn't plan to shoot him, of course. We didn't go back to that nightclub to kill anyone. We just wanted to shit them up. A moment of madness cost that bloke his life and me well over three decades.

I felt I had paid my debt to society. But with no end in sight, I started to look for my own way out.

Outwardly, I was doing what old lags do. I had become a mentor to some of the prisoners who had come in for their first stretch. Being an old hand, I found a lot of the younger prisoners immediately drawn to me, especially if they had never been inside before. I was that classic old timer you see in the prison films. I looked institutionalised, well versed in the system, keeping my head down, doing my time. I was respected and well liked by the other cons. I certainly had their respect for the time I'd done. A lot were curious about why I was still inside and felt that it was no longer a case of justice being served, but an act of revenge on the part of the system.

One day, I got an offer that was to set me on my way out of the roof and over the wall. The screws needed someone with woodworking skills and they came to me. The prison wanted a new workshop – it was a project to train cons in the basics of wood and metal work, electrics and plumbing. I'd been tasked with putting up partitions, installing work benches and sorting all the equipment needed.

For the first time since I'd been recalled, I actually settled into the routine of the prison. I suppose having something to do gave me a sense of purpose, however brief and fleeting it would be.

◆ ◆ ◆

Pentonville, or the Ville, as prisoners call it, opened in 1842. It took two years to build and had a central hall with four radiating wings, all visible to the staff based at its centre. This design had two purposes. All four wings were easy to keep an eye on at the same time and it meant groups of prisoners could be kept isolated from one another.

The Ville's twin aims of keeping bad people away from good people, and punishing them for their low moral threshold, were amply fulfilled by this horrible place. And in its 170-odd-year history, it had only ever declined.

In May 2003, a report by Her Majesty's Chief Inspector of Prisons blamed overcrowding for the poor standards at the Ville. Basic requirements for inmates, such as telephones, showers and even clean clothes, were not being provided regularly. There was a lack of access to education, to courses, and the report said it had 'inadequate procedures for vulnerable prisoners'. You could fucking say that again – the place was a badly run shithole.

In August 2007, a report by the Independent Monitoring Board said the Ville was infested with rats and cockroaches. There were three times as many prisoners as there should have been and about 1,000 too many vermin per inmate, as well.

Staffing was bad. They never had enough screws at any time. It made managing the place a nightmare, gave it a jumpy atmosphere, put the screws in a bad mood and kept us in our cells.

I can confirm the infestations, having seen them up close and personal, and the inspectors could hardly fail to notice. I used to search out every single hole in my cell and then find anything I could to block them up with. I would lie awake at night and hear the cockroaches nibbling at the padding I'd squeezed into the gaps.

The report went on, page after page, describing the dump's all-too-obvious failings. Medical facilities were well below par. The conditions for anyone not feeling all right upstairs were laughable – except that having a breakdown in a prison isn't funny. The reception facilities for new prisoners were terrible. Scared and confused, ready to lash out, someone coming in for the first time needs to be eased in a bit, for everyone's sake – a few days, maybe, on a medical wing so they can come to terms with their new reality. The Ville barely managed that. There was a lack of decent facilities, like a library, which helps the days go by. It went on and on – the whole place was unfit for purpose.

And then, in October 2009, gross misconduct charges were brought against the senior managers at the Ville. An investigation found the governor had shipped out inmates to stay temporarily at Wandsworth prison before inspections to hide how badly overcrowded that dump really was. These impromptu and temporary transfers included the more vulnerable and problem prisoners. It was a fiddle, an attempt to make the Ville appear to be a better class of shithole. The basic fact is that the antiquated, overpopulated building was no longer fit for purpose, if it ever had been. After all, the Victorians weren't exactly famous for their enlightened approach to criminal justice.

Three years down the line, when I put the workshop in, it was celebrated as a sign of improvement by the staff and the Home Office. It was nothing more than window dressing, like painting the walls of a house as it falls down around your ears. Some dignitaries came on one of those prison tours they hold to show how good things are and what they're doing to make things even better. These nobs wanted to come in and have a look at the workshop. The prison staff were keen to show it off.

I had no desire to meet them. A faceless, forgettable politician and some quango-sitting do-gooders who smile politely as they're led round to gawp at prisoners. I wasn't going to acquiesce to that bollocks. If I'd complied and played the good, quiet prisoner role, then the system would definitely have got the better of me. I stayed in the background as the party was shown around the workshop and admired my handiwork. I didn't need accolades from anyone to have a sense of pride. I looked at them with cold eyes.

But my diligence was to pay off. My graft was noted, and I was asked to fit out another area. I was approached by the physical education instructors. They wanted their gym, offices and changing rooms converted, so once I'd finished the trades classrooms, I started on the gym.

The screws made me an orderly – a trusted position, as it meant I could come and go when I needed to and crack on with converting the space. Being an orderly allowed me certain privileges that I needed to do my job properly. As well as putting up partitions and kitting out the staff's area, I was about to clean things up, wipe down the machines and benches, put things away.

The gym at the Ville had tall, whitewashed walls with long, deep windows set into them. The ceiling was a pitched roof, with barred skylights set into them. The floor was coated in moulded lino and it held about thirty-five people working out or doing a class. Through a set of double doors was a reception area, and across from there was a hall which the screws decided they wanted partitioned off to make a new office.

Through this hall, another set of double doors led to what used to be a toilet block. The toilets had been converted into shower units some time ago, with space sectioned off for a changing area. There was a toilet for the screws, a small laundry and a store room for cleaning equipment. It held a washing machine and tumble dryer.

It was while I was in there, sizing up the job, that I noticed the false ceiling and the hatch set into it. Looking up, a memory came flooding back to me.

◆ ◆ ◆

Back in 1971, I'd got sent down for twelve months for driving while disqualified. I was taken from Wood Green Crown Court in the back of a police van and dropped straight into the Ville. From the very moment I landed, I was put to work in the shop, sewing mailbags.

There were rows and rows of prisoners, all sat in lines, all doing the same thing. Sitting there, sewing stitch after stitch after stitch, while a screw sat up high in a chair like a tennis umpire, watching over us, his beady fucking eyes looking for any excuse to punish us.

It was regimented. You went in, sat down and started sewing. Eight stitches to an inch. It was enough to crush the soul of the most determined spirit. It was mind-numbingly boring.

As I looked at that false ceiling, I remembered those mailbags, and realised I was standing right where the mailbag sewing room used to be, all those years ago. I could even remember the layout, forty-one years later. And it all came back to me – the noises, the smells, the overbearing sense of oppression.

I remembered one day a con set off the alarm bell. It happened quite a lot – anything to break the monotony and stir up the screws. As the alarm shrilled out, I was still engrossed in my own misery, sewing the poxy mailbags in silence, but the screws bursting in got my attention. I looked up and caught the eye of one of the officers. They were looking for someone to blame and randomly selected four of us. The fact we hadn't moved for fucking hours didn't make a difference, and the tennis umpire screw didn't say anything.

'You're nicked,' one said, and all four of us were dragged off to the governor's office. In those days, if you went up before the governor, you were guilty. That was the culture of prison life back in the early 1970s. A governor at Wandsworth once said to me, 'If my staff tell me you were riding a motorbike along the landing, all I want to know is where you got the petrol.'

I was strip-searched, put into a Seg block and ended up doing three days on bread and water.

For those of you unacquainted with the prison lexicon, 'Seg' means the segregation unit. It's solitary confinement, and used as a punishment. Under Prison Rule 45 – and Young Offenders' Institute Rule 49 – you can be placed in confinement for breaching good order and discipline, or for your own protection, or for the protection of others. Over the course of many decades, solitary confinement has become notorious as a cover for extremely sinister behaviour. Unimaginable things have happened behind the closed doors of Seg blocks, away from witnesses and cameras. Prisoners have been brutalised, tortured and starved, and have even died.

The 1970s and 1980s were particularly dark times for prison brutality. Segregation units and close supervision centres (CSCs) used isolation, sensory deprivation and violence, causing multiple mental health and physical issues for prisoners. These blocks and centres are still in operation throughout prisons today.

◆ ◆ ◆

Standing in the hall, I remembered back four decades, remembered the feeling of being taken out of that mailbag row and thrown in Seg. I could see that old mailbag room clearly, and as I stood in the gym, sizing up the work that needed to be done, I could see how that old mailbag room had been altered over the years. The ceiling had been lowered, and a loft – a hidden, forgotten loft – had been added at some point. I noted it, and filed it away for further investigation later.

As well as the structural work I was asked to do, I had other tasks to tackle. There was a load of old equipment in the sports hall and I was asked to recondition it. Vault horses, benches, badminton and football nets. I tried to estimate how much it would've cost them to get someone in to do what I did. And an outside contractor would have had access to anything they needed – tools and materials. I had to work with what I could get hold of inside. On top of that, I wasn't getting paid for my labour.

But I wasn't doing all this solely out of the goodness of my heart. I started by repairing the bits of equipment that got used most. I found bits of old mattress, rubber canvas and other surplus materials that I recommissioned. I revived the equipment, gave it all a new lease of life. The only two things I requested were a pair of scissors and a staple gun. I built a sit-up bench, which I believe is still in the prison today. I am not going back to check.

It was around this time I got the news that my mum was too ill to come and visit me. The thought of her, just a few miles away but too frail to make the journey, played heavily on my mind. My parents had visited me up and down the length of the country. Wherever the system had slung me or dumped me, they got there. Relentlessly, over the course of three decades, they'd make a journey to see me, no matter where I was. Now Mum was too ill to make a trip from Barnet to Islington, a bus ride away. It broke my heart, the thought of her slowly fading, so near to me, yet so far away.

I had a parole hearing coming up in a few weeks' time and everyone around me felt sure everything was in place. It was a racing certainty, they assured me, and themselves. I wasn't so confident. I'd had too many knockbacks down the years. But my key worker arranged to take me to a new hostel, which I would stay in when I got the golden ticket. If this happened, it would mean I'd get to spend some precious time with Mum. I knew she hadn't got long. Every minute now was crucial, and each one that went by with me inside was another wasted minute I could be spending with her. I had to get out, by fair means or foul.

When the news came, I realised I should have expected the decision. It wasn't like they'd ever acted differently. This was how they worked. The Parole Board gave me a knockback.

I had recommendations for release. My probation officer, my key worker, everyone whose views needed to be taken into account said I was ready. But the bastards turned me down. They didn't know me from Adam, so they were obliged to go on the recommendations put forward. But, as before, they made this seemingly random decision.

I thought to myself, 'What have I got to do to get out of here?'

I'd been recalled to prison for breaking my parole conditions. I hadn't committed another crime, so it wasn't a matter for the courts. This was to be dealt with internally by the Ministry of Justice. I hadn't done anything against people or property. I'd breached my parole and it was a straightforward Prison Service matter.

After the decision came through, I went to see the number one governor, a bloke called Kevin Reilly, and requested a home visit to see my mum. She had been coming up in her wheelchair to see me – she would have walked across broken glass, so when visits became too much for her, I knew it was bad.

I went through the rigamarole of why I needed to visit her. She was, by now, completely bedridden.

They said no – it was a point-blank refusal.

'No, Mr Massey, it's not possible.'

'Why?'

'Because your record suggests you can't be trusted.'

'That's nonsense – I did a runner years ago. I've been given parole already and I am on recall for reasons you are well aware of.'

'No, Mr Massey.'

'What about with a guard, then? She's dying.'

'No, Mr Massey.'

'But why?'

'Look, it's a no, John. And to be frank, if it wasn't, we don't have the staff. You can forget about it.'

'So because you ain't got the staff ...'

'The matter is closed. Thank you, Mr Massey.'

They said they couldn't trust me. I said give me an armed escort, do anything they wanted, just let me see her. Even the Krays got out to see their mum. I never had any of that. In my mind they'd damned me worse than the likes of the Krays. It just didn't make any sense – how could I be considered a higher risk than these types of people? It felt like a diabolical liberty.

'Well, fuck that,' I thought. 'I'm off.'

◆ ◆ ◆

My mind was made up that if I wasn't going to walk through the main gates with the blessing of the Parole Board, I'd find my freedom in my own way. I began planning. It gave my days purpose, helped break the monotony of prison life and calmed down my thoughts during long, dark hours.

You pick your places and your moments. There are times when you get to walk from place to place inside, and you use it wisely. You are out and about when you are going to the doctor's, the gym, the library. You are constantly surveying your surroundings and you see things that normally you would not. Escape was always in my thoughts and I had created a 3-D image of the building. Every walk from cell to shower, to canteen, to gym, every step. I scanned walls, windows, ceilings, doors. The fabric of the place was stamped on my imagination.

I kept my eyes open. I knew the building's layout, the systems the screws used; I was always scanning, always searching for possible weaknesses and possible opportunities.

Some people could look at the same landmark every day but not describe it, because they haven't really seen it. Not me. I soaked it up, every inch.

As I said, my good work hadn't gone unnoticed, and soon the screws had another job for me to do. They had this little office next door to the gym, and it was really noisy. They wanted a false ceiling built to give them some peace and quiet.

And it was when doing this job that I saw an opportunity. I decided against the trapdoor in the shower block because there were cons using that block all the time. I couldn't be seen tampering with it, so I went to look at the private block for the screws that only gym orderlies could access.

At that point, it was not even a formulated plan. It was just curiosity. I thought, 'Could this possibly be the way out?'

I knew roughly what was likely to be up there. I'd gone to the upper floors of the cell block next to the gym, which looked down on to it. I could see a skylight that must be above the new toilet block. I noticed a flat concrete slab with glass bricks set into it, and I worked out it must be where the screws' shower cubicle was. It looked difficult to shift, but that could work to my advantage. No one would expect it to be a possible way out.

From when I was in the building trade, when my dad was a plasterer, I knew the concrete slab would be held down by just a piece of mortar. It looked heavy — but what if I could chip the mortar away? Maybe I could work it loose enough for my purposes.

The viewpoint at the top of the block revealed a tantalising route towards the walls — and I noticed another handy defect in the security that would work in my favour. For some reason, all the cameras were pointing the wrong way.

There was razor wire around the edge of the building, but I knew I could get past that — and it didn't cover all the wall. It wouldn't have been a problem for me, anyway. I'd get through it somehow. It's not nice stuff, razor wire. It shouldn't have been there in the first place, as it was supposed to have been outlawed under European human rights laws. It'll rip you to pieces if you don't know how to handle it. Nowadays, since my little trip, there's a double roll of it round the top of the Ville.

While I now had a possible way from my cell to the outside world, I knew there was plenty more work to be done before I could say any of it was viable. It was all conjecture at the time — I had no idea it would work.

Firstly, I had to find a way of opening the padlock on the drop lock on the trapdoor. Because of my time in the building trade, I knew how it could be done.

I tried to pick the lock. I had to stand on the sink to reach it and couldn't get it open that way. It was too hard, stretching up, to get to the lock and work at it. But I was determined to see if behind the trap-door lay a loft space that I could quietly convert into a small workshop to gradually chip my way out on to the roof.

I decided to recruit some help. There was a mate of mine on A Wing and I asked him if he wanted a job in the gym.

By now, I had been working there for several months and had earned a bit of trust among the screws. I got my friend a job helping about the place. He kept lookout for me while I messed about with the trapdoor.

As I had the job of maintaining everything – looking after all the gear – this meant I had access to the security cabinet. These lockers were found in each workshop and held a few tools, things best kept stowed away from the lags. I liberated a small claw hammer from the cabinet and set to work. I knew the padlock was made of soft steel because of its colour and texture. I thought, 'Can I open it up? I'll need some force to do it.'

With my pal keeping an eye out, I jemmied the end of the claw hammer into the padlock's U bend and worked it loose. It finally sprung open. I pushed at the trapdoor, keeping as quiet as I could, and lifted it a little higher so I could squeeze up through the gap. Using all my strength to pull myself through the opening, I was up among the rafters. The first part of the plan was complete – but there would be plenty more to do before I could taste freedom.

◆ ◆ ◆

As my eyes got accustomed to the gloom, I knew my hunch was right. It was musty, full of cobwebs, dust, grime … but there was light coming in from the glass bricks. I knew I was in the right position.

My first problem was that the skylight was too high up for me to reach and there were bars across the gap leading up to it. I looked at it and wondered how I was going get past them. Should I saw through the bars? How long would that take? What could I use to cut through the solid, 3in bits of metal?

They were bolted to the ceiling, so that gave me a weak point to exploit. I had a eureka moment – 'I'll go and get the socket set they use for the dumb bells,' I thought.

The security cabinet contained a set of Allen keys and a spanner socket set. They were used to alter the weights on the gym's old-fashioned dumb bells – and they would become a key component in my escape.

I measured the bolts holding the bars in place and I only took what I needed. I couldn't risk taking the complete set because the screws would notice and questions would be asked. One afternoon, I made out I was tightening up the dumb bells and, while I was doing it, I slipped the right-sized socket into my pocket and put the rest back. I could now go up into my hideaway and start undoing the bars.

◆ ◆ ◆

I had to use the trips through the hatch wisely. Each time I disappeared into the ceiling, I was all too aware there was a chance I'd be discovered. Now I knew my guesses about a possible route out were correct, I was still acutely aware that the gap between success and failure was extremely slim. One little hiccup and my jailbreak would be over.

I needed something to get through the mortar, once I'd managed to get the bars off. We had a set of 25kg hexagonal weights and I put one of them up there. They were covered in rubber, which would soften the noise I was going to make. I thought I'd use one to chip away at it.

Next up was the question of how I could reach the concrete lid with glass bricks set into it. It was still out of my reach as I balanced on the beams.

Lying in my cell each night, I knew at any moment my attempt could be discovered. I was aware that time wasn't on my side and felt that, now I had started, I had no option but to see it through, one way or another. I created scenarios, solved problems, worked out what my next step was and how I could achieve my goal.

The answer to reaching the skylight came again from gym equipment. Prisoners used sets of steps for aerobic exercises. The steps slot together, neatly on top of each other, for storage. It gave me another idea.

They were kept in the prison hall and I asked the screws to help me carry them over to the gym. I said we needed them for circuit training. I smuggled five of them up into the loft and they fitted together to build a platform. I could now get into the void and get to work on the bars.

As well as the mental strain, it was physically tough. The weight of the bars, when I got them off, nearly crushed me. On top of that, the work had to be done in complete silence. I had to gently take the weight of those bars and put them down on the false ceiling, so they wouldn't fall or cause any debris to clatter.

And I had another problem. In the ceiling was a mesh grill looking into the screws' toilet. Sometimes they'd come in for a dump, just a few feet below me. I had to stay completely frozen until they had flushed and gone. It was so nerve-wracking.

My mate from A Wing helped out when he could. He'd be standing watch for me when I was up there, but trying not to arouse suspicion. He had a mop and he'd bang it on the ceiling if he thought there was a patrol heading our way. I'd come down sharpish.

As I continued working away at the skylight, I had a few hairy moments. The trapdoor lid was heavy and a tight fit. I had to lift it from the inside of the loft using just a small screw I had put in – and it lacked purchase. One day I had massive difficulty shifting it after I'd finished for the day and was due to be at a roll call. I was stuck. It seemed only a matter of time before my absence would be noted and an alert sounded. I thought I was done for.

I was shouting down the vent shaft to my mate that I couldn't budge it, that I was stuck. I tried everything to get his attention, but he didn't notice. Thankfully, he knew roll call was approaching. He eventually heard me stage whispering through the vent. He pushed the trapdoor far enough open with his mop, and I squeezed my fingers through the small gap he'd made.

Despite the scare, work continued. I made progress into the mortar, and started thinking about what I would do once I was on the other side of the wall. I knew getting out of the building was just the beginning. Where would I go and how would I get there once the breakout was done? How could I get messages out to people who might be able to help me? I knew it was likely my disappearance would be quickly discovered; I didn't fancy trying to get too far on foot – but I knew I could jump on a bus if I could get to the Cally Road without an alarm being raised. And once on a bus, I could blend in and head for a safe house until I'd worked out my next step. Top of the list now was paying a visit to Mum somehow before striking out for another country.

Such thoughts were put out of my mind when fate dictated when I would have to make my move. We had had a lot of rain, a real monsoon summer through May and into June. I noticed water seeping into the mortar where I had been working.

The rain had got behind it and big chunks would fall off on to the ground. It meant there was debris falling into the toilet and showers through the grill. I had to clear it all up sharpish so they wouldn't look up and investigate – or, worse, catch me up there. It went on for about three weeks, but it felt like a year.

Other factors also put the escape in danger and made me hurry. The governor decided, out of the blue, to do a security audit. They go round testing everything, trying all the locks, the bolts, the bars, the lot. The gym was no exception – except the lazy bastard checking out the showers and toilets just gave the padlock on the trapdoor a rattle with a night stick. They didn't bother to undo it and look up there. If they had done their jobs properly, they would have found the set of bars leaning against the wall, clocked my progress and it would have been all over.

I redoubled my efforts, spending as much time as I could finishing the job as the rain fell steadily. For days and nights on end, dark, heavy clouds hung over the Ville and London was hit by downpours.

I had chipped away all the mortar by now and I gave the slab a few thumps – but it was so heavy I couldn't physically push it. I used the weight to give me extra leverage, and it had a big, soft rubber covering. It made a soft thud and moved a tantalising fraction of an inch. Ever conscious that I could be heard, I got the music in the gym turned up a fraction and my mate on watch would make a point of rattling his bucket around.

I was living on a wing and a prayer. I thought maybe, because of the rain, they would have to get round to doing something about the roof because the building was leaking so badly everywhere. I fretted about leaving my escape too long. I decided I'd go a couple of weeks earlier than I had planned.

◆ ◆ ◆

I still hadn't been able to shift the loose panel and turned once more to the sets of steps for the answer. I now had six of them, and they were high enough for me to reach the skylight. I piled the steps up beneath the exit I had created. I lay flat on my back, put my feet up on the slab and found I could lift it like a leg press.

I thought, 'Right, I'm all set.' They'd called a security audit a few days before and it was freaking me out, so I decided I'd go at 6 p.m. that night, 17 June 2012. Time to say cheerio. There was no point waiting for them to discover my work. I should go as soon as I could.

◆ ◆ ◆

The Ville's regime saw the prisoners locked down at 6 p.m., cell doors closed until the morning. It makes for easier handling for the screws. The day crew have gone home and the night shift are just settling in. There are fewer people on patrol and keeping an eye out, a skeleton staff.

A few prisoners are given permission to be elsewhere for a while – evening classes, meetings, that sort of thing – and there was a night class on in the gym, so I had a good reason not to be in my cell. I could say I was clearing things away to be ready for the following day. It would be the right time to make good use of my handiwork.

I had a clean suit, shirt and shoes delivered to a pub a couple of miles away, so I had a change of clothes waiting. Otherwise, I didn't need any outside help. I knew the less I had to rely on others, the better the chances that things would go to plan.

I had to work out how I would get down and over the wall, once on the roof. It was a drop of 35ft, too far to risk jumping. I found the answer in the gym – the nets from a set of five-a-side football goals. The netting was quite strong, and there was plenty of it. As the day approached, I quietly cut lengths from the nets and tied them together.

It was time to go. I moved swiftly into the shower block, climbed up on the sink and hoisted myself through the gap. I quietly closed the hatch, hoping that would be the last glimpse I'd have of the inside of that fucking place. I was on my way.

I got up on the platform made by the sets of steps, lay flat on my back and pressed the slab with my legs. I moved it bit by bit to the side. A space opened, little by little. Sky appeared above me. I squeezed through the gap and slipped out into the heavily clouded early evening sky.

I took a carabiner clip from one of the weight-lifting machines and fixed it where I had removed the bolts for the bars. It looked pretty solid. I tied the rope off to it and then wrapped the other end round my arm.

Speed was crucial. I couldn't turn back. Every second, once I'd decided it was time, had to be used to put distance between myself and my captors.

I had to be fast. It wasn't easy – I don't like heights, and here I was, clambering across a roof to a wall, holding on to this bit of rope and about to throw myself over. I thought I'd put my foot on the ledge and just go for it, leap out and take a chance. I took a deep breath and dived over the edge of the roof, out across the wall.

I fell 20ft as my rope paid out.

I was hanging there – the rope had tightened round me and I couldn't work it loose. Then, suddenly, away it went and I fell the rest of the way.

I had tumbled a further 15ft onto paving stones. I broke a bone in my foot as I landed, but the adrenaline masked any pain and I didn't feel a thing. I found myself in an alleyway that snakes along the northern side of the prison – a small, rarely used path that leads to a set of wardens' houses in the outer grounds of the prison.

And it was here that my luck almost immediately ran out.

I landed, got myself up, and there, standing just 10yd away was a screw I knew called George. He'd clocked me and with eyes like saucers, he said, 'John, what the fuck are you doing here?'

I didn't want to have to tackle him but I was now way beyond the point of no return. I'd have chinned him if I needed to. I liked the bloke, in a way. He was one of the better ones, but he wasn't going to come out of it well if he tried to stop me.

I said, 'George, I don't have time to rabbit.' He just stood there gawking. I set off as quickly as I could in the opposite direction and leapt over the next wall.

I stopped for a moment behind a set of garages on a housing estate that borders the Ville. I caught my breath and changed into a jacket I had wangled off a bloke on remand.

I had managed to scrape a few quid together, a valuable fund, by dipping my hand down the back of a row of armchairs in the gym that the screws used for a lie-down and a kip. I'd give the chairs a clean every day and I'd scoop up the coins I found down the back.

I had a £1 coin I'd got there. I went as fast as I could to catch a bus on the Cally Road to Chapel Street.

The bus pulled up and I handed him the quid. The driver said to me, 'Sorry, mate, it's more than £1.' I didn't have any other change except a tenner and so I went to hand him that, but he didn't have any change.

A woman behind me said, 'Hey, it's ok, I'll get that for you.' She was more impatient than kind, wanting to get out of the rain that had begun to fall and get home. I was standing there obviously looking very flustered. She had no idea where I'd just come from and why I was in a bit of a hurry for the bus to get going.

I had to keep it down, keep it calm. The hot sweats, icy chills, the rubbery legs, the laborious breathing, the temptation to run, the temptation to grin – I kept a lid on it and kept myself cool.

The storm created by taking my freedom off my own bat and ingenuity, my daring and risk taking ... its intensity was familiar because I had broken out before. And, as before, after I had completed the first stage – the task of removing myself from the jurisdiction of prison wardens – my next step was to get out of north London, away from the manor I was known to frequent, head to a safe house and then smuggle myself across the English Channel.

There I was, John Massey – serial prison breaker, convicted murderer and notorious bank robber – on the run again.

◆ ◆ ◆

As I stepped on to the number 259 heading south down the Cally Road, just a few hundred yards away George the Screw was turning back on himself, frantically fiddling with his ID card at the gates, buzzing repeatedly on a staff door, shouting to be let in, trying to sound the alarm as quickly as he could.

I thanked the lady who'd paid for my ticket and made my way to find a seat, hoping the rush-hour bus passengers would provide the camouflage I sought. The next stage was to get to Chapel Street, about ten minutes or so away down by the Angel, where a suitcase would be waiting for me at a pub by the market.

The bus driver had shaken me up when he'd said he couldn't change the note and I thought I'd have to get off the bus. Yet I'd been rescued

– and here I was, looking out the window on to streets, trying to keep calm with people, oblivious, all around me.

I could see and hear London going about its everyday business – people heading home from work, going for food, whatever – and I was in the middle of it. It was so strange. I was dizzy with it, but trying to keep my wits. I sat back as the bus slowly made its way towards Upper Street. I got off at the Chapel Street stop. I'd got that bit planned, and it helped me focus.

I went to the agreed pub, trying to be as natural as you like, where there was someone I knew. I had arranged to go to the bar, buy a pint and ask for the woman I wanted. Her reaction was absolute shock. She quickly ushered me behind the bar and down into the cellar. There was a suitcase ready for me. In that cellar, I ditched my prison clothes and began a long chain of staging points to a destination out of the country where I could fade from view.

I knew the next twenty-four to forty-eight hours would be crucial: it was a high-profile escape from a well-known prison in the heart of the capital. There was embarrassment for the authorities, and they would use every trick in the book to get me back. They would throw all their resources at that task, enlist the help of every civilian I'd pass on the street. What I had done was big, big news. Everyone who saw me could potentially be my nemesis.

I'd be painted as a dangerous criminal, a lifer with previous. They had a horrible mugshot on file, one used to portray me as a cold-blooded killer, a label I'd been given a long time ago. It would be circulated. My face would be plastered all over. The tabloids would lap it up, the rolling news channels enjoying the air time they could fill with this yarn. All I had was my wits and the aid of a select few.

Back in the Ville, things were hotting up. The escape caused uproar. No one knew how I'd managed it. Fingers would be pointed, heads would roll, but before the inquest, before the fallout, before a screw noticed the dodgy lock on the trapdoor, found the skylight, found the football net, clambered across the roof – before all this, they wanted their man back in custody.

A London-wide alert was issued, the Metropolitan Police scrambling. Squad cars were out in force. Every copper had my name and face at the front of their minds. My phone record was scrutinised. Known acquaintances and my family were checked out.

I contacted my sister Jane and we arranged to meet at a friend's house in Kentish Town and then to drive together to Faversham, Kent, where I could lie low for a day or two.

◆ ◆ ◆

Before I could leave London behind, I needed to be off the streets and well hidden while the first wave of searches played out. From Chapel Street I headed across to King's Cross on another bus and from there would make my way to Kentish Town.

I had to get to a friend's house as soon as I could. I was just going to turn up and knock on the door. No one was forewarned. From there, I was going to call another contact who had somewhere out of London.

Still looking over my shoulder, suspicious of everyone I saw, I urged the bus through the evening traffic. I was so worried, I stayed on the bus too long and missed the stop. I knew it would all be going off around me by now, that they'd be after me, and the whole of London would be on lockdown and high alert.

The person I had met at the pub accompanied me. She thought that if I wasn't on my own, it was likely to arouse less suspicion. We got off just past King's Cross – I was terrified they'd already be watching all the train stations – and we jumped into a cab.

I had grown up in Kentish Town and still had a strong network of old friends and trusted acquaintances. I knew there was risk of capture and that the police would know where I had previously frequented.

But I felt I had little choice. I could draw on crucial support, and it was worth the risk if I didn't hang about for too long.

I had one overriding mission to complete before I got out of the country. I knew someone who lived in the flats in Harmood Street and that was where Jane was going to be waiting for me.

When I'd called her from the phone box, I'd told her to get a shift on but to take care, and make sure she wasn't being watched. She knew what to do. I could rely on Jane.

She was quite shocked. 'Oh, you've come early,' she said, trying to be all deadpan about it. I explained I'd had to bring the breakout forward because I was worried about being discovered, and the rain had frightened me, with the roof of the gym leaking and lumps of plaster falling down.

It had been a snap decision but one that needed to be made under the circumstances – and one that meant I hadn't been able to help out anyone else in the Ville. There were people there I knew and liked doing heavy bird. They would have given their right arm to come with me and there is nothing like giving someone their freedom. But as well as the risk to my escape – the more people involved, the greater the chances of a security breach, or being caught in the act – another factor played on my mind.

I thought about it for a long time. Should I let a couple of the lifers know? There were some doing thirty-five-year stretches. Afterwards, some of those I'd done bird with asked why I hadn't told them and given them the chance too. But I was worried if I got them out and they did something terrible on the outside, I would have that on my conscience.

A storm had by now broken over the Ville. The place was in lockdown and the wardens were giving my known associates inside a going over. A furious discussion was taking place at senior levels in the Ministry of Justice, the Prison Service and the Met Police. How did I escape? What were the failures of the system?

While an inquiry was to be launched on how I had managed to get away, more pressing was my recapture. The embarrassment was huge, but those in charge knew it could be tempered by me being swiftly apprehended. With the press eager for a story, the authorities didn't want the narrative to be how a 60-something-year-old had made the Prison Service look stupid, but how well the forces of law and order had done in getting me under lock and key again.

The Metropolitan Police pulled out all stops. That meant using the media to enlist the help of the public and also, more importantly, putting me under pressure to give myself up – or forcing me into making a mistake that would lead to recapture.

My escape was everywhere and that made the situation intimidating. There was a picture of me on screen every two minutes on *Sky News*. The news channels were going on and on about it. The newspapers were ready to print any old nonsense about a so-called dangerous criminal on the run.

The adrenaline had not stopped and it was exhausting. Real freedom would not be mine to enjoy until I was across the Channel. But before I could head out of the country, I had my important mission to accomplish.

I was extremely emotional. I had to see Mum. I was determined I wasn't going to leave the country without holding her in my arms. We made some plans. She was in Barnet, so we arranged for her to travel to relations in Kent, near the safe house I was heading to.

I got word she had arrived and hadn't been followed, so I stepped out into the streets and started another risky journey.

She was sitting on the couch when I walked into the room. She didn't notice me come in. I quietly sat down next to her, and put my arm round her.

She looked at me and screamed with delight. She just clung to me. It took time to recover, for us both to comprehend that we were there, in the same room, having a cuddle. It was really something.

Looking into Mum's eyes, holding her on the sofa, hearing her say my name over and over … it was what I had dreamed about for years – but it was also tempered by the knowledge of how I had got myself into this position. I wasn't there with the blessing of the state, which for so long had denied me this simple pleasure.

It was a heart-breaking moment – I knew I couldn't stay for long. I had to arrange to get somewhere safe. The manhunt was in full swing. Mum begged to come with me. She said, 'Take me with you, son. Take me with you. Don't leave me behind, Johnny.'

I risked taking her out for a couple of hours, thinking a bloke pushing a wheelchair with an old lady in it wouldn't attract attention, but I had to go my way and she had to go hers. I just couldn't see any way round it and it broke my heart. She started crying, and I said, 'Give me two weeks and I'll send for you.'

It was now twenty-four hours after the breakout and I needed to get my head down, rest up and work out my next move. I had an idea of how I would get away from England and strike out for Belgium. I could get Mum to join me later, once the trail had gone a little colder.

I stayed at a relative's house overnight and didn't get any sleep. The news was on all the time with my picture on it, and I didn't want to look at the newspapers.

With the family high on the list for the police to visit – and the danger of them being arrested for harbouring me high – it was time to make a move to another safe house, where I could start putting together my escape bag. I needed a false passport, cash, clothes, perhaps a disguise and, crucially, help with travel – by car, train, boat or plane. I was still in a state of shock that I was waking up with clear blue skies above me, not the grimy cell ceilings – but to keep it that way meant finding a decent hideout.

I contacted a friend who lived in Faversham and he took me to a builder's yard down a secluded country lane. Here, there was a ramshackle Portakabin and I was given a key to it. It was enclosed by a tall, corrugated-iron fence and in the middle of nowhere.

I spent the night there. It wasn't exactly comfortable, but it was a relief to be on the move, hiding somewhere I was pretty sure wouldn't be searched. The Portakabin had a bed and a portable cooker I could heat up a kettle on, make some basic grub. On reflection, I should have stayed there longer. The friend who put me there was surprised to see me – I was two weeks earlier than he expected. He was going to arrange transport for me to get me out of the country, but being early meant he still had details to finalise.

Things were going pretty much to plan. I just needed not to make any silly moves and I'd stay at large. I was torn between a natural urge to get moving, to put as much distance as possible between myself and the British authorities, and the need to be patient.

Finally, everything was sorted. I was going to smuggle myself out in the back of a lorry owned by a firm whose drivers I knew. The trucks went back and forth to Europe all the time. They were searched on their way into the UK, but not so much as they headed abroad. It offered a good chance – but my early breakout had put the kibosh on the idea that, twenty-four hours after hopping the wall, I'd be enjoying a cold lager in foreign climes. I still needed to wait for the guy who was going to take me to return from a trip to Holland.

I had the choice of going to Belgium or Spain. I had, after a previous escape, been extradited from Spain. It was a possible destination, but my previous meant there could be complications if I headed south. There would be the chance of meeting people I knew who didn't have my interests at heart, or Spanish police on the lookout – and then there were some painful personal memories I would have to deal with too.

The Low Countries had numerous advantages, not least because of the place I had my eye on. A friend had a big château he was renovating. I could live and work there, see my days out. It was a lovely place, secluded, in the middle of the countryside, with plenty to be getting on with to help earn my keep. There was loads of room and a really interesting job to do. Plenty of carpentry, building, all sorts. It would have been ideal. I could have brought Mum over. The heat would have been on her, but there would have been ways to get her there. I'm good at losing tails and throwing the authorities off the scent. We could have got Mum there and looked after her for the rest of her days.

◆ ◆ ◆

While I knew I was as safe as was possible holed up in the draughty Portakabin in the Kent countryside, I was uncomfortable and felt cut off, adrift. Every noise I heard made me start. With the reality of the escape now sinking in and the thrill wearing off, my isolated position was making it tougher. When my friend who had left me there told me his daughter lived nearby, but was off on a two-week holiday and I could house sit, it seemed like a fairly safe move to make. At least I could take a long, hot bath and have a TV to watch – as a tennis fan who had played endlessly in prison and, with the Wimbledon championships on, I could happily while away the hours catching the games until the lorry I'd chosen was ready to head back to the Continent.

I spent another night in the builder's yard and then the friend who arranged the transport came to visit me the next day. He said things were still not quite ready, but it wouldn't be long. I had some breakfast with him, then we drove to his daughter's house and settled down to watch Wimbledon.

Little did I know that, due to an unrelated quirk of fate, my bid for freedom was about to be dramatically curtailed.

My mate had a court order hanging over him relating to the Proceeds of Crime Act, and to give the Ministry of Justice the swerve, he and his wife had pretended they had split up so their shared assets were no longer in his name.

They were trying to steal everything from him, take the lot. He had squared it so it would look like he and his missus had gone their separate ways and she owned everything, so they were not entitled to take diddly. That was where it all came unstuck.

His wife didn't know about me. The police were looking for me, and they were also looking for him. They went to his house where his wife was and she told them, 'Oh no, he's not here, he doesn't live here no more. We're through,' thinking she'd better stick to their story. They asked her where they could find him and she said, 'Oh, he's been staying at our daughter's.'

To compound matters, my mate's name had been on a special 'persons of interest' list kept at the Ville. It showed who I had been in touch with – which made him someone the police were going to get round to speaking to at some point, as they cranked up the hunt.

They knew his name, they knew his previous, and they knew he was connected to me. It didn't take them long to make their way down that list. Looking back, I was a little bit green about it.

So there I was, settled in an armchair, sipping a cup of tea, dipping a biscuit in and watching the Wimbledon final on the telly when my all-too-brief sojourn on the outside ended.

They had a team of a properly tooled-up police coming in through the front door. I heard them and went straight to the back door to make a run for it. They were already coming in over the garden fence. They had me surrounded, and that was that.

No Belgian château with my mum for me. No – it was back to porridge.

TWO

My earliest memory – when I sit back and really think about the little me of seven decades ago – my earliest memory is walking along a country lane. I was 3 years old. It has stuck with me, this scene. It has been embedded in my brain. I've always been able to see it.

I was walking along this country lane, holding my mum's hand, and we came to a fork in the road. There was a bit of grass in the middle, with a little pond, reeds and lilies, and there were frogs jumping about. We stopped and I was absolutely absorbed by them. These little frogs, leaping about in the water.

We eventually carried on for a bit, down this same little country lane with cowslips in the verges and fields behind, walking along in the sunshine, until we came to a big house. There was a cracked tarmac path and an unkempt privet hedge – a detail my young mind logged and I can recall perfectly seventy years later.

There was a tall, thin woman coming out, striding down the path to meet us. I have a vivid memory of her. I can see her right now. I can remember not just how she looked, but how I felt, how she made me feel as she walked purposefully, so determined to do her task, which happened to be something to do with me that day.

She was wearing a big, starched, fly-away collar, sticking out like an Elizabethan ruff. It ringed her neck and made her look even skinnier:

elongated, like a wading bird on a marsh flat, with a long, angry beak to peck her sharp words out from. We called her Mrs Fly Away, because of those collars. I used to wonder, after I'd been there for a bit, whether she had a whole room full of them or if she sat alone in her lodging each night, a day of brutality towards 100 random children completed, and scrubbed her one starched, white, fly-away collar in a small sink with lukewarm water spurting irregularly out of a wall-mounted immersion heater.

That was all to come. That morning, I thought this was all a big adventure, walking there with my mum, basking in the sun and the grass, and the skylarks or whatever diving and dropping over the fields. I'd only ever seen fields of bricks and debris, and things that were harder than me, things that hurt you if you knocked against them — sharp edges on bomb sites and other people's fists. And here I was, in an environment where everything to my left and right, front and behind, looked good to flop down on.

I was so happy. A lovely summer's day in the countryside with your mum all to yourself. What could be better?

We walked up the path, but we didn't go into the house. I was led round the side and into the garden. There was a big row of windows, with kids' faces staring out at us.

I didn't think anything of it, especially as my eye had caught sight of this big, red trike sitting there on the lawn. It looked like the best toy ever, the most enchanting thing I'd ever seen. It beckoned me over and the adults encouraged me.

And of course it was there to distract me. They asked if I'd like a go. Would I? Not half. 'Go on then, Johnny, have a go.' I jumped on it and started enjoying myself. I did a circuit of the garden, and when I came back, Mum had gone.

◆ ◆ ◆

It is a memory seared in my mind for a good reason – May Massey, my mum, had taken the difficult decision to leave me at a children's home. It would be the first of a number I found myself in over the next three years.

This first home was in Henley-on-Thames, and I'd been handed over. Mum had filled in a form and left me riding off on a red trike while she disappeared, not for five minutes, not just round the corner with the lady with the big collars, no – for an unspecified period of time.

I know how hard that must have been for her. She was pregnant with my sister Jackie and Dad had been given a short prison stretch for a minor crime. Mum was under pressure and couldn't cope. Someone she knew told her of how a Catholic charity for Anglo-Irish mothers could help – they'd take me in. Mum, as she proved later, was full of motherly love, a matriarch for seven children who all loved her dearly. It wasn't a callous act, rather an act of desperation brought about by her bad situation. It must have killed her – and is perhaps part of the reason that later on in life she was so loyal to me – but it was a decision that has lived with me too, and it seems obvious these early, formative years and this huge dislocation had knock-on effects that echoed down my life.

From Henley-on-Thames, they moved me about, from one home to another, and then another; each transfer, always unexplained and unexpected, added to my sense of confusion and homesickness. I remember some dump in Margate where they would force us to drink down curdled milk with a skin on the top – disgusting stuff. There was a place in Broadstairs, with small, barred windows that had eerie shadows across them, and another in St Leonards-on-Sea where older kids bullied us younger ones mercilessly. I wet the bed every night, making me miserable and those bastards meant to be looking after us poor kids furious. It was a condition I had right from childhood and through my teens, and only stopped when I was about 20: it must be a sign of the psychological trauma inflicted by being placed in a children's home at such a young age.

◆ ◆ ◆

I was born in 1948 to Jack and May, a couple who had met as war enveloped London and its population lived on a Blitz footing: every moment was important, no one knew what tomorrow would bring, and relationships were forged with a different backdrop to that of the previous generation. There was urgency in the air. Mum had been married before, in her late teens – a short-lived betrothal that begot one son but ended when her husband, Brian, left for a new life in Australia. A vague plan was made that May might one day follow, but leaving her family behind, to pursue a relationship first forged in youth and without any real basis, was never going to happen.

Then Dad came along. Whatever the background to the first blossoms of their meeting, six decades of marriage would later prove it was a match that worked.

The couple came across each other one evening as Jack used a phone box in Ferdinand Street, Kentish Town, and May waited patiently outside for her turn. I was their third child of seven.

The family had settled in Ferdinand Street to start with. It was a working-class district made up of back-to-back, two-up, two-down cottages originally built for the railway workers of the Victorian era – this was before Camden Council started a sweeping social housing building project that would change the neighbourhood in the 1960s.

The Irish diaspora, to which my dad belonged, was large. Many worked in construction. Others got jobs in public services, nursing, midwifery, teaching, the railways. The area's street markets gave opportunities to young men as porters, as did the borough's meat trade. While the immediate post-war years I was born into saw plenty of poverty amidst the slums, there were improvements coming. The world they'd fought for was being forged by the Attlee government: universal healthcare, new schools with school dinners, free milk, vaccinations … and there was work to be found by our parents, returning from the war industries on the Home Front or from abroad in the services, rebuilding the bomb-damaged city.

My mother, full name Elizabeth May Easterbrook but always called May, was born in Wickford, Essex. She was one of seven children and the family moved to Kentish Town in the 1930s.

Mum had left school when she was 14 and got work locally: with her sister, my Aunt Hilda, they found jobs in what had once been a false-teeth factory on Highgate Road near Parliament Hill Fields. Before the war, the firm was called Shand Kydd and made wallpaper. When hostilities started, the print production line rolled to a stop and May and Hilda were put to work next to each other, making components for bombs. They were the girls Gracie Fields sang about, who made the Thing-Ummy-Bob that was going to win the war.

Mum was a worker. She grafted all her life, never moaned, never took a day off. As well as bearing and raising eight children, she worked as a chambermaid at hotels and as a cleaner and a nanny.

At the weekends she'd take my little sisters Jane and Kim on a train from the old Kentish Town station to Southend. When she became a grandmother, she and Hilda would take the six grandchildren down to Butlin's in Bognor Regis.

They'd head to Clacton, the kids, my mum and Aunty Joan squeezing into the back of Dad's work van – an old *Evening News* delivery rattle trap, painted in the company's livery of bright yellow and navy blue – sitting on an old mattress, and Jack and Uncle Dennis up front.

May's father, who we called Pop, lived nearby in Grafton Road and had found work at a slaughterhouse on Market Road, which runs down from York Way towards the Caledonian Road, where decades later his grandson, that's me, would spark a national manhunt after escaping from Pentonville.

The Market Road cattle traders and slaughterhouses were famous. Livestock would come in from the counties on the north side of the capital to be slaughtered and sold to butchers. It was an important meat-processing site. The local trade had a number of Irish butchers, and the Queen's Crescent area, which my family knew well, was renowned for it. The street once boasted multiple butchers and the local pubs held meat auctions every Saturday night to get rid of unsold cuts for the following day's roast. I remember people queuing up to get into the pubs along there on the Saturday evening to take part in the auction or raffle. And once the joint had been roasted and everyone's fill eaten, Mum would make lovely bubble and squeak the next day with the beef and spuds and cabbage left over.

For Pop, long hours, low pay and poor conditions were the order of the day. Pop's life at the slaughterhouse came to an abrupt end when he was in his 40s: he was tossed by a bull that had worked itself loose from a tether in a holding pen. Mum said the injuries he suffered were severe enough for him never to be able to work again.

◆ ◆ ◆

I don't know too much about my dad's early life or the family background on his side. I know that he was born in Birmingham, near the Bull Ring, in 1925.

He was an only child. He never knew his father, but he did tell us both his parents were originally from Cork, Ireland. In his later years, he revealed he had long dreamed of returning to Birmingham and tramping the streets of his youth. He saw Harry Houdini perform in the Bull Ring street market, showing off his escapology tricks and also his prowess as a boxer. He spoke about returning to Ireland, as so many of his generation did as they reached their older years, to see a country they'd either left as youths or had heard of through the songs sung by relatives round pianos in parlours and pubs.

He would wear one of those cheesecutter flat caps and knew his way round Birmingham. Perhaps he'd been a Peaky Blinder and that's where my taste for that life came from?

Despite not talking too much about it, we all knew he had an emotional commitment to his past and was quite nostalgic. It would come out when he'd had a drink or two. My sister Jane, her partner Roy and Mum decided one day they'd take him to Ireland for a holiday.

They hired a five-berth campervan and all bundled in, and took Dad to see his roots. My mum even climbed up the steps to kiss the Blarney Stone. Jane and Dad couldn't manage the steps, so they stayed at the bottom and smoked a few fags. Jane said she would never forget Dad telling her it was the best trip of his life. It was a special time for him.

Mum had had my older brother Brian with her first husband. Then came Carol, followed by me. Terry, Jackie, Susan, Jane and Kim followed at regular intervals. Mum and Dad loved each other – and seemingly had a bit of a deep-rooted cultural, Catholic-influenced aversion to contraception.

When I was born, the family lived in Ferdinand Street, Chalk Farm. It had a set of London County Council blocks, red brick, six storeys, balconies and communal gardens, drying areas, pram sheds: Edwardian civic sensibility, solid, imposing, symmetrical, a step up from the Victorian industrial workers' back-to-backs. The Ferdinand Street dwellings offered a more secure tenure and therefore a more settled community – midnight flits to escape rent arrears, with goods loaded on handcarts and prams, were to become a thing of the past.

Yet the Ferdinand Street home did not last. It isn't clear why we upped sticks from an area where Mum and Dad had friends and family. It can't have been for reasons of space, as we moved to a house less suited to the growing Massey family. Soon after I was born, we moved to Westland Place, Shoreditch, off the City Road, and it was here I spent some of my childhood.

Jack was working as a plasterer and he'd start early so he could knock off at lunchtime. Dad was still drawn to Kentish Town and his mates round there, and would head to the old Mamelon Tower pub on Queen's Crescent, a lively meeting place for the building and butchers' trades, a place where jobs could be picked up, tips offered, goods bought and sold, fortunes and misfortunes shared.

Dad loved to unwind after a busy day at work, plaster dust in his hair, have a few beers and games of pool. He was excellent with a cue. His friends still say what a great player he was, and the more pissed he got, the better he played.

But life was hard for Dad. He had so many of us to feed and keep clothed and straight, with little help from elsewhere. His work as a plasterer, while consistent, did not always bring in quite enough.

It was at the turn of the 1950s when Dad was caught pinching lead from the roof of a bomb-damaged church, a place called St Silas, whose tower had been knocked off by a Doodlebug in 1944 and whose roof had not yet been repaired. For this minor crime he did three years and that was how I ended up being placed for an unspecified length of time at a children's home, a chilling portent of what I would face in later life.

◆ ◆ ◆

The moment Mum left me is still crystal clear, more than sixty-seven years later. I'd had her to myself all day, and it was lovely. Then it hit me: it was over, she had left.

The children's home held around 100 of us, between the ages of 2 and 12. The building – something like a former poor school – loomed over us, its high-ceilinged corridors and draughty dormitories lacking domestic warmth.

I stood in that garden and I remember all these faces pushed up against the windows, staring down at me in silence; these children, brutalised, watching, looking at this bewildered little boy in scruffy, long shorts. I thought, 'Hello, who are they? What is this?'

The tall, skinny woman took me inside to this room. It was like a hospital ward, with rows and rows of beds. Then I realised what was going on and, believe me, I screamed blue fucking murder.

I was there for a while, a year or so, then moved, and then eventually brought back. I remember they gave me a sixth birthday party, so it must have been three years I was away. I hated the place. Every day it was a fight, and every day I was taught I had to play the system by the older children.

Attending a church service on Sundays was compulsory – a chore I didn't enjoy but it was an integral part of the regime. We had a choice between church or chapel and we worked out the church had a shorter service, but even then it seemed to go on and on and did nothing but bore the fuck out of us and make us think these adults were a bunch of crazy hypocrites.

I didn't settle. I hated the staff, hated the food, hated the rigidity. I missed my family and was deeply resentful. It manifested in a stubborn will not to conform, not to give in – and to show my displeasure in any way a boy barely out of toddlerhood could find to express himself. And my 'misbehaviour', which with the benefit of hindsight was simply a form of expression created by the experience, led to increasingly tough sanctions from those in charge.

There was no love shown, no maternal figures to offer comfort. They were tall, angry-looking people walking through cold corridors.

While my memory of the place is a bit patchy, I can sometimes sense the atmosphere, see images of it, and I don't remember happy times, though I suppose there must have been some. But I do remember the bad times. I remember them clearly – they have haunted me, never gone away or faded.

The adults there, led by Mrs Fly Away, used to make us go to sleep after lunch. I suppose they wanted some peace and quiet for themselves,

I don't know. But I just couldn't do it. I was always hyper as a child, one of the reasons Mum had found me a lot to handle when she was on her own. It wasn't me trying to be difficult, I just couldn't get to kip in the middle of the day.

With a belly full of food, I didn't fancy the compulsory post-lunch lie down and let those in charge know. The House's way of dealing with me would today be recognised as the horrendous abuse of a small child. I was restrained against my will – an experience that would become familiar in later life.

They would carry me, one grabbing me under my arms and another taking my legs, and drag me into a cold, whitewashed room at the back of the building. I'd kick and struggle, and it aggravated them and made them grip me tighter, give me a slap or two. The place they dragged me to was used for medicals. It stunk of disinfectant and nit lotion and castor oil.

In this Room 101, up against the back wall, was a hospital trolley. They'd grip me by the arms and then roll it out in to the middle of the room, its fat rubber wheels squeaking as they jostled it into position. Then they would strap me down so I wouldn't run about, and give me a few slaps too for good measure. When I had been tied down, they'd leave me – turn off the lights, close and lock the door, give me a warning.

It was horrible, and it was this method of incarceration that prompted my first ever escape. I'd wriggle free or find a way to undo the straps. Then I'd run around until they caught me again. I'd force a window, rush out the back and hide in the garden, and give them the run about. They'd eventually catch me and give me what for.

I was a prisoner at a young age. It wasn't called child abuse then, not like it would be now. It was just the old system – accepted. We had no advocates, no value, no recourse.

You wouldn't dream of tying a kid to a trolley and hitting them nowadays. Can you imagine? It was a restraint table on a medical gurney, the sort of thing you see in *One Flew Over the Cuckoo's Nest*, and it was absolutely terrifying.

◆ ◆ ◆

For a long time after, I did wonder why Mum had left me there and whether she loved me. I only found out some years later that Dad had been inside. It was never spoken about at home. Dad had been ashamed. Later, he would have a strong aversion to prisons, and visiting me when I was behind bars was always particularly tough for him.

I came home to a crowded household full of siblings. By now, besides Mum, Dad and me, the family included my brother Terry and my sisters Jackie, Susan, Jane and Kim, all sharing two rooms.

We lived in Westland Place, Shoreditch, a row of terraced homes off the City Road. The street led nowhere, with one end still full of debris from the bombs that had fallen during the Blitz. We lived on the top floor of one of the dilapidated four-storey houses.

I remember Dad leaving early for work each morning – something I hated, as Dad would take his heavy overcoat off the bed, which I would be curled up under. I always knew Dad had gone to work because I'd wake up with cold feet and nothing covering me.

We cooked on a gas stove that stood on a landing. A coal bucket was kept on the stairs, which was our only source of heat. We would take a shovelful up to our rooms to get a fire going, or burn whatever we could find outside. That was a permanent challenge – find something worth burning and get it home and enjoy some warmth.

I used to love building the fire in the grate. Mum and Dad let me do it. That was my job: clean out yesterday's ashes, sweep the hearth and scrape the charcoal from the firebox, often covered in a sticky resin from whatever we'd burned the night before. When they dug up the old cobble streets, you'd find big blocks of thick, heavy, tarry wood beneath them and you'd slice them up like bread. They were lovely for starting a fire and burnt slowly and steadily for hours. Whenever we saw a road being relaid, we'd be there with sacks and wheelbarrows, taking as much as we could carry and then going back for more.

There was no bathroom. Washing was done at the sink, and once a week in a tin bath or at the Vestry communal bath and wash houses in Shoreditch, where entry was 2*d* for children and 6*d* for adults – a treat we children would take in fortnightly turns to enjoy, three going one Saturday morning, followed by our other siblings the following week.

With no indoor plumbing except a faucet with low water pressure, there was no flush toilet. Having a piss or a crap meant going outside and into a small brick shed with a modesty door that showed your feet off and offered little privacy. The drain ran out into a main sewer behind the houses that each house on the terrace was connected to, and which had been damaged during the war: it led to regular blockages and a build-up of methane that created a stink. The sewer was especially bad in the summer months, and in the winter would fill up with rain water and not be able to drain away, backing up and occasionally spilling over.

You had to go all the way down the steps and into the basement and then out the back to use the toilet, and because of that, none of us ever wanted to use it at night. We never wanted to venture out in the cold and dark, treading in God-knows-what, knowing there were spiders and rats and flies and all sorts waiting. Instead, we had a piss pot in the bedroom, a china bowl with a picture of a man on a horse in a red hunting tunic surrounded by hounds. We all used it, and we'd all wake up as each of us relieved ourselves, trying not to splash. It would be overflowing by the morning, and we'd give each other bother about whose turn it was to take it downstairs, carefully balancing it as we'd go. I remember feeling extra shame if someone had left a crap floating on top.

The other floors were occupied by a variety of characters. On the middle landing, below us, were the Scrutton brothers, Ernie and Ronnie. Ronnie was a bit of a tea leaf – actually, they were both as bad as each other. On my way to and from school, I would see Ronnie going in and out of derelict buildings with a crowbar after some scrap. He was always after scrap, always after anything he could get his hands on. A regular totter. Saw value in everything.

On the ground floor there was another family, and the man there was the landlord. I don't remember much about him except my dad avoiding him on a Friday night after a few beers when it was payday and there were arrears to be sorted. In the basement was an old lady called Emma. She was very quiet and kept herself to herself. Her place smelt of cooked greens.

The house had been condemned, the Abercrombie plan for London drawing a big red line through the neighbourhood, with plans to decant those living there out to Essex, or find them prefabs, while new concrete blocks were laid out for the Londoners who had survived the Depression and then the war, and who had, in the eyes of Beveridge and Bevan and Attlee, earned the right to have an indoor loo.

The landlord knew the house was fucked and wanted rid of it, and no doubt his occasionally paying tenants too. He tried to sell it to my dad for £7. Dad didn't fancy it, it was in such a poor state of repair.

When I got back from my extended children's home tour, Dad gave me a dog. We called her Susie and she was very nervous when she first came to live with us.

Dad brought her home one day and I got up nice and early to see her. He'd got her off a mate in the pub. She wouldn't come near any of us. She would hide under a chair, scowling. She must have had it rough off her last owners. The simple fact was she didn't like and didn't trust humans when she first arrived. Eventually she came out to see me, all friendly. She must have been very lonely.

Susie wasn't the only companion I had. She was joined by another dog who became inseparable from me. I called him Micky and he was the same age as me – a little black mongrel with a curly tail. He had these very big paws. At the time, I loved the Tarzan films with Johnny Weissmuller and I'd pretend Micky was a lion and we'd wrestle together – we'd roll about all over the place.

He was always happy and he went everywhere with me. He'd follow me to school. He knew his way about as well as I did, and if we got lost or separated, he'd always find his way home, no matter where we were.

We were a tight-knit family and we found happiness in being together. We found escape by entertaining each other and we stood together in times that were not easy. But it made us feel together and strong. We played together, kept house together, looked out for one another.

Even though money was tight, cash could be found for adventures: bank holiday jaunts to the fairs on Hampstead Heath and excursions to catch minnows and sticklebacks along the canal, and gather up horse manure from the dray horses that still plodded along the towpaths. We'd learned to keep eagle eyed for rogue pieces of anthracite coal, and shoved them in cloth sacks that were covered in years of dust.

There were trips to the cinema, too. I'd go up to Hoxton every Saturday morning to watch the films. It cost us 6*d* to get in. You'd see Flash Gordon and Dan Dare, you'd get a cartoon and then *Pathé News* before the feature film started.

Dad loved watching Westerns, and so did I – Tex Ritter, Roy Rogers. Now and again they'd have a yo-yo competition on the stage for the kids before the films started. I always wanted a go, wanted to get hold of one of the prizes – a free pass for next week's programme, a bag of roasted nuts or toffee, and the kudos amongst your peers – but I could never master it.

Dad had settled after his spell inside, learned a harsh lesson, and was earning money. He was known as Jack the Plasterer, and was renowned among the trades for his work: so much so, people would hold off getting their rooms finished until he was available. He was known for making his own cornicing, being able to copy the ornate Victorian and Arts and Crafts motifs on ceilings and round the edges of rooms in homes knocked about by the war. It was a job that required skill and care. He took pride in what he did. While he was primarily a plasterer, he was well versed in all sorts of decorating. He really was handy at all the facets of his trade, practical and methodical. I remember thinking how skilled he was, the best in the world. He was a no-nonsense guy, took nothing from anyone.

Mum was by now working as a chambermaid in West End hotels and her shifts saw her leave to catch the bus into town long before school started or return late at night when we were in bed. A loaf of bread would be left for us to cut, marge, salt and jam on the side, with Carol in charge of the bread knife and dishing out the rations.

Mum and Dad brought in money and showed us the value of work – but still, times were tough.

By now, I was enrolled at the Moreland Street Primary School. There was a headmaster called Hodgkinson and he loved the kids to feel the wrath of his authority. He would take an assembly from the stage in the hall, stand there in his gown, and scowl down his nose at us. God only knows why he'd become a teacher – he hated children. I think he'd been knocked about in the war and had shell shock.

He was an evil bastard. One time, he called me up in front of the school and asked me where I'd been yesterday. I didn't know where I'd been. Had I been at school? Had I been truanting? I froze. I wasn't quick enough on my feet to say I'd been sick and you can ask my mum. I stood there and, before I could react, he caned me. He pulled my trousers down and absolutely walloped me.

The adults were still coming out from the torpor of war, trying to make sense of life on Civvy Street, trying to move on from the horrors of Dunkirk, the Atlantic convoys, the campaign in North Africa, liberating Italy, D-Day in France and the liberation of occupied Europe. All that generation went through, the ghosts that haunted the dreams of those who made it through the war, some of it was inflicted on pupils.

I had little interest in the lessons dictated to me as I sat squashed behind the cramped, ink-stained desks, and I didn't enjoy the strict discipline. Instead of facing this daily battle of wits, I just didn't turn up. I'd set out walking to school and then would swerve away from the gates. At an early age, I set about exploring London. I'd been playing truant from the moment I realised I could, walking the streets, knocking about, exploring bomb sites. There was so much to see. The city was like an adventure playground, a wide-open place with no one in charge.

When I was 11, I left Moreland Street Primary and enrolled in a secondary modern called Northampton School. I don't remember taking the 11-plus. Maybe it was assumed I wouldn't pass, so they never put me forward for it. Maybe I took it. But regardless, I wasn't much interested in these things and no grammar school would've wanted me.

I started at Northampton School, which was round the back of Ironmonger Row in Islington, in 1960. It was here I made a really good childhood friend, a bloke called Steven Georgiou, the son of a Greek restaurateur. They lived on the Gray's Inn Road and my mate Steven would later earn fame as the singer Cat Stevens (now Yusuf Islam).

We'd met in the playground on our first day. I liked him instantly, and he liked me. We got on. He was my mate, he laughed at my jokes and I found him good company. He was non-judgemental, never thought bad things, always saw the best in people. Looking back, I kind of knew he had something – he wasn't like any of my other friends. He was hard, no one messed with him, but he was hard because he was clever, different, confident, and he knew how to get along with everyone.

We were a pair and looked out for each other. His dad's restaurant was called the Moulin Rouge and he would give his lad two bob a day pocket money. It was a fortune, and he'd always share it. He was never bothered. He'd be, 'What we doing, Johnny? Where we going? What's the plan?'

We'd bunk off and ride the Tube. He had this trick, like tagging, graffiti: he was a great artist, and would get these big inky pens from a place up Charing Cross Road. He'd have a load of them stuffed in his trousers, leaking everywhere, and he'd pull them out with a mischievous smile and get to work. I'd keep an eye out and he'd go and write on the Tube maps and change the names of the stations to hilarious things, rude stuff. I would laugh till I cried, watching him come up with all these creative new double-entendres and all sorts, like something out of *Carry On*. It was all done in a beautiful script so you could hardly tell the difference. I loved the idea of a bloke getting on the Tube in his bowler and heading into the City, starting at Look At Your Barnet, changing at Wank, and then going to a job at St Smalls or being asked to change here for the Mouldy Bailey.

The Tube didn't just offer free travel for us youngsters to explore London, or the enjoyment of minor vandalism, it offered warmth. I learned I could jump the gates, get on a carriage and stay there all day. We'd say to the guards that our mum had the tickets and she was just coming behind us, and we'd whizz through.

It wasn't always straightforward, though. There was one day my absconding attracted the attention of a pair of police officers. I was accosted by two men and they flashed a warrant card at me. I was taken to West Central police station, near Saville Row. It was hours before I gave them my name, I was so frightened. I was scared shitless of what my dad would do when he found out the Old Bill had found me riding without a ticket and playing hooky.

I cracked when the two male officers were replaced by a nice-looking, kindly WPC. She got my name out of me, all gentle and reassuring. They got hold of Mum, who was working at the old Strand Palace Hotel, and when she finished her shift she picked me up. I thought Dad would kill me, so I ran away until I was too hungry to stay out. But though Mum knew I'd been playing truant, she never told him.

Me and my mates filled the streets after school, dusk and hunger eventually dragging us home. We'd play out and use a fence as a goal or for cricket. Behind our house was a bomb site, full of spiky, sharp wrought iron and bricks, big slabs of timber at angles, lead pipes, slate, guttering, the detritus of a life wrecked by the Luftwaffe. Our world was covered in debris. It felt like most of London was still bomb sites, or building sites. Everywhere you went – all debris and dereliction. There were disused factories and old waterworks and we'd spend hours building camps in them. In the places they'd got round to fixing up, there would be tools we could nick and sell on with no questions asked

('We found it, this old chisel ... worth a shilling down the Mamelon Tower?') and there would be wheelbarrows or porters' carts we could use for races along quiet streets.

If there were a few of us, we couldn't bunk the Tube or a bus, so we'd walk – walk for miles and miles. I remember we went all the way to Crystal Palace to see the park with the dinosaurs. I was horribly disappointed – I'd gone to Regent's Park and peered over the fence to look at the giraffes, and someone said he'd heard of a park where they had dinosaurs. I believed him and thought there would be proper monsters. We jumped a tram southwards, went past Victoria and then over the bridge, through Stockwell, Brixton, out of our manor. We got there and they were just these models.

The gang I was with were really impressed, but I got the hump as I'd been convinced they'd be real, like crocodiles or emus or something, so I clambered all over them and smashed up the horns of a triceratops. A parkie chased us out. I spent a long journey home berating the others for being gullible, believing these creatures were alive and living in south London, but it was me who'd wanted to believe it, not them.

We'd walk all over. We'd go along the river to Trafalgar Square, which had really taken a beating during the war. There were all these bombed-out places to explore, completely infested with pigeons. We'd climb up, clamber over the debris and get into what was once someone's house, or an old factory, make our way up wonky stairwells or piled-up masonry, waiting to be cleared, and collect the pigeons' eggs.

They were dangerous, these decaying bits of wasteland where tragedies had happened, where people had been blown to smithereens, but that was the point to us – it was so exciting. I couldn't help but love the decay: the buildings where, four storeys up, you'd see a wardrobe attached to the walls with no floor and someone's clothes still in there, the old iron bedsteads balanced precariously on half-blown floorboards, the detritus of a domestic life interrupted by high explosives. You'd go across floors with these huge drops and big holes: lethal, lethal gaps. There'd be pits full of dark, black water, ringed by buddleia, bracken, evening primrose and rosebay willowherb, which covered everything in a carpet of red flowers. It had been totally taken back by Mother Nature.

It was a wonder we survived – but we did. We came out unscathed. You could play out in the streets completely unchaperoned, and we never felt in any danger at all. We just ran about all over the place.

◆ ◆ ◆

That was our childhood. We took to the streets looking for innocent, and sometimes less innocent, adventures.

We used to do some shoplifting together – nothing serious but for the fun of it, really. We'd filch chocolate bars from the counters, one of us distracting the shopkeeper, asking them something stupid, silly, to get their attention while the other stuffed whatever they could grab down their shorts.

Steven was great at this: I'd have to try not to listen to him as he worked a number on some shopkeeper, standing there with a beady eye in a brown, knee-length smock, behind an old-fashioned till with big, chunky levers ready to ring up a sale. Sometimes Steven would go in first, make the bell above the door ring, innocently ask for something – a quarter of acid drops – and while they were measuring it out, he'd reach up and cut the string that attached the bell to the door so I could come in undetected. We'd pinch chocolate bars of all kinds and brands … We'd hide them in the school desks the next day if we'd got a good haul, more than we could comfortably eat, and we'd sell them off to other kids. Everyone was perpetually hungry and we'd all grown up with rationing, so chocolate was a valuable commodity.

My post-war generation discovered English pop in the form of skiffle: Lonnie Donegan, followed by guitar lead groups like The Shadows, Joe Meek and Tommy Steele. American artists also made their mark: Buddy Holly, Eddie Cochran, Chuck Berry, Gene Vincent, Jerry Lee Lewis.

I loved them all.

Steven and his family lived above their restaurant and he had his own room – something I found impressive – and so I'd go there and hang out with him. He had this guitar, a proper, real acoustic, bought by his dad down Denmark Street and something I could only dream of … It sat there on a stand and I was fascinated by it, but he was too shy to play it in front of me. I'd been desperate to play music, consumed by it, and had seen my dad singing Irish songs in the pubs with fiddle players, banjos, and watched carefully what they did. I yearned to join in, and wanted to play guitar. I tried to teach Steven how to play the D chord and always wanted him to let me have a go, show him what I'd picked up. I played 'Everyday' by Buddy Holly and the Crickets, and coaxed him into singing along.

We were close friends through our formative years. So much so that when I decided, aged 11, to run away from home, it was Steven's house I headed to.

I can't remember why I decided I'd had enough. Maybe Dad had the hump with me; maybe I just fancied a change. Things could be fraught at home, with discipline meted out by a belt and no jury to decide if you deserved the occasional thrashing Dad would decide to give out. It was always cramped there, never enough space, and I used to look for places to have some peace and quiet – that's why we loved the bomb sites so much, I suppose – it was about getting your own space, finding somewhere you could be the master of all you surveyed. So I ran away, and Steven's house was the only place I could think of going to.

I turned up one evening and knocked on the door. Steven's dad opened up and said, 'Hello, Johnny, what can we do for you? Bit late, isn't it …?'

I said, 'I've ran away, I ain't going back.'

He took me in, held my hand as I walked up the stairs, ever so gentle, into this room full of all these Greek Londoners, wizened old ladies gossiping over a table full of grub. He cooked me a steak and chips and then sent me home to my mum.

◆ ◆ ◆

Despite Dad's regular work, and Mum's work as a cleaner, we still lived
hand to mouth. I remember my mum had bought a pair of shoes off
the old lady in the basement. I was mortified. I was ashamed to go to
school because of the clothes I was wearing – it was one of the reasons I bunked off so often, I just couldn't face it. I was always wearing
my shoes out, scampering about, scuffing them up – it was a constant
annoyance for my folks – and I hated the short trousers they put me in.

I once found a blue suit in a bag on a dump and I took it home,
patched it up and it fitted me. I was about 12 and I thought it was
very trendy.

I remember feeling perpetually hungry. Much of my daily roaming
was in part, subconsciously, driven by hunger. Opportunities to eat
something were always seized on. Meals at home did not fill the hole in
my stomach and my adventures always had an underlying purpose – to
find something, somewhere to eat for nothing.

There was this shop on Pitt Street, up in Shoreditch, which I loved
the look of. They'd sell round teacakes in a red and silver foil wrap-
per. Sometimes I'd manage to raise the money I needed and I'd walk
in, bold as brass, go up to the counter and put on my best la-di-dah
voice, thinking if I talked like Burlington Bertie they wouldn't notice
the stick of sugar candy I'd filched on my way in. I'd eat it all before I
got home.

Mum used to send us down the shops to get things on tick. A
quarter-pound of ham or corned beef, with the promise we'd pay up
when Dad got in. It was too embarrassing for her, so she'd get us to go.
It was a bit of a dirty stroke, as we'd nick the shopkeeper's cakes as well,
but I didn't think of it that way at the time. He might've known and
taken pity on us. Anyway, he never refused us. I think he knew Dad
was in a trade so his money was safe, and if we owed him something,
we were sort of honour-bound to shop there. The bloke who ran our
local store had a whole neighbourhood in his pocket.

Each week, the milkman would come round to collect his bill, and Mum's would be significant, partly because me and my brother Terry loved to eat caramel wafers. The milkman sold them – and we would wake up early, catch him at the top of the street, and get them on tick, aware that at the end of the week there would be hell to pay when the bill arrived, tucked into the neck of an empty milk bottle.

Then there were school dinners – I loved them, I really did. You can't really, truly understand how much a kid looks forward to a hot meal if he isn't getting all he needs. It was a joy. My favourite was shepherd's pie, as you'd get lots of it, and then you'd have treacle sponge and custard. You'd get lots of that, too – and Mum would also make it at home. She'd wrap it up in a tea towel and steam it, and then pour golden syrup over it. It was gorgeous. And on a Sunday, she'd always lay out a nice spread for our tea.

The cockle man would come round with his barrow on a Sunday, too. I'd eat the winkles, picking them out with a safety pin. It reminds me now of snot. You'd get whelks and cockles and some salt and pepper and vinegar. For me, pie and mash was the really big treat. You could get it for two bob and there was a place down Nile Street, East Road, which was terrific.

We'd go up the Chapel Market and Mum would get us to carry her bags for her. We'd go to a place called Cheap Jacks and buy their broken biscuits off them.

Other establishments were out of our price range and, looking back, we already had a keenly tuned sense of a world of haves and have-nots. We'd go up to the Star Café on the corner of Westland Place and Lyle Street, but we couldn't afford to go inside. It was always full of people, well-turned-out office types, and we instinctively knew it wasn't for the likes of us.

We'd press our noses up against the window and gaze longingly at the cakes. There was a van that delivered their cheesecake. We'd queue up outside the van with milk formula tins in our hands and the driver would see us and he'd tip all the desiccated coconut off the trays into the tins, all the bits that had fallen of, the toppings ... and there would be these big blobs of cream. It was delicious. It was such a treat.

We were always after ways to turn a few bob from somewhere. Finding ways to earn money came naturally. There were opportunities known to every kid on every street.

There was the Corona pop man, who'd come round on a Sunday delivering. The bottles had a metal stopper and you'd get thruppence back on them. It was the same with the Tizer bottles, so I'd go out hunting them, gather them up and take them back to the sweet shop.

And there was still some rationing in place when I was a nipper. Mum would receive meat coupons. We would also buy cheap cuts of horse meat from the butchers to feed the dogs. I remember seeing the tripe laid out there on the butcher's slab – horrible-looking, rubbery stuff. I hated it, loathed it. It looked so disgusting.

But our family table couldn't be choosy. The things we used to eat, or Mum would try to feed us – she would cook up pigs' trotters for us, and I hated them too. Micky would hide under the table and I'd slip him the bits I didn't like.

Later, when I got back from a spell at a reform school, Dad and Mum had moved the family out to Leyton to a house with more room. Things were looking up. Dad bought a van, a 5cwt Thames van, which he used for work, and we had the house to ourselves – I shared my bedroom with my brother and that was OK.

My schooling was always troublesome. I was expelled from North-ampton when I swung a punch at the headteacher, Mr Hodgkinson. The abusive bastard had singled me out for some licks and I'd had enough. I didn't see why he should be allowed to thump me without any comeback. Something snapped and I decided, 'Fuck it, I'm going to get the first blow in.' I reached upwards and landed a punch on this coward. I was expelled and given an extra caning for my troubles.

Corporal punishment might have been legal, but it never sat right with me. You'd take it from your mum and dad, but not from anyone else. Not from some stranger. What right did he have? I wasn't taking it. They used to give you a slap around the face and it would set off the red mist. Sometimes it was a rap on the knuckles with a ruler, or they'd get out the strap or cane. They were all so sure of themselves and they felt they could do what they liked. That was my first impression of how authority was able to take control of you – they thought they were omnipotent. That's how I would describe it – they thought they had this innate right to behave like this. I couldn't understand that.

From there, I went to a secondary modern called Rising Hill. It was while at this school that I first handled a gun. I had joined the Air Training Cadets at the school. They had a hall in Rosebery Avenue, near Sadler's Wells, which they used for training. I went once a week for a time, enticed by the promise that the recruits would get to have a ride in a glider as part of the training – a promise that typically never materialised.

But I did get to handle and strip machine guns, an experience that stayed with me for many years. We'd be given Bren guns and Sten guns, and we'd learn to fill the magazines with bullets. They were the main two guns of the British Army and they were very basic. There is nothing more basic than a Sten gun. It has a lever, a spring and a magazine slot. That's it – that's all. Brilliantly simple, really. They either had a side magazine or a long, slim magazine. The Bren had a curbed magazine and the end of the barrel opened up.

I could fire single shots off them, or automatic ones. The Bren was meant to be mounted on a tripod, while the Sten was extremely light and had a skeleton frame.

I also got a bit of experience handling firearms when me and some mates signed up for the Territorial Army in Finsbury Park, on the understanding we'd get to shoot some rifles at a firing range. It sounded fun. We used a .22 rifle called a Martini. It was a single-shot rifle with a bolt. They taught us target shooting, showed us how we had to look down the sight – and I was a good shot. I enjoyed it for a few months.

We were given a very basic uniform and you'd have to Blanco the belt and polish the brass. They had gaiters and tunics. You had to buy boots in order to keep them, so I never got a pair of my own, but I loved to spit and polish the toe caps. There was a drill hall and I remember the noise of people stamping in unison – it was like a thunder clap.

We also went camping with the TA, but never much one for being told what to do, I found that the nonsense about army discipline ruined what should have been an enjoyable jaunt in the countryside for a load of London urchins. Laden down with duffel bags full of kit, we spent nights in tents at Dibgate in Kent. There was lots of parade, drill, awful boring bollocks, giving some bigger kid the chance to shout at little boys – that was what it was all about.

They had this punishment they called Jankers, which was marching up and down with your kit on, and then they'd make you stand guard and do guard duty right through the night. But the shooting range was fun and it made up for some of the more annoying things they got us doing.

◆ ◆ ◆

Despite my parents' careful eye, I managed to get myself into enough trouble that at the age of 13, in September 1961, I was sent to St John's Approved School in Tiffield, Towcester, for breaking into a shop. I stayed there for two years and left when I was 15.

The crime I committed to earn this detention hadn't gone the way my 13-year-old brain imagined it would. I had been caught in the act. I did it on my own. I didn't want to tell anyone what I was planning, and I thought I'd get a bit of a score off it, all to myself.

I'm not sure why I thought it was a good idea, but it was something I had heard discussed numerous times by boys I hung around with. The difference was they would talk about things, and I would go right on and do them. It's a part of my character that would have long-lasting impacts on my life and others' later on.

I chose a store in Haggerston, a tobacconist and sweet shop that looked easy enough to get into and would have rich pickings for my hot little hands. I'd got it worked out – I was going in through the roof. I went round the side of the shop and shinned up a drain pipe. I got on the roof – a semi-derelict mess that didn't look like it would keep the rain out, much less hold my weight. I made a hole to climb through.

I thought I'd been sneaky as fuck, a mastermind, and I'd soon be enjoying the proceeds, living it up with my ill-gotten gains, stuffed with chocolate and armed with plenty of fags and a load of other stuff I could sell to my mates. But I didn't get away with anything. I got caught pretty quickly.

The shopkeeper was in when I clambered through the roof. I'd chosen the place because it was a lock-up – it didn't have the owner living above. But there he was. He'd been done before and had decided to sleep overnight on the very night I decided to rob him. Maybe he'd had a row with his bird. Anyway, my first attempt at cat burglary ended the moment it began. The shopkeeper heard me coming and called the police, who showed up so quickly I'd hardly managed to clamber back out before they were on me.

The coppers chased me through back gardens, up and over walls, across flowerbeds and lawns and behind sheds as I tried to get away. They said I was like a Jack Russell, I was so quick and slippery. But they got me eventually.

By this age, I had already been convicted of three previous offences, which due to my tender years are no longer noted in my records, and I'm not entirely sure what they were. One entry does say I was fined 10s at Old Street Juvenile Court for attempted theft, but what theft I attempted no longer stands out in my memory when put up against all the others.

For my attempts to knock off the Haggerston tobacconist's, I was charged with being 'found in an enclosed yard for an unlawful purpose' and shop breaking. Before I was sentenced for this, they charged me separately with driving a car whilst under age – a conviction that saw me banned from driving for five years. It was an order I broke repeatedly once I'd been shoved through the juvenile criminal justice system.

So, this attempt at taking the untold riches of a rundown and dingy shop saw me moved to the approved school in Towcester. It was when I was at this school that I was given my first lessons in carpentry – but not before I had shown them my absolute determination that no one could hold me against my will.

Before they sent me to the approved school, they put me on remand in a place in Shepherd's Bush called Stafford House. I escaped from there – it wasn't too difficult. It was hardly Colditz. I climbed out a window and legged it.

But I did get caught quite quickly, which was all my own fault and hardly required a sleuth in charge of the manhunt. Of course, I went straight home, where they knew they'd find me – and I was put in a secure unit instead. It was horrible. They would only feed you bread and water.

I look back now and I realise, compared to other institutes I have graced with my presence, the experience at Tiffield was not wholly negative. My talent with my hands was recognised and respected for the first time. It gave me self-respect, something no one had ever told me I could have a piece of for myself.

I learnt some carpentry there. I made a pair of stepladders – decent job it was. We had a fellow called Beanie, who was the carpentry teacher. He took me under his wing. He was very nice to me. He knew I had an aptitude for it. He showed me how to sharpen chisels, how to take care of my tools and take pride in my work. He was a stern man, but he treated me well and I responded to it.

I suppose the introduction of an authoritative figure in my life, someone who offered me respect and earned it back, made a lasting impression. Beanie was certainly an inspiring teacher, no doubt working in trying circumstances in state-run approved and reform schools in the late 1950s and early '60s. He did something I can never forget – he ignited my lifelong passion for and ability in woodwork, something invaluable and which I nurtured during long years inside, later in life.

One project from my time with Beanie stays with me. Beanie decided to show us youths how to make canoes. I thought mine was a real work of art. I put this blue canvas round a wooden skeleton frame. We took them on a canal trip. We went 60 miles in them. I also helped Beanie build a double canoe. I'd paddle it with him and we'd go in the wake of a barge – and that was terrific, great fun. We'd camp out in the evenings. I loved it. We could stay out all night and then get back in the boat the next morning.

I actually quite liked that approved school, despite the pickiness about certain things and the shitty conditions. We stayed in these draughty old dormitories, where all the windows were broken. It was freezing. I remember I liked my blankets to be heavy and I always wanted to sneak an extra one from somewhere if I could manage it. They'd come round and check your blankets and strip them back – it was bloody cold in the winter.

But there were also weekends out in the countryside, fresh air and nature to commune with – something all new to the likes of me. We'd go out to a quarry and pick rosehips. We'd have these little bags you'd fill up, and whoever picked the most would get a prize. We'd go and find blackberries, clambering into the bushes, and in return we'd be given tickets you could cash in for what you'd gathered. They'd use the rosehips to make a syrup that you could pour over your rice pudding. It was delicious.

◆ ◆ ◆

When I was released, I went back to live with Mum and Dad, but again my time with them was going to be short. In September 1965, I was sent to a borstal in Rochester – a secure unit in the grounds of Rochester prison, where I would serve time fifty years later.

I was sent there from Bow Street Magistrates' Court. It was pretty soon after I'd got back home. I can't remember why I'd been nicked – it was something petty, stealing lead off a roof, I think.

In later years, I got my records from that time and saw the Rochester borstal staff called me 'extremely immature and resentful of authority'. They didn't hold on to me for long. About a month after I'd got there, I got away. I hopped it over a wall and ran and kept running. They didn't catch up with me until the following August, when I thought I was in the clear.

Whatever lesson it was I was meant to absorb, whatever it was they were trying to drill into me, it wasn't working. Despite being given what my records describe as a 'severe warning', I took off once more in September 1966 – though this time I was caught the same day – and then, the following April, when some other inmates and I were taken out for the day on a working party at Portland borstal, I scarpered again. I'd been moved to the south-west, in the belief that the further away from London I was, the less chance there would be that I'd get itchy feet and do a runner. But they were very, very wrong. I wasn't hanging around, ever.

And looking back, I know why. It was absolutely inhumane what they did to kids then. Rochester borstal was a brutal, horrible regime. I wouldn't hack it, I wouldn't do what they ordered me to, I wasn't having any of it from them.

I remember I was put on fifteen days of bread and water for escaping from Rochester. There was a punishment regime of ten weeks I had to complete, and then I was sent on to Portland Bay, Dorset, and ended up doing a year there.

I wasn't going to let them think they'd won, so I escaped from there too. I decided to go and have a look at the seaside when I was on the other side of the walls, and that's where they caught me – when I'd gone down to sit on the beach.

I was then sent on to another reform school, the Reading corrective centre, as a punishment – and it was a place you only got transferred to if they wanted to give you some severe straightening out. It was a tough place. You had to run about at 6 a.m. in the freezing cold. You had to do it in time, in step, and if you didn't, you got a whack. You had to do circuit training there, three times a day. Everything was physical. It was harsh. They thought by smashing the shit out of us each day we would somehow be born again into decent citizens, not fucking massively resentful about everything in society they represented to us. Reading was an awful place with nothing but horrible memories, a place whose regime was based on the most brutal of Victorian prison systems and was urgently in need of reform.

There were other reasons I hated it. The Reading borstal was right next to a biscuit factory, and the smell that wafted in over us was an awful thing to suffer when you were as hungry as we were. It was fucking torture, the smell of baking and chocolate and sugar melting. It was almost like a deliberate challenge to our state of minds.

It was closed in 1968, which goes to show what a horrible, brutal regime it was inside. The fact it was shut then – in 1968, when the standards for these things were nothing like they are meant to be today – speaks volumes. The place was a dangerous shithole run by abusive, bullying thugs.

I was given what was called a 'written discharge' from Rochester, which meant I had to stay at Reading for the remainder of my borstal sentence. By that time, I knew their regime and how to duck and dive. The one thing about Reading was there was always someone weaker than you, and if you were training in the gym or doing anything physical, like running round in time like soldiers, you would hold out for someone else to flag first, to start feeling the pain of the exercises, so the guards would clock them and you could avoid the heat. I can't stress enough how the staff's brutality caused everyone so much suffering and there was very little reform.

Reading had a really high suicide rate. Can you imagine? We are talking about a place for juveniles – and these youngsters, not much more than children, were killing themselves at a rate of knots.

The kids just could not hack it. I remember seeing a kid hanging off a window. The screws kept saying, 'Don't look, don't look', but you couldn't help it. There were people who would lock the doors of their cells from the inside and block them up so no one could get in – and then try to set fire to themselves. It made no difference. The staff were absolute fucking savages. They took pleasure in trying to outdo each other for their viciousness and bullying.

This old Victorian jail had doors with heavy old locks on them everywhere. One of the screws' favourite things was to take these big sets of cast-iron keys – it always struck me they were like the sort of thing you'd get at the Tower of London. They'd make you bend your head down and they'd whack you on the back of the neck with their bunches. It hurt so much. You weren't allowed to talk, to smoke, to do anything without risking some kind of physical violence as punishment. Later, I learned some of the guards got nicked for what they did – but as ever with these things, it didn't result in any convictions. No one has, as far as I know, been made accountable for the abuse they dished out to vulnerable young people.

◆ ◆ ◆

It was at Rochester that I met a boy who would become a close friend and later a close associate when, as an adult, I expanded the type of work I did on the wrong side of law. His name was Terry Harper. He was shrewd and clever and would think things out, while I would go crash, bang, wallop. That's why we were so successful later as bank robbers. We complemented each other.

Terry, or Hardy, as he would later be called by police, was also sent to Reading while I was there, and became a comrade in arms against the injustices of the system holding us. We looked out for each other, made sure the other was safe, and also, occasionally, made each other laugh – a vital thing to be able to do in hell.

Terry had grown up in Green Lanes, near Manor House. He was my age and we both recognised we possessed a similar outlook when it came to rules and regulations. I don't know why he was in borstal, but he came with that nickname 'Chopper', so it must have been some-thing to do with that. Doesn't sound great, does it? But he was my pal and I didn't care.

I was released from Reading in December 1967. Staff described in my records at the time of my release that their charge 'kept himself to very much to himself and was determined not to co-operate and benefit from training'.

I got home, got myself sorted out, said hello to the folks and my friends, and got to work. Dad gave me a job as a tiler. I managed to keep my nose pretty clean for the next two years, having Dad on my case with his work ethic, getting me up, getting me out, teaching me the tricks, giving me a wage. It was OK, and I stayed out of prison until I was nicked for a number of minor motoring offences – some linked to the fact I was disqualified while driving under age, some-thing I still scratch my head about. If I was under age, how could I be disqualified? I shouldn't have been behind the wheel in the first place. Anyway, as I was to learn, the law can move in mysteriously opaque ways when they think you're no good.

I had a happy homecoming after I'd served my time. My dog Micky pined for me and the family were thrilled to have me back. When I came home from borstal – and I'd been gone for nearly three years – we were out in Leyton, a place called Linley Road, a big, long street. I got to the end of the street and there Micky was, waiting for me out-side the house. He spotted me and he went absolutely berserk. It's one of my favourite memories. It took him an hour to calm down.

I got stuck into work for Dad. I was his labourer and I knew what to expect. I'd done weekends for him already. He was a hard taskmaster, but it was OK and the best offer I had. I didn't immedi-ately decide to work with him, though, maybe because I knew there would be no fucking about. I did a couple of other jobs first: I'd been an apprentice cabinet maker in Old Street, but I soon lost patience with it because all they wanted me to do was melt horse glue, sweep up and do a bit of beading. But I did pick up a few tips, watching the cabinet makers. I stuck it out for about three months, and then went to another cabinet maker in Hackney Road. Then I worked at Woolworths in Mare Street as a storeman, until I broke a pallet load of soft drinks and they sacked me. They gave me a week's notice. Whenever I got notice from one place, I'd just line up another job. There was plenty of menial work going. I got a job delivering the *Financial Times* in the City to offices and banks. I earned a few quid, so I bought a Lambretta scooter for £60 from Pride and Clarks in Brixton. I thought it looked great.

I was a bit of a Mod. I liked to listen to the Yardbirds, the Swinging Blue Jeans, The Hollies, The Who. I loved Otis Redding and Aretha Franklin, and loads of obscure British and American rhythm and blues. I loved The Shadows too, and The Supremes. I had their album *Reflections*. I was into guitar music and later on I gravitated to Creedence Clearwater Revival.

I had found and reconditioned a turntable to play my growing collection of music on. It was this old radiogram I'd spotted on a bomb site one day and so I took it home and got it working. That was something else. My own record player. It had one of those automatic playing arms, so you could put multiple records on at a time. I'd go to a bike shop called Beazley's in Murray Grove that also sold records or the stalls at Hoxton Market – they'd be selling singles for 1s 6d. I bought The Hollies' 'Just One Look' and rushed home to play it – I nearly wore that one out: we played it over and over.

I was an avid record collector. My mum and dad would get dolled up at the weekends to go out, and they'd get home invariably pissed with some friends, and they'd get me out of bed and make me DJ because I was the only one who had any records. I'd love it when their drunk mates would come back, as they would slip me half a crown.

I did other jobs too. I was a carpenter's mate for a bloke in Kilburn for a brief time. He was a funny old guy who smoked a pipe and he spent most of his time lighting it rather than working. It meant I didn't learn too much from him.

I think my later work as a getaway driver partly stemmed from an early appreciation of cars – and how to drive them fast – which definitely grew stronger around this time. I loved a good-looking car that had a bit of welly. Who didn't?

The first vehicle I ever drove was a tractor on a farm. It was on the Isle of Wight, and we'd gone there for a school trip. I was about 12 years old. The farmer asked us if we wanted a go, so I had a drive over some big open fields. You couldn't go wrong, there was nothing to crash into, and I remember the feeling – it was just so wonderful to be in charge of this great big bit of machinery, to be trusted. You weren't going to go anywhere fast on that. The steering was very heavy – you had to be pretty strong to steer it. And there was no throttle as such – there was a brake held on with a clip, and when you pressed it down and released it the tractor started moving. It was a single-gear thing.

Cars appealed to my sense of adventure, my interest in how things worked and my love of making mischief, of breaking rules that I didn't want to adhere to. I got banned when I was 15 – when I wasn't even at the age when I could get behind a wheel legally anyway. The ban was five years and I couldn't see the end of it – and I couldn't think of staying away from a car for five years, so I chalked up the motoring convictions, one after another.

Later, I would become very adept at taking cars that weren't mine, but I bought my first car for £15. Aged 16, I was still without a licence and still banned, but such legal niceties weren't going to stop me getting behind a wheel. It was a Vauxhall Wyvern. One of my dad's mates had a car showroom in Regent's Park Road, up Primrose Hill. I worked for him for a little while, tinkering under bonnets, and he sold me the car. Remember, this was an era of British car production, when the engines didn't need computer diagnostics to fix them, when your average person could pop up the bonnet, peer inside and fix mechanical issues as and when they emerged, which they frequently did.

I was no different to other men of my generation, people who didn't just like the look of cars, or just enjoy driving them, but understood how they ran. They had great old cars you could pick up for very little in those days. Big engines, leather seats, big sofa seats back and front, column shift gears. They were lovely to drive. I was always fiddling with my car, taking things apart, cleaning it. It was a big interest of mine. I had to know how things worked. I used to take everything apart – watches, TVs. That was how I fixed up my own record player – by being curious about how it worked, fiddling about with it, finding what was broken and fixing it up myself.

I later had a driving job – above board for once. I got a bit of work as a minicab driver in Weedington Road, Queen's Crescent, from a mate of mine called Charlie Howlett. It had a garage next door, run by a man called David Romaine, which was handy for fixing things. I bought a Humber Hawk. A lovely car, it was. Two bob a mile, we'd charge. By the time you'd paid rent to the cab firm and put your petrol in, it wasn't a great earner but I enjoyed driving about. It helped me learn a lot about London, about the streets, shortcuts and quick ways about – so it helped me in my later trade. It's all gone now, all those streets, all the freedom to drive about – it's all one-way systems, cameras, bus lanes and restrictions today.

So I had a clean nose, a good car and a record collection. I felt I could start enjoying life as a young man in Swinging London.

I used to go out picking up girls: we'd go to the Monarch and the Crowndale in Camden Town, get on the booze and have a laugh. There was the White Swan in Tottenham, the Duragon in Hackney. There was another pub in Hoxton also called the Monarch where we could drink into the early hours, and I'd often go out drinking wherever my dad was. By now, the family and I had moved back to Kentish Town and we had a place in a block of flats in Islip Street.

Criminality was not part of any long-term plan I had. I didn't set out to be fucking Thomas Crown or anything. I had dreams. I loved tennis and was bloody good at it, so I wanted to be a tennis player, but I was never encouraged. My dad once asked me on my birthday what I wanted as a present, and I said a tennis racquet. He said, 'No, that's a posh man's game – here are some boxing gloves.' He wanted to get my face punched up at Shoreditch Town Hall. They held matches there for 30s a bout. I didn't fancy that much. Dad wanted me to get in the ring and get stuck in, but I said, 'No thanks. Fuck that.' Seemed a mug's game, getting walloped for others' satisfaction and other people's wage packets. Not for me.

Later, as my skills behind a wheel saw me in great demand, I harboured dreams of being discovered as a racing driver. And I was soon to know what it's like to have to drive a car fast with others in pursuit. It came about when I had a chance meeting with an old friend.

I bumped into Terry at the City Club – it was off City Road, and a bloke called Bruce Greenfield owned it. I was about 23 or 24 and hadn't seen Terry since borstal. He rocked up into the club with a fistful of cash and a proposition. He was making good money working for a gang who held up payrolls on a Friday night, did post offices and knocked off the odd bank van. He trusted me. I was in.

My first ever stick-up job, not long before Tel and I met up, was relieving a factory owner of the week's wages. This bloke had a place round Fitzrovia. I'd heard from a girl I dated and who worked there that her miserable boss drew money out of a bank on Tottenham Court Road towards the end of the day and then made his way through the back streets to his office above the factory floor. I'd found out my target went to the same bank each Friday afternoon and then divvied up the wages for his staff into brown envelopes.

I waited for my chance. I watched him a couple of times, knew where he was going, and also eyed him up and down. I was confident I could take him, no problem. And I did. I jumped him on a cold winter's Friday and made off with a bag containing around £600 – a fortune for me back then, but probably more importantly, I'd broken my duck and got clean away.

From here on in, I decided to earn a living taking other people's money with menaces. Meeting Terry came at a good time. It was the start of a new life forged by guns and danger, of high living, fast cars and dreams of an early retirement with pilfered riches beyond my wildest dreams. It was the start of my life as a career criminal, as one half of a duo the police would dub Laurel and Hardy.

THREE

Robbery with the threat of violence was a frequent occurrence on the streets of London in the 1960s and '70s. When I was a young man, there were various gangs operating across the capital. The allegiances between these gun-toting stick-up merchants were fluid enough for joint operations to be launched by different configurations.

Work was offered if someone had proven themselves to be good under the stress of the job. Recommendations were made, character references crucial, in the high-risk world of robbery with the threat of violence. My way in was through Terry. He knew me and trusted me, and he had proved himself already, so his word held weight.

But the idea that the 1960s and '70s were when it all started, as some of the fresher bandits I met in prison seemed to think, was absolute nonsense. My generation wasn't the first, and won't be the last, despite how it's changed, what with all the different security methods.

Basically, armed men up to no good were not a new phenomenon in London. It had a long history and had been a form of crime that was rampant in the immediate post-war years, when I was a kid. This was fuelled by the availability of weapons from the stocks of the war industry, and people who had been shown how to use them in the name of King and Country. These were hard men who had been to the Continent and shot up Nazis. They had seen things and tested their courage. They came back knowing how to handle themselves, handle fire arms, and with an idea that life was very short, very cheap, and you should try to make the best of it.

But London's gangland culture, looking back now through the prism of time, looked particularly prominent in the 1960s. Maybe it's that a good robber is never known about, so those who came before were excellent blag merchants. Maybe it's because it was a period that has been glamorised through the telling of the stories of people like the Krays, the Great Train Robbers and Billy Hill.

And in those early days, before I got properly started, I was moving in a world where every so often you'd hear a tale or two from a bloke at a bar who would be flush and buying the rounds. It was common knowledge that commercial robbery was good for those looking for a score, and some of the close-to-the-wind blokes around our way were at it.

I'd tried my hand at it as a youngster, when I broke into that tobacconist's and got nicked, but premises, locked up at night, were easy enough pickings if you did a bit of homework. Find a way in when the staff have left, take whatever isn't nailed down, and off home you go.

But when a burglar or robber is on to a good thing, eventually the law and insurance firms get wise. After a year-on-year increase in burglaries, the falling cost of buying a safe and the insurers' diligence in apportioning blame changed the game for us. It added a new element of skill.

The professional safe breaker, who could take on sophisticated locks, was a respected underworld figure. It was after 1945 that the cracksmen emerged as a force. The generation who had gained experience using explosives during the war thought, 'Why fiddle with locks when you can quickly remove the back with a well-placed bang?'

The margin for error and the danger of blowing up more than you'd bargained for meant that burning holes with an oxyacetylene torch then became a popular method. But the manufacturers got wise to that, too, and safes became further reinforced: it was a race between those hoping to relieve a business of its takings or a bank of its deposits, and those seeking to scupper criminal intent.

And with this, by the mid-1960s, the scourge of the stick-up hit London like never before. There had been that spike in armed robbery after the Second World War, but it had been a speciality for the select few and was a fairly insignificant racket in terms of income for the gangs. As I said, back then, for the ones who came before me and my mob, commercial burglary was big-time stuff. Black marketeers would raid warehouses for cigarettes, alcohol, meat, nylons and anything else they could sell on quickly – and they would sometimes be armed. But they didn't walk up to a security guard and use their weapons as the first port of call. They would much rather go in through a loading bay that an insider had made sure wasn't properly shut and be well away when the raid was discovered the following morning.

But the change in culture saw brazen gunmen walk directly into a bank, wave a weapon about and demand their bag be filled. It would take two minutes of high risk, another five to get clear in the high-powered stolen car outside, and then it would be lazy afternoons in dark pubs to spend the takings. The stick-up craze was helped by the fact that all you needed was something that looked a bit like a handgun and some desperation mixed with bottle. It widened the field.

By the 1970s, when I was active, armed robbery in London had risen by 350 per cent in under a decade. It wasn't helped by members of the Metropolitan Police's Flying Squad often being in the pay of those lifting bank notes from cash drawers. Some of the crews barely bothered loading their weapons, as they knew the police weren't going to be arriving pronto, because if they did, someone wouldn't be getting their bung.

And the game was further skewed in the favour of the gunman if they could put a few streets between themselves and shocked bank staff without being apprehended. There were no DNA tests that could reveal the identity of those behind the discarded stocking. CCTV was in its infancy. There were no time locks, no dye to make notes unusable, no GPS tracking systems, and so it was no wonder that criminals of my generation thought the odds were worth a go.

As security has improved, it's also worth noting that the friendly neighbourhood building society is pretty much a thing of the past: in thirty years, around 10,000 high-street branches have closed, and a similar number of post offices too. It means there are simply fewer to target, and the ones left standing tend to be bigger and offer higher levels of security. I noticed that after I got out. I'd walk up and down the high street and, by habit, the banks and building societies used to stand out. But they all seem to have gone – swallowed up by internet banking and the banking executives' greed, cutting costs to pad out their own fat backsides.

The loose gang of around eight people I worked with were professionals. I didn't do any work with someone I didn't like the look of, or didn't trust. It meant we really didn't need to use our firearms for anything but to deliver a very serious warning to whoever was holding the bag of money we had designs on. I told the jury in my murder trial I hadn't shot a gun on a job before 1975. But at the time, there were plenty of others willing to use their weapons – and it enhanced the risk, as the Flying Squad saw it as a further escalation of the war taking place on British streets.

Our place in the public mind was interesting. It was affected, I reckon, by the American gangsters of the 1920s and '30s, who were ingrained in the British cultural imagination through Hollywood. This type of crime was also glamorised by British crime capers such as Michael Caine's turns in *The Italian Job* and *Get Carter*, and celebrity figures like the Krays. It meant some muppets did try to get work, thinking it was all fun and games, guns and glory, but of course it fucking wasn't. I hated that – I thought they were muddying the waters a bit, queering the pitch. But then again, it gave the Old Bill more people to chase, so maybe it took the heat off us.

Despite the hype, and professionals earning headline-grabbing paydays, genuinely large scores were rare and required detailed planning and, more often than not, inside intelligence. Yet that encouraged a plethora of one-off desperadoes who fancied having a go themselves.

This rise in armed crime was a mixed blessing. The Old Bill were now increasingly under the microscope and the Home Office were after results, but it also created a welcome distraction. The one-off armed heist merchants would get hold of a gun and try their luck, seduced by the idea of lifting a sack of currency from their local high-street branch in the morning and swanning about the French Riveria behind a pair of expensive sunglasses by dinner time. They might have been game, but they were always such amateurs, who only did one part of the job – brandishing the gun and grabbing the loot. They didn't think through the details – the trustworthiness and bottle of the others involved, the sourcing of weaponry from someone who won't squeal, the stealing of a high-powered car, the getaway route, the safe house to lie low in and the laundering of the cash. These people gave the Flying Squad better arrest figures, but also frustrated the police, as they knew for every Johnny-Come-Lately they nicked, the real big timers were gathering their wits for another operation and were still at large.

London was a nest of criminals, and the police were reacting. Across the nation, the Old Bill were getting uppity and more aggressive. The police were becoming less likely to enquire the purpose of your business and more likely to just fucking shoot it out with you.

I followed the trial of Howard Wilson, a former copper-gone-rogue and his two accomplices, Jon Sim, another former plod, and Ian Donaldson. They were behind the Linwood bank job in Glasgow in 1969, a crime that made headlines about a new wave of gun slinging. The trio robbed a branch of the Clydesdale Bank, lifting £14,000, and in the process shot three police officers – killing Detective Constable Angus Mackenzie and Police Constable Edward Barnett, and seriously injuring Inspector Andrew Hyslop.

Wilson was a policeman of ten years' standing but had quit under a cloud over missed promotions. He was running a greengrocer's, but this went belly up and, facing bankruptcy, he decided he'd make money in a different way.

Their first job was a success. Using a pistol acquired via a contact at a shooting club, they lifted £20,000 from the British Linen Bank in Williamwood in the summer of 1969. They had recruited a young man called Archie McGeachie as a driver. They got away, and laid low so as not to arouse suspicions.

But by Christmas, the cash had been swallowed up by Wilson's failing businesses, so they planned a second blag. Before they went into action, Wilson asked McGeachie to join them again. McGeachie refused, and on 23 December 1969 he disappeared from his house. He hasn't been seen since. At the time, the River Clyde's Kingston Bridge was being built. Just like it's said that the concrete of London's A40 West Way flyover contains the remains of a number of people who had crossed gangs, McGeachie's body was rumoured to have been dumped in one of the bridge's supporting stanchions.

The raiders didn't take this as an omen that they should call off the job. Instead, they lifted over £14,000. It went wrong as they unloaded suitcases of cash from a car outside Wilson's home. Opposite, buying a newspaper in a shop, was Inspector Hyslop. He knew Wilson from the force – and had never trusted him. He saw the men and went over to take a look.

Wilson greeted his former colleague and invited him in for a whisky. The officer obliged – and when inside the flat, he asked to see what was in their suitcases. Wilson reacted quickly: he shot Hyslop in the face, paralysing him. As the critically injured officer slumped to the floor, two constables rushed in. Wilson didn't hesitate – he shot both officers in the head. One managed to stagger into the bathroom, while Wilson stood over Mackenzie, who was still alive. He discharged his pistol into the injured officer at point-blank range, killing him.

Wilson's accomplices were found guilty of armed robbery, while Wilson got twenty-five years for murder. The reaction was huge. The death penalty had only been abolished two weeks before his conviction, and a demonstration led by the families of the officers called for Wilson to hang. He escaped the noose, but spent years in high-security cells and earned a reputation as a troublemaker. After serving thirty-three years, he was released in 2002, aged 64. I later saw the man who killed two coppers get parole – it was controversial at the time, and fucked me off massively as I was still inside with no hope of clemency. I was fucking furious, not because I thought he should have stayed in for life, but because I was tormented by the idea that they could let that fucker out but not me.

Such events splashed across the news and with the movement of cash from the Royal Mint to banks and post offices having security procedures more in common with the Wild West than what happens today, it was tempting for anyone with a big pair of bollocks to embark on a career that carried big risks in return for the prospect of huge rewards.

Robbing banks also meant not having to take an item of value and convert it into cash, though my mates and I knew many, and worked with many, who did. If you went down Hatton Garden, and knew where to look, it was a good place to fence, or use hot bank notes to buy gold and silver. These bits could then be sold on, pawned or kept for a rainy day.

There were key players. The famous Moshe Riyb, known as the King of Hatton Garden, walked the streets of London's precious stones and metals district and would pay cash for anything you offered him. Such a character could be helpful when there were candlesticks to get rid of – but also when there was £500 in a top pocket that was best converted into something else of value while things cooled down. He would buy anything, from your grandmother's diamond engagement ring to a crate of bullion lifted from a bank. When he was finally raided by customs officers – the police had a long-standing arrangement with Customs and Excise that the latter could take the lead on crime in their patch – they found around £2 million worth of gold and his office door propped open with a lump of solid silver, the melted-down proceeds from scores of small house break-ins.

◆ ◆ ◆

Over that drink in Farringdon Road, in a quiet corner, Terry revealed how he was earning a living. He told me how he had been introduced to a loose crew of well-organised men who were leading raids against banks and post offices – and judging by the wedge of notes in his inside breast pocket and the 3.5-litre Rover Coupé outside, it was going well.

I was intrigued, and when Terry mentioned they needed someone handy behind the wheel, I was on board. I could drive. I liked to drive. I could drive fucking fast, well and safe. And I needed some money, adventure and a purpose. I liked Tel. He was my kind of person.

To the modern ear, my short career as a bank robber sounds like something from *The Sweeney*. I prided myself on my ability as a getaway driver, combining skills behind the wheel with a cabby's knowledge of the streets that my crew and I would prowl.

As I said earlier, because of the spike in hold-ups that I was no doubt partly responsible for – with places getting knocked off on a weekly basis – the police and the banks were doing whatever they could to try to fight back. The Flying Squad were driving fast cars and were armed, too. They were getting better at it. In the early days I could leave them for dust, but later they got a bit more adept at handling their motors and gave us a bit more of a challenge.

But they couldn't be everywhere at once, and intelligence-led policing could only go so far. The robbers' code meant that if they did get a tip-off, it was often a red herring, a wild goose chase, to draw attention away from where a real heist was due to take place.

We knew that confronting a guard carrying someone else's cash across a pavement with a handgun and a well-barked order usually ended in our favour. The question was how to get as much of it as possible in the shortest amount of time. The banks would split their cash up into different bags, and they brought in a new rule a while after Terry and I got going. We were hitting them so hard that only a limited amount was being carried. For a time it was £25,000 – and then they cut that back to £15,000.

We lived with a constant eye out for a possible job, alongside the ones that we spent a good deal of time planning. Our state of prepared-ness – and the risks we were willing to take – made it even harder for the police to react. Randomness acted in a bank robber's favour more often than not. If we had no idea when we'd do our next score, how could the Old Bill know?

On our daily excursions, driving around, we got an eye for the vans we were looking for. They were managed by Securicor, Security Express, Group Four and Brinks Matt. They were the major money carriers for the banks. All had different vans and we could recognise them, spot them from miles up the road. And when they parked up, you had to know if they were either picking up or dropping off. You had to work out if they were going in or out, or there was a risk you'd jump them and end up with an empty box.

We didn't wear masks at first. We had this barber who'd make us wigs and moustaches instead. They were terrific, really lifelike, and could be removed pronto once the bags were safely in the back seat or boot.

It was a good way to earn money, and Tel and I caught the eye of some respected firms. It was this track record that led me to play a key role in a job that would make headlines. In the summer of 1973, a group of accomplices and I decided to hit the *Sunday Mirror*'s payroll.

Every Friday was payday for the staff at the newspaper's offices and print works on the Gray's Inn Road. We knew that they paid in cash. We knew that inside that block was a serious amount of money and that, with thought, care and a pair of bollocks, it would be ours.

They had a security guard on the door in a uniform and we studied people going in and out. We saw that if the people going in acknow-ledged the doorman, he didn't challenge them. It seemed like if you said, 'Hello, mate', he assumed he knew you, and you were waved past. He must have seen thousands of people walk through the doors each day, nod, and that was that. It was too easy.

My four accomplices and I decided to hit as stacks of cash were being counted out and placed in pay packets in the cashier's office. We had to get a big holdall through that front door, full of guns. We had to get up about five flights. We'd been watching and we knew the money went to an office upstairs – we saw a guy go in and take a lift, so we watched where the lift stopped.

But our secret, careful reconnaissance was a waste of everyone's time. We found out that everything was literally signposted inside, like an invitation to make yourselves at home and take whatever you fancied. There was a big sign saying 'Cashier's Office'. Come along this way, it seemed to say, and take your fill. So we did.

◆ ◆ ◆

Getting hold of shotguns was relatively easy. I'd buy them off people with country properties. Handguns were harder. They had to be bought through word of mouth. I once got myself a Beretta. I bought it off a bloke who worked for the council. I don't know how he'd come across it – maybe it was nicked from the army. It had a proper little leather holster, too, and a spare magazine. I used to have a drink with him at the Tunnel Club in Belsize Lane, Belsize Park. It was a good little bar – in a basement and visited by people of interest. A good place to let your hair down if you fancied it, or have a meeting that wouldn't be noticed. And that was how it was – you'd be having a drink with someone, they'd get a bit loose tongued and friendly, and then such things would come up in conversation.

That Beretta was lovely, and very easy to conceal. He told me he'd take £200 for it. I thought, 'Deal.' I'd probably have given him a bit more because, once I'd held it, I had to have it – it was fantastic, light, reliable.

There were handguns to be had back then. Now you'd have to pay thousands of pounds. They were also proper originals – nowadays they're usually something that has been adapted, messed about with, designed to fire blanks, so worked over by some backyard gunsmith, which itself holds a number of dangers. First, there's the risk that the bastard might have done something wrong to it – you don't want a gun to go off without your say-so, as I was to spend the majority of my adult life cursing. Then there's a good chance a gunsmith is known to the police, or will eventually become known to the police. They aren't crooks normally, just nerdy blokes who have a shed and a workshop and like to play toy soldiers. If the police put on any heat, they usually spill what's what. The ones who don't are cherished and looked after by the fraternity – they are rare and vital to the trade.

It's surprising how many people have a load of armaments secreted about their houses. They'd be wrapped up in an oily rag and then buried under someone's floorboards. It wasn't just crooks like me. Like my council worker mate, people came across weapons from all sorts of places and picked them up off all sorts of people. Sometimes you'd buy one from someone who'd had their dad's old army revolver tucked away in a bureau and realised it shouldn't be lying around there, and that it was worth the price of a week's holiday. So they'd ask about and eventually word would reach the likes of me.

And you would have what was called a 'rest up' – it was a flat which you had for the sole purpose of storing guns. My sister Jackie would hide some behind a panel in her bathroom. I used to give her a little cut every time we took them out or put them back again.

For the *Mirror* job, we'd retrieved our guns from various spots on the morning of the heist. We didn't want to have anything incriminating on us until the last possible moment, knowing how much the plod liked to give one of us a tug if they saw us out and about. Tel and I got ours from a lock-up on an estate in Holloway and were ready to go.

A fresh car was waiting out the back of the *Mirror*'s headquarters in Holborn. When we thought it was time – mid-afternoon on a Friday – we just walked brazenly in with our bags. We said, 'Good day' to the person on the door and made out we knew where we were going. We timed it for when we'd seen the cash going into the offices. They had a special knock they used so the staff would open up – and we would be waiting. We went into a toilet and stood on the seats of the loos so no one would know we were in there, and one of us kept a lookout. We had him at the door, listening, counting the steps, waiting to hear the knock. We didn't want to strike until we could get all of the money. The lookout came back and said he wasn't sure how many times the bloke carrying the cash had been back and forth. He'd lost count.

So there we were, perched on the bogs, getting cramp, the nerves jangling and adrenaline shooting through us. The lookout sounded like he'd lost his bottle as well as the count. We'd seen it before – someone you've brought in on a say-so starts twitching, talking fast, finding excuses why the stars aren't aligned that day. We looked at each other, cramped up in the loos, and said, 'Right, we know there's a big number gone in, whatever the weather.' We made the decision – 'Fuck it, let's just strike now' – and we timed it just right.

We appeared on the guard's shoulder, armed to the teeth. As the bag carrier knocked on the door, we all pushed into the office and they had all the money out on the desks, ready to be put into packets.

'Bingo,' I thought as I scanned the room, checking out the old biddies we were about to rob, sizing up if there were any among them who might need to be brought down a peg. No – to a person, they were shitting themselves, eyes wide open, rabbits in headlights. They all had a strip-light pallor, looked like they'd caged up together in this office for decades, waiting for something like this to happen. It no doubt helped that none of them seemed to care we were taking all those little brown envelopes full of notes they had been filling.

I looked at the cashiers filling up these packets, carefully ticking off each receipt, and I had one of those moments of pure clarity. For me, those small pieces of paper with the queen on them represented something deliciously macho, something irrepressibly attractive. In the faces of those terrified bean counters, I saw a bewilderment, as if each frown was asking me directly what on earth could possibly be so valuable that I was willing to threaten someone I'd never met before with a deadly weapon and risk my own freedom to satisfy my thirst for what they had.

I soon snapped out of this train of thought, came back to the real world. We told everyone to get down on the floor – I remember how slowly they seemed to follow our instructions, as if they'd all lost control of their motor skills and had bad backs, hips and knees. I watched them lower themselves down, pinning their faces to the carpet tiles, shaking as they did so. We were their masters, like a pack of lions snarling round some knock-kneed grazer we'd taken down: perhaps I didn't understand it so much back then, but the feeling of authority when you reach this point is overwhelming. I came to identify this later as a key reason I was addicted to the blag: that moment when the person in front of you says, 'You win' and you are in complete control, which translates into you walking away, unchallenged, with a bag stuffed full of tickets to daydreams.

We scooped up all the cash laid out on their desks and what was in the safe, too – it was at the back of the office, completely in view, tucked into what had once been a fireplace. 'Hello,' I said. 'What have we here …?' Its door was half open, and I noticed it as we were about to leave. Inside were bundles of £50 notes and I was almost overcome with sheer wide-eyed greed as I pulled them out and shoved them into a bag. Genuine buzz. Makes me laugh now, thinking about it – one of the others came and gave me a hand and lifted a sack out onto his back, like a regular swag man. He was ecstatic – thought he'd landed us a serious contribution. Turned out that bag was full of luncheon vouchers, worth 20p each. We never let him forget it.

We gathered up all the cash – bundles and bundles and bundles of notes, and even rolls of coins – and were in and out in about three minutes. As we left, we yanked the phones out of the walls and locked the door behind us, taking the key. It was a pretty pointless thing to do in hindsight, as they must have had another key inside the room, but if it bought us another two minutes, that could make all the difference between living it up on the proceeds or getting your collar felt.

We had recced the building and we knew we could take the back stairs out to our second car. What we didn't know – couldn't have known – was that, as we left, there were loads of workers coming up the other way. The stairwell was packed.

But nobody challenged us or hassled us; no one paid us any attention. We just looked like a group of blokes in a bit of a hurry.

We got to the ground floor, found the double doors out into the fresh air and went across to the loading bay where our car was. The first leg of the job safely completed, we all piled in, me behind the wheel. I drove about fifteen minutes to our next stop, where we changed cars.

After putting some distance between us and all those shocked *Mirror* cashiers, the gang split and we went our separate ways. One of us had been charged with taking the cash to a safe house, and we had agreed to stay well away from each other for some time, until a prearranged meet-up to sort out the proceeds at a later date.

It was a really great feeling, knowing we'd hit payday. I know some people think it's an easy way to make money – wave a gun about – but a lot of the time, it took a lot of fucking bottle to do it. I remember a couple of guys had to sit on the loo for thirty minutes beforehand because they were shitting themselves so much. It was never a coward's way to make money. You really had to steel yourself. You were putting your life into the lap of the gods.

And you really didn't want anyone you were with losing their bottle when you were halfway through a job, as it would be a liability for you and everyone else. But all these feelings evaporate when you've reached the point of no return, so you'd work efficiently, without fear. When you got the money, there was a real buzz about it, and when you got the money home safely – well, you can imagine. There's the adrenaline come-down that hits you, and then the idea that you've actually gone and done it and the thought of all that lovely lolly to fill your pockets with.

Weeks later, we all met up again and sorted out who was owed what. It was about £50,000 in cash, and my cut was about £12,000. We'd gone to a workshop on a little road off the North Circular, and we used it to divvy it up. We didn't stay long – just enough time for the take to be counted and cut into five parts, minus any general expenses, and then you'd split. You'd knock on the door, they'd hand you your cut and then you'd go, no questions. That was how it worked.

◆ ◆ ◆

But once the money was in my hands, despite my earlier caution, I wasn't one to sit quietly on what I'd made. I was young. I did lots of things. I'd go and buy a nice car, or a gold watch. I bought a house in Walderslade, down in Kent, with some of the proceeds. I used a mate's dad to buy the property. He knew where the cash was coming from, but his wife didn't have a clue. The house was only £14,500, so I handed him the notes and he sorted it out for us. It was quite sad: he was very ill, on his way out, but he was willing to help in return for a little touch for his trouble.

I liked a decent car. I had a Corvette Stingray, a two-seater, bought out of a newspaper. It was 7½ litres, so it was really powerful – you could get a wheel spin out of it at 130mph if you put your foot down. Metallic blue and left-hand drive, it was an American car someone had imported. I liked that sort of thing.

I part exchanged it at an Aston Martin showroom owned by a man called Arthur Mafia in Barkingside. That one was maroon, a second-hand Aston DBS Lagonda, leather and a wooden veneer, with a big engine – nice car. One of the novelties was it had a built-in phone. I used to phone my girlfriend Marilyn on the way home to ask her to get the dinner ready! We thought that was a hoot.

That was what I wanted to do – buy a good house and good car, and find a way of making my money work for me so I wouldn't have to be out on the blag long term. The house was in a nice area. It had a lovely garden with a 12ft wall round it and an arched doorway leading out into some woods. It had all the lights, fittings, fixtures. It had two big lions at the top of the stairs going down into the front door. I even thought about buying out the people next door and turning it into one big house.

I had plans. My girlfriend was pregnant with our daughter Sarah – she was born in that house. Despite what you might call an unconventional way of earning a living, I started to settle down into a pattern of domesticity, when I wasn't holding up banks at gun point.

◆ ◆ ◆

I didn't always work with the same people in my career as a bank robber. I met new parties, forged alliances across London's underworld. We worked with some people in north London, but also in the south, too. We didn't stick with one firm. When the word got round that you were good, you'd get offers from others. We went where the talent was.

But I did forge a special relationship with my main man, my main accomplice, Terry. It isn't easy to work out quite the number of jobs we did together as a pair. I'm a bit shy about it and still don't want any comeback, and the fact is, it was some time ago now, even if they are moments you think you'll remember for ever. But let's say it was a good number – well into double figures. I just had complete trust in Terry, and that made it much easier to work.

I knew I'd never leave him on the pavement. There were some times when the balloon would go up and the heat came on and you'd just go into survival mode. Our maxim was never leave anyone behind. It was like being a soldier. You would never leave a soldier, your pal, in a combat zone.

Terry and I had a particularly strong bond, and that's what made us so successful as a two-man team, which we became when we split from bigger, major gangs. And it meant we could work all year round. The work was there and we were hungry for it. We thought, 'We might as well make hay while the sun shines.'

There was this thing among the fraternity that working in the summer months had in the past been seen as especially risky for armed robbers. Security guards would become suspicious if they saw someone loitering in a trench coat, overdressed for a hot day, which could mean they were concealing a sawn-off shotgun.

The guards weren't armed. They had truncheons, big fucking mahogany sticks that would break your skull if you got a whack, but they never drew them. We used to say to them, 'It's not your money, mate. Don't get involved. Just hand it over and we all go home smiling.' And the shock of someone pointing a gun at you had a pretty decent impact, to say the least.

Once in a while we would find someone who didn't want to roll over – and when that happened, we had to prove to each other we were good for this line of work, not just mouth. There was this one guy at Clapton Pond, up in Hackney, who came back at us. It was just me and Terry. I was in the car with the engine running. He got out to tackle the guard. There was a scuffle and so I thought, 'Fuck this, I'm wading in too.'

He shouted at me, 'Just get back in the car, get back in the car – I've got this!'

He did as well. Gave the fucker a good smack, down he went and off we went with his bags. Terry was a good friend. He knew what he could do and didn't expect anyone else to cover for him.

It only made us more confident, and it showed as we got more brazen. We once did two vans in a day. We were coming back from doing a bit of work down in the south-west of town and it had gone perfectly. We saw another van as we headed back to north London and we thought, 'Fuck it, we'll have that as well.'

We made more money than we knew what to do with. We had it stashed in a fridge full of cornflakes boxes. I had a suitcase of cash which I left with a friend and he started dipping into it. I'd given him a bit of it anyway.

But after a long series of blags, Terry and I did start to think about retiring. We'd made a fortune and spent a fortune, and then made it back again. It was time to seek a new way to earn a living and enjoy the proceeds, rather than risk it all on another spin of the wheel.

We decided to quit at the beginning of 1975. We'd been at it for about three years and, while we knew the Old Bill were after us, they hadn't got enough to act. We were set up now, so we chatted about it and agreed, 'Yeah, time to pack it in.'

Retirement sounded weird but that was what it was. We'd bought nice houses – he had one in Enfield, I had mine in Kent – we had good motors and large stashes of bank notes to spend. So we quit. I did my house up, landscaped it, made it lovely. I decorated, I did the shelves, I tinkered and all seemed well for a few weeks.

But we got bored. Tel phoned me up and said, 'You all right?'

I said, 'Yeah, I'm all right, I suppose.'

'What you up to?' he said.

'Nothing,' I answered, and he said the same.

We were both OK, but we were fucking bored. So we thought, 'Let's get the tools out' and off we went. The retirement lasted bugger all. Let's be honest – robbing banks was an addiction. It was a habit we couldn't kick easily, just like that. It was about adventure and adrenaline and we were bloody good at it. To be honest, we couldn't keep ourselves away.

◆ ◆ ◆

I suppose in those two years of really intensive activity, we must have done one every fortnight. There were a few times we'd come away with nothing but that was the luck of the draw. There were a couple of times when we weren't sure if they were picking up or dropping off, but we thought, 'Fuck it, can't wait around all day. Let's get this one done and move on.'

We hit a bank in Mitcham, Tooting Bec, one September morning. A large secure transport van would pull up on a regular basis and they would do a big old drop. It was worth about £150,000 and for this one we were with a gang made up of a couple of north Londoners and a couple from south of the river. It was a big packet of money – you could hardly get your arms round it. Sometimes the workers would carry boxes or they'd use carpet bags. The manager would come and open the side door and the guard would carry the cash in. We could see the office through this window and we were puzzling how we could get at all this money – we'd seen them make several drops and we decided we wanted all of it, not some of it. We realised we could get in through a window rather than in through the front door.

We opened the window with a scaffold pole and climbed in – and there it was, wrapped up in cellophane for us to pick up.

And then the alarm went off.

Outside, guards were alerted and came to investigate. There was a van with a couple of Alsatian guard dogs, and their handlers came too. It didn't end well – the guards found us and told us to stop where we were. We raised our handguns and a stand-off ensued.

It got bad. Lots of shouting and threats, and we said to them, 'Whatever you do, don't let those fucking dogs go. You let them go and we're not responsible for what happens next.' The guards disobeyed that order and one of the guys I was with fired at a dog.

I remember the guard shouting, 'Fucking hell, you've killed Satan!' That dog was the only thing that ever got hurt. I still think about that poor little sod now.

We'd showed we meant it and the guards backed off. So we pegged it with the cash and bundled into a van we had waiting. We screeched off, drove as fast as we could to a small street that had a pedestrian railway bridge. We dumped the van, grabbed the cash and legged it over the bridge where we had a car waiting on the other side. Then we calmly made our way back into town and everything went fine from then on.

◆ ◆ ◆

The death of Satan didn't put us off for any length of time. Tel and I decided to hit a bank on Muswell Hill Broadway. It was a small one – a little branch. As you came up into Muswell Hill, it was on the right. It was a busy shopping street, but with nice clear roads coming off it we could make a getaway down the hill. We were going to take out a vault.

That day we made an error, though. We thought it opened at 9 a.m., but it was 9.15, because of its size. We pulled the car right on to the pavement, smashed the windows with scaffolding poles and climbed in to get to the vault. We screamed at the guys there to open it and they said it had a time lock of 9.15 a.m. It wasn't advisable to wait, of course, so instead we blew open all the tellers' drawers with a shotgun. We only got away with about £2,000 – and we knew they had a lot of money in the vault.

By now the Old Bill were calling us the Laurel and Hardy gang, as Terry was short and fat and I was tall and skinny. The police always thought we must have had some inside information, some help, but we didn't. We just knew what we were doing.

◆ ◆ ◆

In 1973, I had fallen in love. I'd been working hard and partying, and it was while drinking in a pub called The Carlton on Grafton Road, Kentish Town, that I first set eyes on Marilyn.

She was at the other end of the bar with a mate. She was a brunette. I spied her and thought, 'She looks nice. I wonder what her story is?'

Our eyes met and that was that. I bought her a drink and we started dating. At the time, she lived near me in a place called Athlone Street and I'd see her mum about as she also lived nearby, in Queen's Crescent.

We'd go out to clubs and restaurants and hang out together. As things were going well, we decided we should move in with each other, get a place and start making ourselves a home.

We found a flat above a doctors' surgery in Crouch End in a road called Weston Park. The landlord charged us £15 a week, which was reduced to £12 after we took him to a rent tribunal.

Marilyn worked on a counter at a bank – and wasn't happy with my chosen occupation, understandably. She knew all about what I was doing and she wasn't thrilled. Far from it.

She used to say to me, 'Don't go today, John. I have a bad feeling about it.'

This wasn't the sort of thing you wanted to hear just before you went out on a job. It was bad karma, and I'd tell her not to worry, that it would be all OK – but when she said things like that, I couldn't help but wonder if she was right, if it was a sign, if I should back out. But I never did.

I felt powerful and fearless. I had money and I liked spending it. The money I was bringing in allowed me to indulge.

There was a Christmas when my kid sister Jane had gone to another sister, Carol's, for the holidays – a place down in New Cross – with Carol's three kids. Jane had gone down there to help out, look after the children, enjoy the festivities.

I decided to surprise them, so I went out on a massive spending spree and bought the children a load of presents. I filled the car right up with these beautifully wrapped gifts, all in gorgeous paper and with ribbons and everything. I felt like Father Christmas.

I liked to treat Jane – I remember buying Jane her first Elvis LP. I was her big brother, eleven years older, and I wanted her to be all right. She was living with our sister Kim and Mum in this house in Islip Street. I'd long moved out by then. I remember there was this hut on the estate which they used for the kids, a youth club. They'd take Jane and Kim and their little gang out for trips, take them swimming, up the park, all of that.

One holiday, the youth workers said they were going to take them all for a little break, a canal boat holiday. Kim was so excited – she ran home to Mum and said, 'Can we go?'

The thing was, Jane knew the trip was going to cost a fiver each, and it was a fiver Mum didn't have. Mum couldn't afford it, or at least couldn't pay for both of them. Jane, being Jane, pretended to Mum and Dad she wasn't interested, said she didn't fancy it, so Kim could go. She was properly gutted. There was a big gang of her mates all going, and she was going to have to stay home at the weekend.

So Kim went off in this minibus, waved the family goodbye, and Jane stayed home. She was going to go up the Prince of Wales baths and help Mum do the weekly laundry instead. Jane had no clean clothes, so they were off to do the wash.

Then I showed up and said, 'Hello, Titch. Where's your sister Kim then?'

She replied that she was on this barge trip, but she didn't want to admit she was missing out, didn't want to admit she had actually wanted to go too.

I said, 'Oh you silly thing, Titch.' I gave her a big hug and asked how long ago they'd left. It was about an hour before. I said to Jane, 'Right, pack a bag. You're going, darling.'

Jane looked gutted. 'I can't, John. I've got no clean clothes! They're all dirty and we have to go and do the washing.'

I looked at her, pulled out a fiver and said, 'Go up Chelsea Girl,' a shop on Kentish Town Road, 'and buy a new set of clothes.'

When she came back I was having a cup of tea with Mum and Dad. I had this blue convertible Triumph Stag, a lovely car, great to drive and really eye catching. I said, 'C'mon, hop in Titch, let's go,' and I drove like the wind to catch up to that minibus and get Jane to the barge. When we pulled up, Kim and all their mates saw us and broke out into cheers. They had a marvellous holiday.

I didn't want my family to get involved with my work, but there was one time I knew my brother Terry was short of cash. Terry, who was usually as straight as anything, didn't really want any involvement but he did need some money, so I offered him a little job.

I said to him, 'Go and nick me a car, Tel. Find me a car we can use' – and waved a big wedge under his nose. I really just wanted an excuse to hand over some money to my brother, but he was the type who wouldn't take something for nothing. I didn't think he'd manage to blag me a motor, and if he didn't I could just say, 'Oh, no worries. Hang on to that cash as a retainer,' or something.

So Terry goes out and nicks a car. In he comes all pleased with himself, saying, 'I've done it, Johnny. I got you a great car – a Mark V Cortina, really chunky, lots of poke, great acceleration, great handling.'

I could tell Terry was chuffed with himself, so I said, 'C'mon then, let's go and take a look.'

'You'll love it, John. It's a proper beauty,' he said as we went down the steps at the back of the flats.

And yes, it was lovely – too bloody lovely! I saw it immediately among all the other cars parked up and couldn't stop laughing. Terry, in his wisdom, had nicked a beauty, nicked a car with the same approach you would have if you nicked a necklace – get something gorgeous, something that stands out, something of quality.

He'd only gone and nicked a brand-new Mark V, with amazing metallic green and red paintwork – a real customised job, with every bloody accessory you could think of.

It was the last sort of car you'd do a bank job in. In fact, it was the last sort of car you'd nick for any reason at all. You'd have to give it a spray job before you could take it out again. It was a real head turner. Within three minutes of driving off, you'd have a hundred witnesses saying what way you were heading, as no one could possibly miss it.

I couldn't let my darling brother know what a balls-up he'd made, so I thanked him, paid him some dosh and drove it back to the street he'd nicked it from. I parked up pronto and didn't fuck about waiting to see if anyone was about. I didn't even close the driver's door – I pulled up, screech, opened the door and then legged it. I had thought that maybe I should roll it into a lake up the Welsh Harp, or shove it in the River

Lea, or torch it round the back of King's Cross. But it seemed like such a well-loved car, I couldn't bring myself to destroy it. Stupid really, considering what we were hoping to use it for – stupid to risk getting a tug simply for returning someone's stolen property.

Terry was a good honest bloke, but he also liked a squeeze if he could get hold of one. He was working as a tiler with Dad once and they had a job in a primary school. After they'd done it, Terry came home with these two big orange space hoppers with smiley faces on them for Jane and Kim.

Looking back, he must have pinched them from the school when he was doing the job. It made me chuckle, thinking about that. There's me doing bank jobs, and then there's my brother nicking bouncy space hoppers for his kid sisters. I guess I was the real wrong 'un.

◆ ◆ ◆

Such fun and games weren't always going to be par for the course in our line of work. We had other close shaves that were pretty uncomfortable.

There was the time Tel and I ended up getting a lift from a job in a police car – but thankfully without any coppers in it. I can still recall the look on the police officers' faces as I opened the driver's-side door of their squad car. I slipped in behind the wheel, revved the accelerator and crunched the gears into reverse.

I smiled at them as I slammed the door shut, and then glanced once more in the rear-view mirror as Hardy and I took off. It had been an eventful day, lifting £25,000 from the hands of a guard delivering to a bank in East Ham, picking up the four cash bags the panic-stricken bloke had dropped and throwing them into the back seat of our getaway wheels.

And now this – handcuffing two officers to a set of railings on a quiet housing estate off the A12 near Barking on a sunny Tuesday morning in June 1974, jumping into their marked car, turning the lights on and hoping to find a way past the rapidly closing jaws of a snarling Flying Squad. It was a close call, but these were the moments we knew we were cut out for. We enjoyed an unswerving loyalty to each other, underlined by our trust in our partner's calmness, mixed with sheer brutality when it kicked off.

This was the fundamental reason why Laurel and Hardy were successful bank robbers, and why the police were desperate to get us off the streets – and, once apprehended, keep us there for as long as possible.

By the summer of 1975 the Laurel and Hardy gang were being mentioned regularly in morning briefings across the Met. The Flying Squad were trawling their grasses, pressing club owners to let them know who was coming in and spending, asking door staff for info about the tippers, threatening anyone they knew with a minor criminal record to come forward, to offer help or face pressure.

It was the same with the drug gangs that the Vice Squad and others kept gentle tabs on, often for either a cut of what was coming in or reliable information that would let the Met feel the collars of the criminals who weren't onside, weren't willing to hand over the heavy brown envelopes.

I was known, a regular suspect, and Tel had also done enough time and cropped up in enough conversations for his name to be underlined in red ink in any copper's notebook. And things were going to get even more intense that summer. We'd been working quite consistently through the spring and into May, June. We'd done a few jobs together, but also helped out a couple of teams elsewhere – we'd had a good payday after nicking some cars to order, getting hold of some clean weapons and even helping map out a route away from a bank for a gang we knew.

We didn't even go on the job, but we got a cut for finding a decent car and driver, getting the heavy weaponry sorted out and sourcing two of them a safe house they could use for a fortnight. It was funny – we were joking we'd moved off the factory floor now into middle management. But it was a joke, as nothing could really get in the way of me and Hardy when we smelt a job to be done.

So it was a Friday morning in early June when I picked Hardy up from his flat in Enfield, where his girlfriend and daughter were staying. It was Tel's family home, but he kept a couple of other addresses on the go. He didn't much like the idea of returning straight home from a job to a house where his child was waiting. We would discuss this regularly. How, if the police traced us there, they'd come in armed – a risky situation we didn't want to put our children anywhere near. We were meticulous about such details, as we felt police officers would be in a 'shoot first, ask questions later' mindset if they thought they were closing in on the Laurel and Hardy gang.

Looking back, neither of us had any qualms at all about waving guns about in public, where other people's kids were. It's an example of the moral juxtapositions we were constantly making: another element of the Bank Robbers' Code of Conduct – unwritten rules that added a sheen of gentlemanliness to what we were doing.

I'd nicked a Ford Granada, 2.4 litre, a dull brown colour that was as quick as the Rovers the Flying Squad were using. I was always very careful about the colours of cars I stole. It was for a good reason, of course – not being too noticeable – and then it became a bit of a superstitious thing too. If a job had gone really well, you would think about using a similar motor the next time.

After collecting Tel, we went round to the drop where we'd been storing firearms. An empty flat on an estate in Holloway – a mate of ours would often stay there, partly to keep an eye on the weapons, partly to make neighbours think a quiet, hard-working, single man lived there, deterring break-ins and any mucking about, and partly because our friend was trapped in a loveless marriage and had a gorgeous girlfriend he was having a passionate affair with. Tel and I liked the idea that, by giving him the keys to our safe house, we were helping alleviate his domestic misery a bit, helping him to get some relief.

The weather was nice and it was shaping up to be well over 20 degrees. When we got to the flat, we went straight into the bathroom, removed the panels and chose our tools. Because of the sun, we'd have to do this in shorts and T-shirts – so we chose three handguns to take with us, leaving the aggressively customised sawn-offs behind for another, rainier day.

◆ ◆ ◆

We had watched a bank in East Ham for some time. We'd driven past it and noticed how busy the high street was. Where the bank sat was always heavy with traffic. But running parallel behind it was a barely used alleyway that was the width of a car and took you quickly out into suburbia. There were loads of half-finished post-war estates around there that offered plenty of badly designed roads, laid out with the aim of getting you as lost as possible, and a network of A roads and dual carriageways for us to really put some distance between us and the shocked, alarm-raising guard we'd just mugged off.

The alley was accessed by a turning 25yd on from the bank – and one that was by a set of lights, meaning we could zip down it if we timed it right, and then cars behind would block up any passing patrol cars giving chase. A hard right into the alley, foot down, 200yd, then a left and into a bypass system out towards the A12.

The job went extremely fucking well. We saw the secure transport van come to a stop. I pulled up just behind and to the right, so we were on its outside.

The guard came out, oh so nonchalantly. We knew this was a drop-off and we watched him as he absent-mindedly tinkered with his keys for the safe at the back of the van. He wasn't hurrying, he was day dreaming – you could see how he was working, not a care in the world, whistling, swinging a key chain, lifting up his helmet and taking it off for a moment to wipe a handkerchief down the back of his sweaty neck. He was doing everything you're not meant to as a security guard. This was a complete eyes-off-the-ball moment.

He was going to make our morning easy, so we didn't hesitate. We swung straight into action. Opening our doors, the engine running, pulling out our handguns before anyone could react, we were on top of the guard, guns in his face, demanding the bags he had. We grabbed the two on the street and I threw them in the back of the car. I was ready to take off when, to our surprise, the guard, who maybe didn't realise the stick-up was about grabbing as much as you could in as short a timeframe as possible, asked us politely if we wanted the other two.

I remember Tel had this priceless look, like, 'Eh, is he serious?' I wanted none of it – we'd got a score, let's go – but Tel said, 'Hang on a tick, hang on.'

With a gun firmly in his back, the guard opened the back of the van again and handed over another two sacks. Seconds later, we were gone.

It was a hot day but, as anyone who has ever lifted a bag of cash from a bank knows, the intense sweat produced on a job quickly begins to turn cold two minutes down the line. Sometimes, I would see colleagues launch into long, confused monologues after a job was complete, their adrenaline still flowing but with nowhere to go. Others would turn ghostly pale and quiet. Often Tel and I would get a dose of uncontrollable post-blag shakes and trembles as the shock of it really kicked in.

We knew each other well enough to recognise how the other was feeling, and we both enjoyed working together for the simple reason that our professionalism remained suitably high in the hours after a job. There were no celebratory thoughts until the guns were back where they lived, the getaway car dumped, the cash counted and stashed away, and a cup of tea and biscuit placed on a side table by my favourite armchair.

That day, after boosting four bags from the East Ham job, I drove while Tel transferred the cash from the bank's sacks into less conspicuous holdalls. One gun went into one of the bags, the others were tucked in our jeans at the back.

We had planned to dump the first car somewhere near the River Lea and Victoria Park, transfer to another and then head up to Holloway to lose the firearms. Then it was on to Tottenham Hale to a lock-up where we could stash most of the money we'd taken, and then drop Tel off in Enfield. That was the plan – until I heard the unwelcome sound of a number of sirens heading towards us.

I couldn't see them but they were making a racket and I got a feeling in my guts. Sometimes it seemed like your sixth sense was kicking in. There was something about the noise coming off sirens in the distance that made me act. I pulled off the main road, skidded the car to a halt behind some garages, turned the engine off and paused for a moment.

Tel and I decided to head off again on foot, so we picked up the bags of cash and as confidently as we could began to walk away, hoping to get some distance between us and East Ham as quickly as possible.

But the police, aware that two men fitting the Laurel and Hardy description were behind a raid in east London, weren't going to let this chance slip by easily. They were going to pour some resources into this one.

More sirens could be heard in the distance, and I had a touch of nerves as we walked down a parade, packed with Saturday shoppers, families, and saw a marked squad car coming towards us very slowly. I saw a turning on my right and, without waiting, strode confidently down it, with Tel following.

We carried on, peering into cars parked along the road, looking for one we could boost without too much trouble, and as we did that, we realised we'd walked into a new estate and had unwittingly stepped into a cul-de-sac.

As we went to turn back on ourselves, we saw the squad car entering from the top, and moving slowly towards us. As it pulled up, the windows went down and the officers politely said, 'Good morning.'

Terry said to me, 'Leave this to me. I'll talk to them.'

The coppers got out the car and came up to us. I could just tell from their faces that they thought they'd got the right people. They were polite as anything.

'Where've you been this morning?' they asked, again as nonchalantly as they could – but I knew, I just knew.

'Oh, nowhere really. Just a bit of shopping,' answered Tel.

Then they asked if they could do a quick routine check through our bags – and I knew one of them had my gun in, apart from anything else. I really couldn't stand it.

'Of course,' said Hardy, and he handed them one. The copper started rummaging inside, and if he was suspicious about what the heavily wrapped block was inside – the cash was bound up – he didn't show it. But I knew that any second now they'd feel a gun and then choices would have to be made.

I said, 'C'mon, I've gotta get home. Have a look and then we'll be off.' As I said that, I found my gun at the bottom of the bag I was carrying and pulled it out. I stuck it in the copper's ear 'ole, and dragged the other copper away from the car. I took their handcuffs off them, pushed them up against some railings and then locked the pair of them to the fence.

The funny thing was, the coppers had driven past lots of people hanging out washing in their front gardens. We got into their car, reversed it and drove back past those same neighbours. What they must have made of the fact two unshaven men were now in the car and not the uniforms they'd seen moments before, God only knows.

We faced an urgent twenty minutes. Driving a stolen police car, having locked up two officers after threatening them with a firearm, and with four bags of bank notes, holding £25,000. The game was on.

We went speeding off down this dual carriageway, and then we hit traffic – proper 'no one's going anywhere' traffic.

I thought, 'Fuck it, let's put the old nah-nah on.' We did and they parted like the Red Sea.

As we made headway, I got the fright of my life. It really made me jump. Silly of me, but suddenly the police radio came alive – it gave me a right shock. It came out with all that Tango Echo stuff, and then said two gunmen had jumped officers and stolen their car. The radio said the suspects were heading towards Canning Town, which was exactly where we were going. Thankfully, the radio announced this as we were on a roundabout, so instead of heading left to Canning Town, I said, 'Thank you very much,' and chucked a hard right onto another dual carriageway, then took the first slip road off we could see.

We were on a bit of land above the Blackwall Tunnel. I took the car down a side street and dumped it by a scrapyard. We pulled out the radio, which we'd been told had a tracking device in it, just to hamper any efforts to start the trail afresh.

Our next idea was a minicab – but before we could reach an office, we saw a bus. We hopped on it and went up to the top deck. We looked hot and sweaty and were clutching holdalls, but no one blinked an eyelid.

Then we got a right scare. It was clear the police were running a huge search operation. The helicopters were up, and the sheer number of cars out showed this was a serious trawl.

I looked down from the top deck, and there was a copper leaning out the window of a Panda, looking back up, staring right at me.

I nudged Terry, told him I thought we'd been rumbled. He looked at me and said, deadly seriously, 'We might have to hijack the bus.'

Thankfully, my worry about the officer's stare was paranoia. The bus didn't stop, and each turn of the wheels saw us move further away from danger and suspicion.

The traffic was backing up as squad cars kept coming past under lights, getting others to move out the way. I remember me and Tel joking about how bad the jam was, how it must be hindering the Old Bill from finding whoever it was they were after.

Eventually, the bus reached Roman Road, and we stepped off and into a barber's we knew. Here, we had wet shaves to remove the beards we'd grown for the heist and trims to smarten ourselves up and take the edge off the day. Finally, we called two minicabs, took a couple of bags each and arranged to meet up later.

FOUR

Charles Thomas Higgins was born on 26 July 1939 in east London. In 1975, he was working as a doorman at a pub in Hackney called The Cricketers.

He was known vaguely to me and to a few of my friends. He worked at the club, and we sometimes went there. That was it. We weren't on particularly friendly terms or anything, but neither of us would ever have predicted, could have predicted, what was to happen. We'd sometimes pop in and that was that. He worked at the place and no doubt was well respected and loved by those who knew him. I found out little about him as the years went by.

At my trial, they produced a police report saying he'd been awaiting trial on a charge of conspiracy to steal. He'd got previous – convictions for burglary, assault, criminal damage and dishonest handling. It was all irrelevant. I knew as well as anyone that the police were renowned for trying to fit up anyone they didn't take a fancy to. The Flying Squad regularly harassed those working on club doors, often assuming (sometimes correctly) the worst. Who knows?

◆ ◆ ◆

Now I'm thinking back to The Cricketers. It was the evening of 23 September 1975. I'd gone out with Terry and we'd ended up having a drink in a basement bar in The Cricketers, a place called Wickets. There was this bloke Maxwell there and another mate, John Dove.

The place had a late licence. It could stay open until 2 a.m., so it was the sort of place you ended up at, rather than started the night at, if you know what I mean. It was here that Mr Higgins was employed to keep an eye on the bar and door, and make sure people behaved themselves.

Looking back, and reading the reports, written during those immediate days, weeks and months after, I can put together a picture of that evening. A police statement says I was with friends, and we were then joined by two others. As the evening wore on, they say our group had become drunk and 'boisterous'.

At one point between 12.30 and 1 a.m., it was alleged one of the party – identified later as Terry – had caused a bit of a scene when he dropped his trousers in front of the regulars. He was confronted by the manager, 'whereupon one of the group threw a glass in his face and hit him in the mouth,' the police records state.

'A melee ensued, during which glasses and bottles were thrown and the licensee was hit over the head; a number of regular customers, including one wielding a baseball bat, together with Higgins, who was the doorman, came to his rescue,' the court report drily notes.

A melee indeed. The whole place kicked right off. Tel and I managed to fight our way out as we got attacked by a furious mob, managed to scrap our way to the door and get up the stairs and out into the street.

But as we reached the top of the flight, we realised our mate John wasn't with us. He'd been behind me as we fended off punches, kicks, blows, bottles. I'd been busy trying to dish it out and thought John had come right with me. Then we heard a bloody horrible screaming coming from back downstairs. John was getting a severe beating, whatever way you looked at it.

The police report continues:

Massey was either called down for or came back for Dove, who was seriously injured to the extent he was later admitted to St Bartholomew's hospital and his right eye removed. One of the group said: 'we are coming back with guns' – a threat that was not taken seriously at the time. The Wicket bar was cleaned up, the licensee went to Accident and Emergency for stitches to a head wound, and Mr Higgins was left in charge of the bar.

What was heard in court – an official version, if you like – sounds pretty straightforward. Detectives said at my trial that Terry, another accomplice and I went to my sister Jackie's flat. Here, I had a collection of arms stashed behind a bathroom panel. Jackie didn't know anything about it. After dropping off poor John, who was seriously hurt – his eyeball was hanging out of his head – at Homerton hospital, we took action. The police said:

> His sister did not know, but they had gone to John's sister's to collect a holdall. Inside were three sawn-off shotguns and a pair of handguns. John, Terry and another friend drove back to the pub, where the friend stayed upstairs armed with a shotgun. John and Terry went back down the stairs of The Cricketers, armed with a shotgun and a handgun each. Moments after their arrival, Mr Higgins would be dead.

According to the police, I went down the stairs first and, as we reached the door to the basement bar, Higgins came out to confront us. The court heard that my gun went off at close range and Higgins slumped to the floor, then Terry and I went into the bar and herded customers into a corner while we searched the place, looking for the owner.

While we were inside Wickets, the police said we 'let off a number of shots at the bar, smashing glasses and bottles while telling the staff they had warned everyone they were "coming back to sort things out"'. After making sure the owner wasn't hiding, we left the way we'd come in.

People in the club recovered their senses and found Mr Higgins slumped in the doorway. An ambulance was called. Higgins was pronounced dead at the scene by medics at 1.38 a.m. A post-mortem showed Higgins had been killed 'due to a haemorrhage from a contact gunshot wound to the right side of the chest'.

I had taken someone else's life.

◆ ◆ ◆

Looking back at that night nearly fifty years later, I remember it clearly with a mixture of deep remorse and regret. I try to understand why I had got myself into such a situation, in such a frame of mind, that someone ended up being killed. How? What was the process? How could it have been avoided? Where could I have turned off?

During the day, Terry and I had met up. We had a problem: what should we do with all our money? We had cash sloshing about from our various jobs and we needed to wash it. We wanted to invest, get it legal, get it out of the cornflakes boxes and earning for us. We had a call from a contact about coming in on a coin-operated launderette and a butcher's shop. It sounded lucrative, a good place to put some money. We had to meet this bloke in a pub in Highbury at 6 p.m. Well, 6 p.m. came and went and he didn't show up … 7 p.m., still no show. We'd been drinking while we were waiting and we got the taste for it, so we decided we'd make a night of it. We went on a crawl and ended up in The Cricketers over in Hackney in the early hours.

The Cricketers was all right – a fairly well-known watering hole where faces could gather and chat without prying eyes or perked-up ears. It looked like a terraced house from the outside and there was a set of steps leading down into the entrance to the basement bar. Once through the door, a bar ran along the back wall, with booths to the left. Another set of stairs behind the bar led up to the ground floor. It was like a converted basement – nothing fancy, but a popular spot for a few jars, somewhere discreet.

After about thirty minutes in there, it all kicked off. We had met John Dove, who was in there with his girlfriend. He was an inoffensive, quiet guy, not a villain at all. We were having a lovely time, enjoying ourselves, dancing about. Terry decided to drop his trousers and dance around with them round his ankles – it was a bit of a party trick for him, a bit of a laugh, nothing more. A guy came over and started a fuss. No one was objecting, everybody was laughing their heads off ...

But then the owner came over too, a bloke called John Cowley, with a face on him. He got the hump. In any other club where management faced this type of situation, they would have known we were good spenders, well behaved. We were buying people drinks and not being disrespectful. He should have handled it differently. He should have said, 'Oi, boys, calm it down there now' and we'd have said, 'OK, mate. Have a drink, sorry ...' But then a drink was thrown – I can't remember who by – and it kicked off big time.

The place erupted like an Andy Capp cartoon. You couldn't see who was hitting who – it was a real bar-room brawl. We soon discovered they had all sorts of weaponry behind the bar: baseball bats, coshes, the lot. We were holding our own. We went into combat mode, back to back, protecting each other, and we fought our way to the door and managed to get out. It was only when we were halfway up the stairs that we heard John Dove's awful screams. They'd set on him like a pack of animals. We went back downstairs and pulled John out of it. His eye was hanging out of his head. We had my car outside, the Aston Martin, so we bundled him in and rushed him to the Homerton hospital and then went away sharpish – we didn't want to be questioned.

Terry, Maxwell and I didn't pause for breath. We set off in the Aston to my sister's house.

Having got what we wanted, we then went back to The Cricketers and knocked on the door. Charlie Higgins opened it. We had intended to get him back inside and then sort out the business we had to sort out. But as I held the gun up – it was about chest height – he threw a left hook and as I staggered back the gun just went off. I was completely unconscious of it at the time – and that's why I haven't considered myself a cold-blooded murderer, as many people have described me.

I didn't have it in me. I'd never shot at anyone before. When a gun goes off at such close range – well, he must've been dead before he hit the floor.

Processing what happened at the door of Wickets bar is the stuff of nightmares. The images the mind conjures up are there for the rest of your life. It was like I was in a role play at the time. I stepped past him and went into the club. It didn't impact on me that he might have died. I just thought, 'Right, he's out the way, I can go in now …' It's hard to describe the feeling. It was like going on a bank robbery. You set your mind on what you are going to do. You don't really think about it. It's like you get tunnel vision. If you aren't like that, you would shit yourself and run – then you wouldn't get the job done.

◆ ◆ ◆

When the police got to Wickets, it was chaos. There were marks on the walls where bottles had been smashed, broken glass strewn across the floor and bloodstains in a number of places. They would retrieve bullets from the bar and forensics experts would later say they had been fired from a gun that had been recovered from a car I owned and had abandoned.

By then, we were long gone. We'd run upstairs, got back into the Aston Martin and returned to my sister's flat to stash the guns. I drove Terry to his home in Enfield, where Marilyn and my daughter were staying that night.

With the adrenaline going, I didn't notice the aches and pains from the savagery of the fight. Neither did Tel. Instead, we needed to clear our heads, shake off the drunkenness, think clearly, and work out what we needed to do in the next twenty-four to forty-eight hours to ensure our safety.

We knew officers would be taking statements. We knew there were witnesses, that there was a strong chance we would be identified. We wanted to buy ourselves a bit of time to get out of the mess we'd made.

After I was arrested, officers taking down my statement noted my frame of mind on reaching Terry's home in Enfield. While being interviewed under caution, I told them:

… me and Terry left and got back in the car and went to Terry's house, where Marilyn was. We went into his house and Marilyn said, 'Have you been in a fight? Why have you changed your clothes?'

I said, 'Shut up and don't ask questions', and I went to the bathroom and sorted some bullets out from the change I had loose in my pocket. She said, 'What are these?' and I said, 'I've told you before, I won't tell you again, don't ask questions.' She saw I was in a threatening mood and did what she was told. I had planned on staying the night at Terry's but he was too edgy and wanted us to go, so I said, 'If I reach home OK, I'll call you in the morning.' I told Marilyn to get the baby ready and we left. There's a part I missed out about the two guns. One was a .38 revolver and the other was a .32 automatic. This gun I placed in the glove compartment, the other I put in my waistband. We got into the car and headed for home. All this time Marilyn was still unaware of what had happened. We were about 3 miles from home when I saw a Panda car tag on behind us. I didn't change speed or course but just kept heading for home. About 2 miles from home another car tagged on behind that one. Marilyn was completely oblivious we were being followed. I wasn't absolutely certain they were after me because the other possibility was that they were heading back to base as it was almost in the same road as where we lived, so it was logical they would be taking the same route. But when we passed the station, I knew we was done for. I thought the best thing was to drive home, so I drove into the drive and told Marilyn to go indoors. At that moment I saw that the police cars had blocked exits of the drive and two policemen were already walking up the drive towards me …

What happened next was described in some detail at the time by both myself and police officers. The thing is, I think the decision I made that night had a bearing on how long I spent inside and how the authorities considered me afterwards.

As the copper came up the drive, I pulled out the gun and said, 'Hold it there.' He ran back down the drive to the car. I said, 'Move the car or I'll shoot.' Nothing happened, so I waited a couple of seconds so that anybody inside would have time to duck. Then I fired.

I let off a round at the police car, striking the windscreen.

Then one of the cars moved back far enough to give me a clear exit. I drove back more or less the same way I'd come until I came to a big roundabout. I missed the turning I wanted to take, so I skidded the car into a U-turn and drove the wrong side up the dual carriageway. I then turned into some back streets and saw that I'd lost the cars that were chasing me.

I sped through the night, aware that there would be an all-points warning as they looked for me. I decided to drive into Dagenham and abandon my car. I stashed my gun – a .32 self-loading Walther pistol with three live rounds in it – under the seat. I stopped the car in a quiet little street, got out and walked to a Cortina that was parked up next to it. I forced open a window and, using a master key I had with me, I started the engine. It worked. I nicked this shitty old Cortina off someone's drive and replaced it with a mint Aston Martin – it always made me laugh a bit at what the bloke in the house must have thought when he came downstairs the next morning. Then I drove back into London. I dumped the car in Chingford and caught a taxi to Shoreditch. I stayed the night at a friend's in east London.

Police notes written at the time tally roughly with my version of how I escaped. Officers noted that a Panda car blocked the southern exit, while another way out to the north was also blocked. I pulled the car over, let my wife and child get out and into the safety of home, before working out my next move. The report states:

> Several officers got out of their cars and Massey threatened them with a revolver, saying 'Fuck off out of my garden' and 'Back off'.
>
> Massey managed to drive his car past the road block to the north, but then stopped and got out.
>
> He faced the police vehicle that had driven across the southern entrance, raised his gun and saying 'Get that fucking car out of the way' he fired, the bullet striking the windscreen at head level, ricocheting and lodging in the rubber beading at the top. The police officer ducked and was uninjured. Massey drove off and escaped.

◆ ◆ ◆

As John Dove slowly recovered from his injuries, he was interviewed by the police. Despite keeping quiet, it was obvious detectives knew who they were after – but Dove never forgot how Terry and I stood by him.

He would write to me in prison, thanking me for saving his life. He was blinded by the beating he took. God knows what would have happened if we hadn't gone back and got him out. We had to fight our way in and fight our way out again – they were like a pack of wolves. It was a horrific scene and we thought someone should pay for it. We didn't contemplate for a moment letting someone get away with administering such a beating on a defenceless person like John Dove. Because it was a gang situation, we felt we had no choice but to deal with it ourselves.

For Terry and Maxwell, the net was closing.

Terry was caught in mid-October: he had gone to sell a Triumph Dolomite car to a dealer in Brixton for £900 and asked a friend to clear the dealer's cheque through the account they held at a bank in Kilburn. A cashier told them the cheque's funds would be good a couple of days later – but, unknown to Terry, officers had been tipped off and they mounted a surveillance operation on the branch, waiting for their quarry to return. He did, on a Friday morning, and they swooped.

Terry refused to speak at first, though later he asked to see the detective chief inspector. He told him where he had been staying 'because I have left my dog there' and he was worried about it not getting fed.

The next day, after intense interrogation, he admitted he had been at the pub – and then that he had been present when the murder took place. 'I was there but I was drunk,' he said. He added that he didn't know what had started the fight.

'Suddenly the guns were there,' he said, under caution. 'Look, I didn't shoot anyone. I don't remember what happened – it was too quick. The one I had didn't work – that's all I remember.'

He declined to say where the guns had come from or whose home we had been to between the fight and the murder. A few days later, police found a shotgun recovered from a flat in north London. He was asked if it was the weapon he had used that night and he replied, 'It looks similar – it could be the one.'

My sister Jackie's boyfriend was interviewed. He claimed the guns had been put in the flat a few weeks previously. After the murder, he removed them and said he believed his girlfriend had then arranged for another person to get rid of them by dumping them in a weighted bag into the River Lea. Jackie was questioned and it emerged that three sports bags had indeed been dumped in the river.

From its cold currents, police divers found a bag containing a police uniform, two balaclavas, four woollen masks and a canvas gun bag. Later, they searched another address in north London and from beneath floorboards detectives retrieved a sawn-off shotgun, a .22 rifle and a revolver. Forensics revealed the shotgun, a 12-bore pump-action weapon with its barrel and stock shortened, had been fired at Wickets bar but was not the murder weapon.

Terry's statement to the police would end with the lines, 'When we went back to the club we didn't have any intention to kill anyone, it was just to frighten them. I don't think we knew what we was doing anyway because we was drunk.'

◆ ◆ ◆

Next to face a grilling was Maxwell. On 22 October, with a solicitor present, he was interviewed. He claimed little memory of the night, refusing to name anyone who was with him. He said he had never met me and had taken no part in any brawl at the bar. The police didn't believe him and formally charged him with murder. His solicitor said his client was innocent and would plead not guilty.

With my friends now in custody, I had a decision to make. Did I try to lie low, wait and see what happened? Perhaps Terry, facing a stretch, would take the blame? Could I get out of the country?

With Dove questioned and Terry and Maxwell in custody, I knew I was next in line. I was hiding out in Cardiff and was safe for the time being, but when I received a chilling message from Marilyn, I decided I should hand myself in. I look back and regret it now, but the police were telling her that, when they found me, they were going to kill me. It was that simple.

My original plan was to let as much time as possible elapse before handing myself in or getting caught. With Terry in custody, I thought, 'Let's see what happens.' If he was convicted, I could put it on him, as he wouldn't give a shit once he'd been sentenced. He got fourteen years, so it wouldn't have mattered to him.

But as the police cranked up their search for me, who they believed to be armed and dangerous, I decided it would be more sensible to take myself to a police station. I went to my solicitor in Clerkenwell and he drove us up Holmes Road nick.

I was told I was being detained in connection with the murder of Charlie Higgins and under questioning I refused to reveal where I had been staying since the night in question. I also declined to reveal any information about where the police might recover any firearms. A five-and-a-half-hour session of interrogation on that first day brought few scraps for detectives to go on.

I claimed I didn't recognise any description of Maxwell, and that Terry was the only person to have got into my Aston Martin. I also said I'd never met Dove, and that I sometimes lent my car to others, though I didn't know their names and couldn't remember any specific dates when I'd loaned my vehicle to anyone. After an afternoon of questioning, in which I tried to decline to give a blood sample and said I had no idea what the number plate was on my car, the session broke up and I was led to the cells to ponder my next move.

Later that night, I told officers I would agree to be interviewed by a detective chief inspector on the condition I could speak with my wife first. Officers' notes also claim I mentioned two other prisoners who had been on remand in Brixton prison for six months after robbing a bank in Hendon. Apparently, they were the culprits, as there was evidence that they had done a 'similar crime'.

After all that, I was transferred over to Hackney police station, where Marilyn was brought to see me and we discussed what I should do. I asked Marilyn if I should tell the police what had happened.

It made little difference. Later that day, detectives decided they had enough evidence to give to the Director of Public Prosecutions. I was charged with murder and sent to trial at the Number One court at the Old Bailey.

◆ ◆ ◆

The day after my arrest, I made a detailed statement outlining the events. The detectives' notes at the time state that I said, 'I didn't mean to kill him. The shotgun had a very light trigger and as I levelled it at him he came forward and I went to push him back and it just went off.'

I then told officers that, if I could make a phone call, they would be able to retrieve a handgun. I called a contact and, later the next day, officers found a pistol stashed in a dustbin outside a block of flats in south London. Almost two weeks later, I was shown another shotgun that they said I'd used, and I admitted that revolvers found in my car and in the dustbin were mine. More weaponry would appear before I stood trial. On a bitterly cold night in early January, officers were directed to another dustbin, this time on an estate in Archway, north London. The tip-off led to another sawn-off shotgun being retrieved.

In February 1976, I was shown the weapon picked up by officers and I admitted it was the one I had carried that night. Later examinations showed that the recoil mechanism had been damaged when the butt was sawn off and that it could not be described as being in working order.

I also made a lengthy statement as I was held at Hackney police station, and it tallies with what I remember four decades later. 'We all got fairly drunk, and then Terry dropped his trousers,' the police tape records.

Then this fellow came over, I don't know who it was, and started to get a bit nasty about it. Then all of a sudden the fight started. The whole lot seemed to be on us, literally every time we stood up we got knocked down again. We managed to get to the door and get out. There were bottles and glasses coming out of the door after us. We were all sort of half naked and had our clothes ripped off our backs. We got to the top of the stairs on to the street and found that John wasn't with us. Then we heard him scream from inside the club so we went back down the steps and managed to drag him through the door. I could see he was hurt bad. We had to carry him up the stairs and took him to my car. I gave him a bit of my shirt to hold on his face and we went to me sister Jacqueline's. I gave her some money to get a cab and take him to hospital. I didn't take him myself because I wanted an excuse to get Jackie out the house because when she first moved into the flat she gave me her key and said I could use it any time I wanted without her knowledge. I went there one day and secreted some holdall bags, behind her bath panel. In these bags I kept guns so when she left the house I took the panel off and got some guns out. We then got back into the car and returned to the club ...

I remember this part of the evening differently today. At the time, I was trying to protect my sister from having any involvement.

We told Maxwell to stand at the top of the stairs while me and Terry went down the stairs. As we were going down the stairs we both agreed if it was absolutely necessary to use the guns that we was to aim low and before we could knock on the door the door was pushed open and the man I now know to be Charlie Higgins came rushing out. Caught by surprise I levelled the gun and went to push him back inside with it. I said the words 'get inside' and the gun went off and we were in the club before we realised what had happened, with that incident not registering. We searched the club looking for the man who had just been shot. Not finding him we never bothered. So out of frustration in not finding the man we shot up the bar. Then we ran out again. Maxwell didn't use a gun so we got back in the car and went back to Jackie's. She was in when I returned and I told her I was in trouble. When she saw the guns she got hysterical. I told her they had been there a long time and threatened her that if she didn't get rid of them that I'd tell the police she knew they were there, and she'd wind up going away for a long time. I said the same to her boyfriend. I kept two of the guns, two pistols and bag of .38 ammunition.

I want to say something about Maxwell, he was led into it and he did as I told him to. He was badly frightened when he heard the shots but he didn't really know what had happened. I said I was sorry for involving him in this and he'd better get a cab and go home.

◆ ◆ ◆

As the Crown Prosecution Service put together their team, and my barristers began to try to build a case for me, I found out I was to be held on remand in Brixton prison – the Victorian place just off Streatham Hill.

First, you'd go from a police station to the magistrates' court, where you'd be automatically committed to be held on remand. They spend a moment to say that they're going to remand you in custody and then they put you into a court cell. That's your first experience, your first step into the criminal justice system, and it's very morbid and very depressing. You feel like the world has ended. It's the start of a journey you don't want to go on.

I'd been taken to Rochester Row – that's where they would gather up all the people from magistrates' courts who'd been remanded. Rochester Row was like something out of Jack the Ripper's time. It was like a big cattle shed and being there always reminded me of animals waiting to be taken to the abattoir. You'd be packed in with people who'd been drinking and you'd all be gasping for air. There would be a little hatch in the door and by now you'd have gone into survival mode. You'd think you were going to suffocate; you'd have to fight for a space to sit and try not to panic. There were occasions when people would talk to each other, but mainly your mind would be too occupied with what was coming next. Some people would act up by being loud, some would be crazy, others would be drunk. I kept quiet. It would be a relief when the doors opened and you'd be put into a van.

You're kept there until the court finishes for the day. Then prisoners are put in handcuffs and transferred to vans for each prison – big, old sweat boxes with twelve cells in each van. The cells are single and small – you can hardly move. The vans are massive flat-ended trucks and they have these little escape hatches on the roof. That's the first thing you do when you're put in the box – you try to test the trapdoor on the roof and you pray for some miracle that they've left it open.

They have these windows that are half-clear and half-frosted glass, and you look out the window like you're a rat in a cage. You look about the cell for inspiration and a way out. Everything is riveted and solid. You're thinking, 'Could I cut through the sides?'

Then you look up and see the escape hatch and think, 'Hello.' Once, I even got myself upside down and tried to force it open with my feet. I stretched up and stamped on it as hard as I could till my eyes were popping out. I tried my very best but it wouldn't budge.

The van moves forward and leaves the yard, off out into the traffic. You look out and the world is going by – people are completely oblivious to what you are going through. Some look at the van out of curiosity and once I even saw someone I thought I knew – that was like a punch to the heart. Slowly, we made our way through the traffic to Brixton.

On remand, you can wear your own clothes and you're allowed one visit a day because you are still technically innocent. All my family came down to see me. I'd been there for a week and because I was on a murder charge I was given a single cell. I was lucky. It was a Victorian cell but it was quite large – 12ft by 8ft – and it had sash windows you could open, with bars on the outside.

This cell's position and the fact I was on my own gave me an idea. The window looked out on to an alleyway and there was a wall opposite. I thought to myself, 'I could leap from the window and on to the wall.' I was sure I could do it if I could somehow saw through the bars. It might sound crazy, but when you're in that situation, ideas like this don't seem so mad – and you find you are brave enough to do something that otherwise might not seem viable. Your courage proves that it is. I thought, 'I could actually get out of this.' I'd heard of a bloke who'd made twelve escape attempts and nothing had happened to him. He'd not been sanctioned, so I thought, 'OK, what have I got to lose? I'm getting through these bars and over that wall.'

Such a madcap scheme didn't seem outlandish as I contemplated my lot behind a triple-locked steel door. The reality, the enormity, was beginning to take root. Everything was playing on my mind.

Before the shooting, things had been so good. I had a little baby girl and a house in Kent with the woman I loved – but now all I could think was how fucking stupid I was. It was so unbelievable what I had done. I couldn't understand how I could even begin to contemplate what I had jeopardised, and the effect my behaviour was to have on others. You don't understand the true value of things until you lose them. I couldn't stop picturing it.

I lay awake at night, listening to the quiet of the prison, my mind churning over and over. I had to accept that this could be the start of a long time inside – unless I took matters into my own hands. I began to formulate a plan.

Being on remand in Brixton meant you could have a meal brought in every day with your visit. When your visit had finished, they would bring whatever had been delivered up to you. It could be a cooked meal from a café or a sandwich. You could have a bottle of beer or half a pint of wine, too.

With this in mind, I saw a weak point I could exploit. My mum's love was unconditional. And I wasn't thinking straight. I was being selfish and, looking back, I wasn't really aware of the full extent of what I was asking her to do. Any other member of my family would have said, 'Don't be so fucking stupid.'

When I first thought of sawing through the bars, the only viable option was to get a blade from a junior hacksaw. I mentioned it to my mum when she came to see me, and I didn't think she would do it.

One day my visit had finished and she said to me, 'I've made you some French stick sandwiches. I hope you like them.' It was the old file-in-the-cake trick. A knock came on the hatch of my cell and it opened up. I went to the hatch very nervously – I was sure what was inside the French sticks would be discovered. As the screws passed the sandwiches through the hatch in the door, my heart absolutely leapt. I could see sticking out of the French sticks two ends of a hacksaw blade. It looked so obvious, but the warden must have been in his own world, or in a hurry. He didn't notice it. I almost snatched the sandwiches out of his hand. It was a big thing, what my mum did.

I didn't eat the sarnie, I was so pleased. I took the blades out in the cell, wiped them clean and hid them. There was a conduit for the wires leading to the light and a junction box. I took two screws out and hid the blades inside the light fitting. I knew I didn't have all the time in the world, so in the next couple of days I sawed through about three-quarters of two of the bars and then I patched up the gaps with some soap so it wasn't obvious. The cell was on the second or third floor and I was almost level with the top of the wall. I did the sawing during the day, when there was plenty of noise, though I had to be careful with all the screws about. It was nerve wracking, the sound of metal on metal, but people around me were playing radios and there was a real hubbub going on.

I was ready to make a break for it, and was contemplating going over the wall at nightfall. But then something unexpected happened.

They came for me to make an appearance at the Inner London sessions of Middlesex court – it was completely unexpected and it was to do with the fact I'd been convicted of driving while disqualified. I thought I'd go to court, hear it out and then be taken back to my cell in Brixton later that day. But when they remanded me back in custody, it was as a person convicted for driving while disqualified, so instead of going back to the cell with the bars I'd been working on, they sent me to Wandsworth. That was a punch in the throat. Those bars might still be ready to be knocked out today – I was good at disguising them. The wardens would come in and rattle their truncheons along them all to see if everything was OK, but I never got any comeback, so for all I know my handiwork remained undiscovered – and the blades are still tucked away in the ceiling light.

As a convicted prisoner, I lost some of my privileges. I was banged up in a convicted cell and was reduced to one visit a week through glass.

◆ ◆ ◆

The trial of me, Terry and Maxwell at the Old Bailey attracted a fair amount of press attention. All three of us pleaded not guilty. Court Number One's public gallery had more than its usual smattering of visitors for the trial's opening remarks, while the court reporters were poised with their pencils and notebooks, ready to fill tomorrow's red tops with what was being sold to the public as a possible gangland feud.

My solicitor was called Jeremy Bayes. He had an office opposite Clerkenwell court in Gray's Inn Road. He was court appointed and I knew him for years. He went on to work for the Howard League for Penal Reform.

I had a barrister called Anthony Glass. He was an upper-crust Jewish fellow who would smoke cigars. At the time he was a junior barrister. He went on to become a judge. I spoke to him in later years and he remembered me well.

I was called to the stand and began giving evidence in front of the jury. I walked through my version of events – the fight in the bar, the chaos that ensued, and how I had gone to grab a bag of guns. I told the jury that I had never fired any of the guns before, but had handled them and kept them loaded, apart from a shotgun which was faulty and I hadn't been able to fix. We had returned to Wickets bar with the intention, I told the court, 'of making a lot of noise and shooting the place up'.

Of the crucial moment – the moment of killing Mr Higgins – the court heard how we had said to each other when we went in that if we did use the guns, we would aim low. That was the plan.

Our friend had had his eyes sliced out of his head. His girlfriend was screaming. He was such a mild-mannered fella – not a fighter at all

– the most gentle bloke you could think of. And like all bullies, they only targeted him. Yeah, we were angry, but not murderously angry.

As we went down the stairs leading to the late-night club, the door was opened by Mr Higgins. The court report continued:

> Massey raised his shotgun and pointed it at Higgins to push him inside; the latter tried to grab the weapon, which went off accidentally, and Massey continued his forward movement into the bar. He fired five shots at the optics, everybody had deserted the bar for the alcoves or the kitchen … and John said the words to the effect that he was looking for someone, by which he meant the man he just shot, explaining 'when we came or when I came through the door and the gun went off I didn't actually think at that time I had hit him'.

When I was quizzed about shooting a pistol at police who had come to arrest me at my home in Rainham, I said how I'd pointed my gun at the police car and seen everybody inside duck out of view. It meant I felt safe to let off a shot. I wanted to make a bang, that's all, just sound effects.

In reply to the question why I hadn't just fired into the air, I said:

> Why, I am surrounded by police officers and I wanted to get away. It just could be – it has happened before – that someone wants to take a chance with me. By firing it into the air they might get the impression that I'm not very serious in my intentions, whereas I could convince them still without hurting anybody.

Later, under cross-examination by my partners' counsel, I said we had been drunk when we got to the bar, and I honestly had no idea who had thrown a drink in the landlord's face, but it was neither me nor any of my mates.

I also said under oath that the guns weren't my property, nor could I recall any discussion about what we intended to achieve by going back to Wickets bar. I managed to tell the court, under cross-examination from Maxwell's barrister, that Maxwell was 'pretty well drunk' and had been extremely scared by the sound of the gun going off. I didn't tell him anyone had been hurt and made sure it was crystal clear he had no part in what happened that night.

The issue of the guns that were used came up again later in the trial – and on reading the court transcripts, and looking back over all these years, it was a moment that swung things the wrong way: it was a damning point in my conviction. I had told the court I hadn't ever fired any of the guns before – but the Crown's counsel begged to differ.

They came up with something I'd hoped had managed to pass them by, a little incident that would have unforeseen consequences. They had noted that, at another trial at the Central Criminal Court just the year before, I'd given evidence in defence of two acquaintances, and my evidence helped them be acquitted of armed robbery. During that trial, where I was a witness, I'd said under oath that I had fired one of the shotguns – the same gun that was used to kill Mr Higgins – in January 1975, when the alleged bank raid had taken place. Both my friends were found not guilty, and the Crown wondered why I had previously sworn I had used the shotgun but now, in a murder trial with me on the stand, I was saying the opposite.

'I lied,' I simply told the court.

At this point my QC stepped in, and asked the judge for instructions. The jury left the court and my defence team argued that I should not be examined over a statement I'd made relating to armed robberies I was not accused of.

Mr Justice Mais overruled their submission and allowed the cross-examination to continue. He stated that the Crown should be allowed to ask me questions over any written statement I had previously given – and, crucially, that it helped establish what experience I had with firearms and highlighted a contradiction in my evidence.

I had to think quickly and make a decision as I stood there in the dock, looking carefully at the faces of the jury who held my fate in their hands. I decided to refuse to answer further questions and reiterated that the witness statement I had made in the previous trial was in no way true.

That trial, which I'd given evidence in while on remand for murder, had seen two men, Tommy Spillersee and Terry Jayes, tried for armed robbery. Friends of mine, they were being accused of a robbery I had committed.

Terry used to work the door at the City Club down the City Road for years and Tommy owned Oscars, a club in Albemarle Street, Mayfair. They knew each other and we used to go to their clubs. They were both fairly good mates. I heard the police were attempting to fit them up for a bank job I'd done in Hendon – not a big score, I remember, but a trouble-free morning of work. Satisfying.

The cozzers picked them for the job because they were supposedly the same size and shape as us – they thought they might be Laurel and Hardy. Terry was tall and thin, and Tommy was short and squat, and just like me and Terry, they had a criminal past. The coppers didn't like them and had a fixation about getting them for something, anything. They wanted to fit them up – but they did actually believe it was them this time round. I got to hear about it and realised they were being tried for something they were completely innocent of. They were desperate for a bit of help – they were clutching at straws, and they would have got fifteen years if I hadn't intervened.

I had communication with them and told them to send their solicitors round to see me in Brixton. They did. We went up the Old Bailey and gave evidence. I had precise descriptions of how the robbery had been done and I stood in the witness box and said I did it. I knew I was facing a sentence anyway, so I said it was me. It's further proof of the miscarriages of justice that go on. I told them exactly how it was done, and made it obvious it was me. The prosecution team were doing their nut – and the pair got off.

But back in the dock and charged with murder, I had to roll back on my previous statements in the other trial and I told the jury I had lied to help friends. I went on to tell the court I didn't know I had shot Mr Higgins and had gone into the club still looking for him, unaware he was injured and thinking he had followed me into the bar. And I also told the jury that sometimes 'guns don't always go where you point them', in relation to firing off a round at police officers outside my home.

My co-defendants' evidence began to cast further light on the evening's tragic events. Terry said he had little to do with what went on. Yes, he said, he was a heavy drinker and had dropped his trousers 'for a laugh' – but he hadn't struck anyone when the fight erupted and instead had been knocked squarely on the head during the melee.

He also said he hadn't expressed a 'particular view' about the righteousness of driving to collect a bag of guns and then returning to the scene to scare those who'd beaten our friend up. He said that, when we arrived, he decided he'd help shoot the place up, but he had no intention of harming anyone. When the fatal shot was fired, he didn't realise it had claimed a life – and once inside, he'd fired a solitary shot into the till and then run off.

Speaking directly to the jury, Terry said, 'It isn't clear to me that Massey is a dangerous person ... I don't agree that Massey is a thoroughly dangerous person to be with. If I thought so, I would have left. If I thought anyone was going to be killed, I would have left.'

The jury thought otherwise. An 11–1 majority saw me given a life sentence with a recommended minimum sentence of twenty years. I was also found unanimously guilty of affray, and the jury voted 11–1 to find me guilty of conspiracy to murder, possessing a firearm with intent to endanger life (unanimous) and attempted murder (10–2). I was given a total of ten years to run concurrently. Terry got a life sentence for murder and ten years to run concurrently for causing an affray, conspiracy to murder and possessing a firearm with intent to endanger life.

Maxwell was handed a three-year stretch for causing an affray and possessing a firearm. The judge instructed the jury to find him not guilty of conspiracy to murder, and the jury were unable to agree whether he was also guilty of murder. My sister Jackie was found guilty of unlawful possession of firearms and impeding an arrest.

In his summing up, Mr Justice Mais told the court:

> I regard Harper as dangerous and vicious. I was not however able to form any conclusion as to whether he was a follower of Massey, who was the leader, or whether they were both equal. I am inclined to the view that Harper was a willing follower and partner though Massey was the leading spirit. I consider however that Harper should remain in custody for a considerable period of time.

I remember it clearly, of course, when the verdict was read out. When the jury came in my knees went all wobbly. My mum was there and started crying. It was horrible.

This jury's verdict was to be my nineteenth conviction for thirty-eight offences, dating from 1960 to 1976.

Some things from my trial stand out, other bits are a blur. I do clearly remember Charlie Higgins' sister. His family were at the Old Street Magistrates' Court for the committal, and she was in the public gallery, which was the same level as the court. As the hearing finished, on the way out, she leant forward and spat at me. I could see the pain in her face. I saw the suffering I'd caused. I understood then what I had done and how it had impacted others.

The experience of being the accused in an Old Bailey murder trial is one way to have a ringside seat at how the criminal justice system works. I instructed my lawyers to appeal, arguing the judge had misdirected the jury when I was cross-examined about my previous use of the 'murder' weapon. Over the last forty years, I've often looked back at how the case against me was built, and have wondered, over and again, if my barrister could have made a better argument about how the shotgun had a hair trigger and illustrated how it had gone off accidentally. Today, a good barrister would have sought a verdict of manslaughter.

Then there was the prosecution. The prosecution barrister bent on putting me away has certainly helped form my opinions about justice. You have a crown prosecutor whose sole duty it is to make sure you're found guilty. He may know you're innocent but he still goes for a guilty verdict. That's not justice. Whoever has the most tricks in their bag comes out on top.

I felt everyone there was playing a role. There was all this drama and posturing that had nothing to do with justice or trying to find out the truth. It made a sham of the whole business and there was something deeply distasteful about it. It was as if it was arranged in a way to make everybody's misery worse.

It's also a fact that the judge presiding over the case had been over-bearing in his directions. I felt the jury had been bullied into making a decision.

Judge Mais was a horrible cunt. They were a hung jury at first – and he more or less threatened them. The jury came back and said they hadn't reached a verdict. The judge began to do this lobbying in an authoritarian way. They think they are the highest power and that people are just in awe of them. Then the jury went back and it was 11–1 in favour of guilty. That was because of the judge.

To me, he was just another person wearing a silly gown and a stupid wig. It goes to show that when people put on a certain attire, they act completely different. What you need to do is imagine them naked and then they just look like any other dozy bastard.

And the worst thing was, I was hopeful during the trial that I wouldn't be found guilty. I knew in my heart I hadn't committed murder and that I'd had no intention of committing murder.

The prosecution were full of subtle tricks to create a picture of me that no one who knew me would recognise. During the trial, they pulled all sorts of terrible stunts. Michael Worsley, the prosecution barrister, laid it on as thick as fuck. I was giving evidence and the judge says to me, 'Would you like a glass of water?' Worsley made a big show of offering me water in a glass and then pulling his hand back and pouring it into a plastic one. He wanted to make me look like a wild animal, someone who couldn't be trusted with a proper glass of water.

Then there was the gun and what the prosecution did with it. For starters, I knew the gun was faulty. We'd bought it from a bloke who had a farm in Essex and we then took it to a barn and sawed the butt and barrel off to shorten it. There's a long tube in the butt that holds a spring that operates the trigger mechanism, and that was damaged. We did what we could, but it still didn't work properly and had a tendency to go off at the slightest touch.

But a firearms 'expert' came into the trial and said there was no problem with the trigger. People took it for granted that he knew what he was talking about — but believe me, he was no expert. I said it was an accident. It was. I went through the procedure of how it came about. The gun had a hair trigger — but the forensics poo-pooed that. It was a Remington five-shot automatic and the spring inside was integral to the working of the breach. We had sawn too much off the butt and the spring was exposed. It flew out and had a tendency to go off without us meaning it to. We had used it for hold-ups. What we should have done was not used proper cartridges. It had been used for bird shooting, and the cartridges were live.

A trick we'd often pull was to mess about with the cartridges so they were non-fatal. We would take the shot out and replace it with rock salt. The rock salt would hit you quite hard, but become powder on contact. It would mean the person would think they'd been shot — they'd shit themselves and freak out — but the injuries, of course, would not be catastrophic. For some reason we hadn't got round to doing it with these cartridges — we rarely used the gun anyway.

Every part of my defence, they found a way to undermine. That Worsley was a sneaky bastard. He got me to handle the gun in the dock. He came over and told me to take the gun, and stupidly I did. He made a big thing of trying to say, 'This is what a killer looks like.' I shouldn't have accepted it off him – it was out of order.

Nearly fifty years later, I still look back and wonder how it could have been approached differently. There's one fact I find hard to understand still.

The difference between manslaughter and murder is big – with manslaughter you get a maximum of twelve years, but with murder you're looking at a life tariff. Anthony Glass was supporting the lead barrister, a man named Richard Lowry.

From the start, I'd put my hands up and wasn't looking to get off. But they said it was premeditated and that was bullshit – it wasn't anything of the sort.

The concept of premeditated murder is one in UK law where certain conditions regarding intent have to be fulfilled. My behaviour didn't show premeditated intent.

I was really pissed off with what they said about the timing: they said if I'd left the club and come back within the next fifteen minutes, it wouldn't have been premeditated – but we came back after twenty minutes, and those five minutes meant they thought it was sufficient time for us all to sober up and be rational, to have a degree of intent you wouldn't have after fifteen. What's that about? We're talking five minutes' difference between manslaughter and murder. I know people who take five *days* to calm down if they've got the hump badly enough, let alone five minutes …

Five minutes – is that really long enough to have a debate about whether you're going to kill someone or not?

◆ ◆ ◆

From the Old Bailey, I was taken to the Scrubs, and after a brief chat with my legal team, launched an attempt to have my case heard again.

I appealed the verdict – but I couldn't appeal against the sentence as it was mandatory for murder. There would be no return to court for evidence to be reconsidered. I didn't even see anybody.

The ruling was upheld and I got a slip of paper telling me so a few weeks later. That was that.

FIVE

Following that moment in the courtroom when I was given the news of my sentence, I was bundled into a 'sweat box' prison van and taken straight to the Scrubs, the west London prison I would get to know well. I was handcuffed and placed inside a cage inside the van, the only window being a skylight above me. That would be my only option for some kind of breakout – that, or the dream that a gang of mates would swoop, armed to the teeth, and spring me. But there was no sawn-off shotgun-toting cavalry on its way. The idea of escape was just a fantasy.

The van picked its way across London, through the traffic, taking me closer to full-blown incarceration. I spent some of that journey trying to work out where I was, thinking of those streets on the other side of the van door, of people going about their lives, free to do whatever they fancied that night. That wasn't going to be me for some time, barring a miracle. I soon lost my bearings, with the stopping and starting and all the turns. It wasn't until the van edged through a set of prison gates into an inner courtyard that what was happening really began to dawn on me.

It was a cold day, but I started to sweat. I was led from the van across a courtyard of cracked tarmac and into a grotty reception area. Here a warden watched as my cuffs were taken off and recorded details from a chitty into the prison book: date of birth, sentence length, all the details that would be scribbled into logs in every prison I was to see the inside of for the next five decades. Trying to keep calm but with the panic inside bubbling up, I pretended to be nonchalant as I went through the customary procedures … all these little steps away from the world I knew and had enjoyed, and was now beginning to realise the importance of. Each one of these little processes was a way of confirming the nightmare was reality. I was going through those locked doors, going behind those bars, and I wasn't coming out for a very long time.

I was told to strip, and was given a proper, full body search – all the bending over, lift your balls, open your mouth – a system that not only triple checks for contraband, but sets out the boundaries and makes it clear who is in charge. It's a handy tool for demeaning any newcomer, designed to put the new arrival in no doubt where his place is.

After this belittling experience, I was led further into the prison, further away from the outside world, into a shower block and told to have a wash. I was given a set of prison clothes – worn out, grey, uncomfortable, ill fitting – before being led to the hospital wing. I would be kept there for a week, not because I was ill, but as a routine for any newly convicted lifers – a system to check exactly how you were going to handle the fact that this was the new reality.

After seven days under the eyes of nursing staff, I was taken back to the reception area and the grey prison uniform was taken off me. Another pair of trousers and jacket, with a scratchy shirt, was handed over – this time the jacket was sewn with the infamous 'patches', an addition I would get very used to over the coming years.

'Patches' is part of the regime for prisoners deemed to be an escape risk or deserving of special measures. You're given this awful uniform. It has a big yellow stripe down it, like a skunk, and a big white diamond on the back.

Nowadays they stick you in green or orange boiler suits. I looked into it and found out it was against European conventions – you aren't allowed to make a prisoner stand out like this among his peers. But the government didn't care. They'd pay a fine instead of implementing changes to make it more humane.

As well as the distinctive get-up, patches meant the prisoner could only move about the prison under guard and was only let out of their cell for work and exercise. They would be regularly moved from cell to cell, limiting opportunities to saw through bars, wriggle windows open or pick locks. Frequent, unannounced searches cut down any risk of plots, but are a form of harassment and intimidation as well. At 7 p.m. each night, clothing would be removed, leaving the prisoner with just a shirt to sleep in. Through the night, the lights would be left on – and the spy holes would be rattled open by wardens on their rounds to check their charges were still where they were meant to be. All these tricks are employed to ensure the prisoner is unable to sleep through.

I was given Category A and Category E status, the highest form of security, which greatly restricted what I could do. Cat. A said I was a murderer doing life and Cat. E meant I was put in patches, mainly for attempted escapes. I went in as a Cat. A and stayed that way for the next sixteen years.

I got to know my new home, the system, the people and the layout. The Scrubs was made up of four buildings with pitched roofs, pandering to the Victorian architect's love of the neo-Gothic.

Modern extensions have been built to link the older buildings with each other and provide extra capacity. The wings were unimaginatively called A, B, C, D and E, and each was made up of four different landings, accessed by steel stairways. One of the first things any newcomer notices is the noise. The height of the wings, around a central hall, creates an echo chamber for the voices of prisoners and staff, footsteps on the stairs, the banging and clanging of cell doors, the barking of instructions, and the sounding of bells and alarms to tell the prisoners what part of the day they've reached.

Later, I would be moved from a spell in C Hall, where new arrivals and those in patches were held, to D Hall. It was a slightly less strict regime, paradoxically perhaps, for people with longer sentences: here, partly due to a lack of staff, the inmates were allowed to enjoy a little bit more freedom.

With the wings well secured from the outside world by a series of double gates and barred doors, cell doors were unlocked at around 7 a.m. It meant the prisoners could come and go about the landings until lockdown in the evening, usually at 8 p.m.

Tables on the ground floor provided space for food, games and gossiping. A big urn of boiling water was always on the go for teas and coffees, and there was a weekly film screening.

I ended up doing three spells in the Scrubs, but I wasn't to know in those first months I wouldn't be allowed to settle in any prison for any length of time. I would be moved about regularly, for no reason except to cause me unease and disruption. Each move would see me lose personal items I'd carefully collected. Possessions would go missing en route or be damaged. It proved to be a source of extreme frustration over the coming decades, and it was a prime illustration of the bureaucratic jobsworthiness of the system I was trapped in: I went through a tick-box induction process every time, and every time something would get lost or broken. I came to hate it.

Maybe it could have been worse: I had friends and contacts across the country. The grapevine would mean, when I appeared at a new facility, there would be a carrier bag of goodies waiting. Reggie Kray, who knew me on the outside because I drank in one of the twins' clubs, would make sure I had a good stock of tobacco, tea, sugar and other cell staples on arrival. He made a point of using his contacts, so I was looked after while the system tried to fuck me over.

◆ ◆ ◆

But there was no comforting bag waiting for me when I first went down. Instead, I arrived at the Scrubs in an unenviable position. Wardens knew I had fired shots at officers and had heard I was a gunslinger with a strong record in hold-ups.

I went into prison with a ready-made reputation. I was a target for every screw with a beef.

Their tactics included slipping a note in a box used to let prisoners anonymously grass up others. They'd be saying I had a gun or a set of keys with me, so they could spin my cell whenever they fancied it. It was a concerted campaign to make sure I couldn't settle and quietly serve my time.

They tried all they could to provoke me. My life was continually uprooted. When they wanted a lockdown or whatever, I was the reason they used.

It went on and on. For the first six years I was treated horrendously. They try to wear you down over an extended period, and it was doubly worse for me, as they weren't used to people having a personality. They aren't ready to have someone who is prepared to stand up to them.

They want you under their thumb, and they had that brashness caused when you put on a uniform. They told me over and over I was just a scumbag, as if the more they said it, the more chance there was I might believe it and break. But I was never going to.

Then there was my brother Terry. Early on, I got some properly devastating news. Months after I was sent down, my dear Terry took his own life. He shot himself in the head with a crossbow.

None of us knew he was in a bad way. We think he'd had an argument with his girlfriend and it tipped him. I was absolutely heartbroken, and it was made worse that I was inside and couldn't see my mum and dad and be there for them. They didn't let me out for his funeral, claiming I was an escape risk.

He was only ten months younger than me. We'd swapped a couple of letters since I'd gone in. We were close, we'd shared a bedroom as kids and I loved him to bits. They took me to a chapel where my family was and I remember my older sister Carol being in absolute bits. She had that same look on her face as Charlie Higgins' sister. They had both lost a brother. I understood now.

Terry's death made me even more determined to survive inside, and come out and look after my family. I never got over his death, never, and it gave me something to fight for – I knew I had to get through this for Mum and Dad. I had to. They couldn't lose me as well.

◆ ◆ ◆

My sister Jane has kept all of my letters – every one I sent her from inside, stretching across four decades. Reading them back, they provide an insight into prison conditions and remind me how an individual copes with facing a life sentence and daily life behind bars.

In a letter to Jane dated 12 July 1976, I touched on how the loss of Terry had hit me and how being inside made it harder to understand. 'I miss our Terry and will never be rid of this deep, hollow feeling,' I wrote. 'Knowing he will never be back is very hard to get used to. I got a letter from Terry just two days before and it was quite cheerful. I'd hate for somethings to happen to any of youse.'

I went on to offer brotherly advice on hearing that Jane had moved out of the family home. 'It's not been a very good year for our family, has it?' I wrote:

> You are my little ol' Jane – you appear never to age, and you probably appear that way to Mum as well. Secretly I think she doesn't want you to grow up. Well, whatever, it is a shame because to me it looks like the family is falling apart. Mum and Dad must be really heartbroken and a little lonely too. Dad will never show or say what he feels yet if you look into his eyes you can see the pain mirrored there. Go back, Jane, and try and make some sort of workable relationship with Mum. Give it one more try for me, huh?

In the letter, I reminded Jane that I'd implored her to learn how to type – 'you could be earning £50 or £60 a week' – or to learn shorthand, 'another skill that will always be in demand'.

I added, 'Even if you had a few O Levels you could have got yourself into a nice little bank somewhere and if you didn't like your boss I could've relieved him of a few grand, ha.'

And then I ended the letter on a brighter note – something I'd always unconsciously do. 'When you are short of money, depressed and maybe in a one sided love affair the world can seem a pretty rotten place to be. Yet you must go on, no matter what,' I wrote. 'I know all about heartache, believe me, and I am still laughing!'

Another letter from the Scrubs as I settled into my sentence is addressed to the whole family: it's full of small talk, an attempt to bring some normality into the situation. I told Dad he should get his varicose veins sorted and revealed I'd met a friend inside, Frankie Abbott, who'd come to the Scrubs hospital to 'get his farmers done'.

I asked them to come to see me on Boxing Day, and said I was settling in, meeting other bank robbers whose luck had run out. 'It is a lot better now,' I said. 'More of my own kind, so to speak, more freedom if that's the word, and better visits.'

I wrote about getting on to a college course and learning some languages – I remember thinking that picking up another language might be handy if I ever made a run for it – 'or they've got a course that doesn't sound bad, antique restoration'.

'I could go on the carpenters or works party, provided they agree of course. Then there's the tailors or laundry, what do you reckon?'

My letters were ways to reassure, let off steam, and try to look at where I was from another angle. I told my family how I'd painted my cell, got some pictures up and had my 'trusty guitar'. Later in my sentence, I refused to make my cell feel too comfortable as I didn't want it to look like I was accepting my lot. I got to the point where I didn't want reminders of what I was missing staring me down every minute. But at the start of my stretch, I did what I could to make my environment as welcoming as possible.

'Looks more like home now,' I told Jane, before referring to friends I'd heard had been nicked for a bank job in Dulwich. 'I heard George has pleaded not guilty, and Jimmy and the others all guilty! Got something up his sleeve, there's no doubt.'

I asked her for an Elton John album for a Christmas present. 'It was still playing when I dumped the Aston! Ha, keep the memories alive, won't it!' I joked.

Other details come back to me when reading these letters: I was docked 7½*d* per week from my wages so I could join a film club, and I told my family all about the food:

> There's eight of us on our table, we call it the bank robbers' table, and we all buy grub from the canteen, like tonight it was Spaghetti Bollock Naked, 'cept me, I had egg and chips, can't get on with that spaghetti, load of stodge. I had a really good curry last week, we have a good cook on the firm! … You wouldn't find better in any restaurant! We buy our own tea as well and brew up properly with a tea pot, all civilised like, ha, must go through about six pounds of tea a week!

The bank robbers' table saw me meet up with others who'd been in the same line of work, and it offered some sense of camaraderie and comradeship.

Inside, I met Peter Coulson, a member of the Wembley bank firm sent down for one of the biggest and most successful heists of the twentieth century – the famous Bank of America job. Coulson had been working as a car dealer when he got twenty-one years for his role in a raid that scooped an £8 million payday, of which only £500,000 was recovered. A gang of seven made off with the sum in 1975 when they raided the Mayfair branch of the bank.

An inside man, Stuart Buckley, worked there as an electrician and had got the combination of the safe by hiding in the ceiling and watching the safe being opened. Renowned safe cracker Leonard Wilde was also involved, while ring leader Frank Maple was never caught, and to this day is said to be hiding out in Morocco.

Peter was a good bloke, and we helped keep each other going by exchanging tales of the crimes we'd pulled off. He was always good to have about, and so was a man we called John the Bosh. He was the key man. Buckley got his idea from him. He would hide in false ceilings and then photo people using security codes. Peter had a mind like quicksilver. Later, after he'd been serving a long stretch, his wife had breast cancer and we wrote to the Home Office to see if they could give him some early remission or at least visiting rights and compassionate leave, but of course that was out of the question.

I remember early on meeting John Sparrow, who was doing time in Long Lartin and was a couple of doors down from me. He was marked – it had been a big case when he went down. He'd been involved in a jewel heist in Blackpool and had shot up a top cozzer, a superintendent, and so he got done big time for that.

There was an acceptance at the time that you were never going to get out for that sort of thing, shooting a copper. We all knew about the cop killer Harry Roberts. He was at Coldingley, on another wing, but we used to chat in passing. If you ever shoot a copper, you can't do any wrong in jail. It's not surprising that prisons are full of criminals who dislike the police, so you were always OK if you were in for that.

They were mates of mine, Peter and Jon and a few others. I hadn't done any work with them but there was mutual respect between us. It was like a fraternity.

I was comfortable being with criminals whose motivations I could understand. Because we were bank robbers, people thought we must be vicious thugs, but that was bollocks. We were just after the money, and money from a system that was stacked against the people. We weren't robbing old ladies: we were robbing the robbers, people who have their hands in all the financial services, insurance, the lot – robbers, all of them.

Bank robbers would no more condone burglarising someone's house than they would paedophilia. There were lines you just wouldn't cross.

They wouldn't hold a Stanley knife to someone's throat. Such a crime would be unfathomable to an old-school bank robber. That code was helpful when we were inside. It was a guide used to separate you from those you didn't want anything to do with – the scumbags, the crazy ones.

The phrase 'institutionalised' is bandied about and usually means someone with grey skin and a pair of dead eyes, who couldn't wipe their own arse if the walls came tumbling down. But there are other ways you get in the system and the system gets in you. Prison slang, for example, becomes second nature (and helps you spot a fellow con on the outside, too). A Parra was a tramp (paraffin lamp), a Steam was your mug (steam tug), Kanga – screw (obvious, really). A Tom Pepper was a liar, named after a tabloid tipster whose horses never won. Being Shanghai'd meant being moved unexpectedly, as did being ghosted.

I soon learned other facets of prison life. I was kept on my toes by the screws, who'd give my cell a spin for want of something better to do. They'd call it locks, bolts and bars, and it's the times they would do it that really grated.

In the old days they would pull their truncheons out and whack the bars with them and then turn the lights on and off. One of the things I found most irritating was when they switched on all the lights and then left them on. You're all ready to put your nut down and go to bed for the night. You get in bed and turn the light out and then you realise the fuckers have left the night light on – you have to ring the bell and get them to come along and turn it off again. They used that as an excuse to take liberties by tossing your cell – they'd come in and disturb your stuff.

They'd wreck your cell with a spin and they never put it back as it was. They'd throw all your legal papers, your personal letters, all the confidential stuff, like legal mail, in the air. Technically they aren't allowed to look at any of that. If they're letters from the probation, MPs or solicitors, you're supposed to get them to you sealed. When you are on locks, bolts and bars, they look at everything, so nothing's confidential.

It's a charade to make the rule that legal mail is confidential if they can then just read whatever they like. You soon find out that when you have two or three screws in your cell, nothing is sacrosanct. All the spiel they give out, one would assume we have certain rights. But in reality you have none whatsoever.

Those first few months became the first few years. Time. Monotony. Time. Monotony. The two things that are abundant inside, and the two things the prisoner least wants. Seven days a week, fifty-two weeks a year, Christmas – there's no day off. Every day is the same.

On a weekend you can't have a lie-in. They disturb you with their locks, bolts and bars. Some prisons you aren't allowed to stay in bed – they make you stand outside the cell. It depends on the regime. If you have a decent jail they may say, 'Oh, sorry John,' and then close the door again, but in general they barge in and do what they want.

There's no etiquette about knocking. You can be standing there bollock-naked and there are women screws who waltz in and don't blink.

Usually after bang up in the night you're meant to be safe till the next morning, unless there's a security thing going on – then they can come in and spin you at 3 a.m. It's something you're always aware might be about to happen. In the old days there were ways to stop them barging in. Those old jails had a lino floor and you could cut a square out and fit a little square battery in, and it would stop the door opening. Or you'd make a wooden wedge – there were lots of ways to balance the scales a little. There were jails where you could get a drill, drill a hole at the top of the door and then drop a bit in it. It would mean no one was opening it unless you said so. That wound them up no end.

Now they have solid 5cwt doors on a spindle hinge and outside they can use an Allen key to undo a fitting. If you wedge up, they just swing the door the other way. But I came up with ways to circumvent that too.

There used to be the old-fashioned trick of just piling up the furniture in front of the door and telling them they weren't fucking coming in. Now they bolt everything to the floor and walls.

◆ ◆ ◆

In a letter written after a few months inside, I asked my family to look out for Marilyn. I explained to Mum I was only allowed to write twice a week, and I had to send Marilyn at least one of the letters.

'It is a small enough thing for someone who is going to stick by me for what could be the next 20 years,' I wrote. 'She is a good girl, Mum, and I wish you could get on better together, it would make me much happier.'

My letters tackled reality, but I also tried to keep the family's spirits up. 'Are you getting any of this lovely sunshine?' I asked Mum. 'I hope you managed to get some sort of break from Kentish Town – I'm having mine, ha!'

I also told them about how I'd been placed back into patches for a misdemeanour I didn't care to elaborate on. 'I promised Marilyn I'd make the shortest route possible in getting out so I must make the effort,' I said. 'I've been told the recommendation is only so much hot air from the judge and that the time depends on me. So for all of us, including me, I'll do my best. With a bit of luck I can cut it in half.'

And wanting to be as conversational as I could, I also gently scolded my mum for breaking down at my trial. 'You let me down at the last minute at the Old Bailey, Mum,' I joked. 'Naughty girl! You looked much happier on the visit here though. Why didn't you show up, Dad? Your old phobia of prisons again? You had better show up next time else I'll send the tax people round to see you!' I chided Dad gently for not writing, adding that I knew 'it is hard to find the right words to say'.

Six months in, I was given access to the woodwork shop and began to pass my hours by making bits and pieces. I started building Marilyn a doll's house, based on a personal vision I kept having of how our home together would have looked if I hadn't returned to The Cricketers on that fateful night.

Keeping things sweet with everyone on the other side of the wall was a constant issue in my mind. I had to show the family I was OK, and make sure they were as well. I had to be a rock for them and repay Mum and Dad and my siblings for standing by me.

'Trust you to create problems,' I jokily wrote to Jane. I was referring to my leather coat. 'You know Marilyn doesn't like parting with anything of mine. You'd be surprised at the things people have asked for since I've been away. It's a wonder that I've got any underpants left, let alone coats!'

I threw in some heavy brotherly advice, warning her not to get pregnant. I wrote:

Under no circumstance can any liberties be taken in any way, savvy? You get hurt other than by normal everyday marital squabbles and I think I have still got enough pull to organise 'hunting expeditions' of my own. Comprende? Clear as glass now? In other words you are like a member of Royalty, whether you be a princess, a pigeon or a swan, you are a protected species!

I also kept urging Jane to get a job: 'Choose a large firm rather than a small one and give your eyes a treat every payday. If there are any firms left in London they would, I am sure, pay handsomely for info …'

◆ ◆ ◆

My time at the Scrubs was brought to an end early in 1977. Without any warning, I was transferred up to Yorkshire, to HMP Wakefield. It's the largest Cat. A prison in the UK, and had earned the unenviable nickname of the Monster Mansion for the high number of murderers and child sex offenders imprisoned there.

They came into my cell and dragged me out of bed at four o'clock in the morning and shoved me in a van – no explanations, nothing. It took me a while to find out what was going on. They were reluctant to reveal anything.

It was the same as the Scrubs – they saw me coming and rubbed their hands. At Wakefield, they also had boxes on each wing where notes could be anonymously dropped for the authorities to read, and they became a regular source of persecution for anyone they didn't like.

My time at Wakefield was marked by tension and confrontation. My reputation was such, anyone could write anything, make it up and put it in a box. Any cunt could make up a story and they fucking did, all the time.

There was this allegation I'd stolen a set of keys, and was planning God knows fucking what, a mass breakout? There was one grass who said I had a set of detonators. Detonators? Fucking hell, I may be connected, but why the fuck detonators? And then there was one saying I had a gun. And you knew screws could use it to tip off. They'd make stuff up and because I was a Cat. A they had to act on it, no matter how stupid it was.

There was this one warden who tried to fit me up big time. This screw was a fucker and he claimed he'd heard there was a handgun in my cell. I was shown a picture of this supposed gun they found and it was totally pathetic – it looked like a child's toy. It was too ridiculous for words, the cunt. Apparently I planned to use it to escape. It was like two cola bottles stuck together. It was ridiculous. They beat the shit out of me and kept me in a strong box below ground, lit with a tiny red light. They would form a gauntlet I had to go through to empty my piss pot, whacking me as I walked past, doing their best to intimidate me, trying to wear me out … It was abuse all the time, being called a Cockney cunt. 'Come up here with your Cockney ways, think you're a gangster, we'll fucking show you,' all that sort of shit. But what they said meant fuck all to me. I was anti-authoritarian. When I got stuff like that showered over me, I didn't give a shit.

I take people how I find them. If a screw said, 'Good morning' to me in a nice manner, it would be the most difficult thing in the world not to reply in kind.

There were some insiders I met at Wakefield who I became friendly with, so it wasn't all bad. It held a high number of members of the IRA, which might have partly explained the way the screws acted. I would come into contact with Irish Republicans over the years, and inside, it was always the case that bank robbers and the IRA got on well and had a sense of mutual respect. When I reached Wakefield, the IRA prisoners were on hunger strike and it would lead to the death of Frank Stagg, a member of the organisation. It gave the prison an ominous and edgy atmosphere, and fostered a greater them-and-us culture amongst prisoners.

I looked out for some of the Republicans, they looked out for me. They liked the idea of me and my mates relieving British capitalists of their wealth. With the Troubles bringing tragedy to Ireland and mainland Britain, there were deep tensions at Wakefield. Wardens were highly strung. Some prisoners were far-right British nationalists. It was mad and also funny: these tough-guy, far-right Nazi weirdos had a face-off in the exercise yard with the Paddies. They shat themselves when it came to tackling real Republicans, real soldiers. After I'd left Wakefield, the deaths of Lord Mountbatten and Conservative MP Airey Neave in 1979 saw many of the Irish prisoners I had befriended face extra persecution.

◆ ◆ ◆

It was, thankfully, a brief spell at Wakefield that time round. In May 1978, I was transferred to Long Lartin prison in Worcestershire.

My prison notes made during the transfer show an early impatience with the system. The hope to get my head down and win remission was already wearing thin. My plans to keep my nose clean and play the system just weren't happening. It was too compromised, there was too much to hate. I couldn't settle and I didn't want to.

'Massey's conduct was characterised by violence, aggression, subversion, disruption and an anti-authoritarian stance,' wrote the Wakefield governor to the chief at Long Lartin. 'He had expressed no regret for the victim and presented himself as cold and lacking in empathy,' the report added.

My letters home also took a darker turn. 'I hate labels – I feel like a fucking item in Sotheby's. I am getting more irritable every day so please do not take me too seriously,' I told Jane.

The strain on my relationship with Marilyn began to tell. 'Marilyn is treating me like a lump of shit and that is more than being spat at by anyone else,' I wrote. 'I just don't know how things are going to work out with us concerning Sarah.'

But the move to Long Lartin worked out well, and is an example of how central the attitude of a prison governor is in creating a regime. I remember Long Lartin with fondness compared to other prisons. I stayed there from February 1977 to February 1982, after which I was transferred to Albany prison in Newport, Isle of Wight.

The Long Lartin governor, a bloke called Jack Williams, encouraged prisoners to find a hobby or a trade, something they could learn and improve themselves with. Jack was progressive. He wanted his prison to be a place of peace and reflection, and he wanted a quieter life than you'd expect of someone who has actively sought control over a large group of convicted men. Years later, I look back at Jack Williams and Long Lartin with a bit of nostalgia and wistfulness. If only all prisons could be run like his.

It was here I befriended a jackdaw. These corvids are, of course, well known for intelligence. The bird offered me comradeship.

It started like this. The jackdaw used to land in the exercise yard, where there was a football pitch. I used to find shiny things and throw them for him. He'd chase them and pick them up.

Gradually, the bird became tamer, and I enticed him inside. There were bars on my cell windows, but you could open up a panel in the glass for a bit of air. The jackdaw would fly in and perch on my knee to be fed. We became quite the pair.

I had another nice pastime at Long Lartin to help make the endless days go by. I was building doll's houses on demand for other prisoners, and I remember the darling jackdaw shitting all over the foyer of one home. I scolded him, saying, 'You dirty bastard,' telling him there was perfectly decent bathroom just along the corridor.

Then, one day, he took off and never came back. He wanted his freedom, I suppose. I missed him, but took comfort in the thought that he was out there.

The contrast between Long Lartin and other prisons was marked. In a letter home ten years later, in 1988, I remembered how Long Lartin had been managed. 'Nowhere seems the same since Long Lartin,' I wrote to Jane:

> That place was a positive hive of industry. Here they won't let anybody enhance their creativity, the arse-holes. For instance they won't allow a prisoner to earn anything by writing a best seller or inventing and painting useful items. If I was to invent an anti-skid device for cars that had the potential to save countless lives, they'd refuse me any kudos or financial gain. Let the fuckers skid to death instead.

Governor Williams was relaxed, and it meant the prisoners were too. Under Williams, the screws were told to turn a blind eye to a lively trade of hash and weed among the prisoners. Cannabis was smoked openly, and it vastly improved the atmosphere. Stoned blokes don't cause trouble. We just wanted to relax, listen to music, sleep well and do our bird. They should give it away with every breakfast tray pushed through a cell door.

Puff and a quiet regime went hand in hand. And in those early days we only had mild hash or grass, not the stuff they smoke now. And it meant jails were much more peaceful than they are today.

Lots of governors didn't give a shit, as long as we weren't smashing things up. I bet they wish they could turn the clock back today. When you were smoking cannabis, all you wanted to do was have a laugh, listen to music, eat chocolate and sleep. There was no violence if you were stoned on the old mellow stuff. They were happy days.

There were all sorts of ways of getting it in and making sure it wasn't found. People would swallow it in sealed bags, or shove it in a bag of chips in the canteen. The most common hiding place for drugs was to grease up your bum and shove it up there – they've been doing that for centuries, of course. Other tricks included getting a piece of rubber, splitting it in two and tucking an ounce or two safely away. Then you'd sew it back together like a bag and shove it down the bog.

Having decent hiding places was vital to improving your lot. Once I bought a mobile phone off someone when I was in Parkhurst. It cost me £50. It meant I could quietly call people at night, which was amazing. But eventually the screws got scanners in to search for phones being used, and they found mine.

I had a decent hiding place when they were doing their security spins. We had big boxes for our paperwork and I made a false bottom in mine. One trick, if you had the balls, was to hide stuff in plain view. Leave it out on your table and the screws wouldn't see it.

Concealing stuff is an endless game of cat and mouse, but it truly matters when you're banged up. A well-stocked cell was a vital tool in getting through the day. You could buy things via mail order, or have things sent in, and you'd filch bits and pieces from the workshops. If you gave me a Stanley knife or a craft knife, I could make anything at all disappear.

◆ ◆ ◆

Sadly for all concerned, Long Lartin with its forward-looking attitude towards work and leisure was in stark contrast to other places.

I was forced into prison employment from the beginning of my sentence and I loathed the sweatshop conditions. They put you in a workshop and I couldn't abide them. You're shut in for a long day. They'd get you making flipflops using injection moulding. Or they'd have you on a job making tags for aftershave bottles and fixing the chain links round the bottles. You'd have to do so many – say, 100 a day. They wanted a certain amount in the morning and then a certain amount in the afternoon. Another job was to shred the coir from coconuts to stuff mattresses with. You'd have to make your own mattress to sleep on. Other times you'd be sent to work in what was basically a General Post Office workshop. They got you stripping telephones, separating the parts and stripping cables for the copper.

It was fucking shit. I went for cleaners' jobs instead, where you could stay on the wing. I couldn't stand those sweatshops – it was like a Victorian factory. It was used as a way of punishing us and making a few bob out of it at the same time.

It meant that the occasional opportunities for more interesting wage earners were always welcome. I didn't mind so much the carpentry jobs they made you do. They would pay a pittance, but in the wood workshops you could pinch bits and pieces for model making, jewellery boxes, Swiss chalets, music boxes, that sort of thing, which I could sell on.

In the early days it was easy. You could have a Stanley knife in the cell, pliers, a little saw and the screws didn't mind that. It was all good, no problem, on you go. It was only later they thought everything was a weapon. It was around that time they introduced drug testing too. People would stop and search you, but in those early years, you could have things in your cell – model-making stuff, and what you needed for a spliff – and openly use them both to help pass the time. I was allowed to enrol on furniture-making courses at Long Lartin and I enjoyed them. Old Jack Williams didn't make you do anything you didn't want to.

I was good with my hands, so I was always making things. It was a good sideline. It kept me from dying of boredom and brought in cash. I'd make jewellery, I'd make Swiss chalets. I spent one year building a doll's house with an internal garage. I had a workbench and a shelf with pots of paint. I found a photograph of a Model T Ford car, so I made a model of it. I had a few quid now and then and a bit of puff, and they didn't have sniffer dogs coming in all the time back in those days. Looking back, this spell was probably when I was happiest inside.

Some prisoners had that inbuilt ingenuity to make the most of what little we could lay our hands on. I used the talents I had. I made a doll's house for my daughter Sarah and sent it out. There was a secret compartment and I'd stashed £250 for her from money I'd earned.

I loved making things with secret compartments. I made jewellery boxes with flowers on the front, and if you twisted them in a certain way, the front sprang open and there was a secret compartment behind. I'd make them, sell them and sometimes for a laugh not say anything and wait till people found these hiding places by accident. I used a spring taken out of a Biro to make a release catch, so it would ping back again. There was a pinhole you pushed something in and then – boing! – it would pop out.

In the beginning I'd get paid in 50p coins for these bits of craft. Then they did away with that and any cash you earned would be put on a balance sheet in the prison canteen. They would have a load of goods on display. You'd buy what you fancied, they'd look up in a little book how much you'd spent and how much you had left, and then you'd sign for it.

It meant tobacco was the main currency, but you could only hold so much at any time. They would say you could only have 2½oz, but most screws would overlook that rule. You'd get your tobacco and then hand it over to someone who didn't smoke. You'd distribute it around the landing so you couldn't be nicked with too much. You could get up to 100oz at any one time. People were always buying and selling things. I used to buy a lot of gifts, especially soft toys for the kids.

In Long Lartin, there was a bloke called Phil Trusty and we became mates. He could take anything and turn it into something else. He was an absolute genius. He had a little collection of hammers and files. He would take a plain old ring and then make it look absolutely beautiful, special and personal. He was very good – a waste of a talent. He should have been on the outside and at a workbench. He made my Sarah a beautiful necklace.

At Long Lartin, we were really industrious. It was a rich jail. Very rarely would someone be destitute or in debt there. Everyone was always painting, drawing, making toys, sewing, making jewellery boxes. It was a hive of industry and on the Friday there would be a big queue of people waiting to claim their wages. You'd come out with a handful of silver, and it was like Portobello Road market. All these prisoners would come out of the cashier's office and they wouldn't be able to resist buying stuff off each other – gifts for their families, loved ones. I was always being asked to make something for someone to send home. I was so busy I had to turn people away. I had a waiting list.

A lot of people today still have things I made for them thirty years ago. I started knocking out 'Fabergé' eggs on little stands. Then there was this guy I worked with who did original oil paintings. We'd put them in the eggs, lacquer them up. When you opened the egg there would be this miniature landscape inside. They looked great, sitting on a silky lining. We'd get the silk by cutting up curtains or the linings of jackets – we always found a way.

◆ ◆ ◆

It was in Long Lartin I met a man called Lenny Kempley, who would become a friend. He was a funny but ultimately tragic figure. We did bird together at a couple of places: Long Lartin and then Albany. I first met him after he'd been arrested coming down the Commercial Road driving a big container lorry full of drugs. He had a massive stash of puff he was delivering, but it didn't end well.

He was stopped. I don't know if it was a random tug, or if the cozzers had a tip-off. They pulled him over and he must have thought, 'They aren't going to take me.' He ended up shooting one of the cozzers, which of course moved it up the scale from importing or supplying cannabis to something else entirely.

Lenny was a nice man, always laughing and joking, and he became a good and reliable friend to me. We'd not met before we were both sent down, but we became mates, looking out for each other and knocking about. He was one of those people who was well liked by everyone he met.

He wasn't averse to playing a few jokes, trying to make the days go by with a laugh. Aware that he was inside for the foreseeable, he held a healthy disregard for prison etiquette – another fact that made him popular.

We met up again when we both moved back across the Solent to the Albany. In the mornings at Albany, you would have a screw sitting at a desk on the wing with his notepad, taking applications from the prisoners for requests like a doctor's appointment or a visit to speak with the governor. Anything you needed, you had to make the application first thing.

So there was this screw sitting at his desk – a right miserable sod he was, always finding a reason to be objectionable or block a request. And Lenny came out of his cell stark bollock naked with a morning hard-on, and he sneaked up behind the screw, who had his back to him at the desk. Lenny, calm as you like, stood right beside him, right at his shoulder, waving his erection. The screw turned round with a start and his nose brushed the length of his dick. Lenny said loudly, 'I'm making an application for you to do something about this here' and there was fucking uproar – the whole wing roared with laughter.

The screw was spitting and spluttering, but what else could they really do to him? He was in for good. They hated anyone who'd aimed a firearm at the cozzers. He knew that. We all knew that, and because nothing could be any worse than the situation he already found himself in, he found ways to pass the time. He was always in good spirits – you never saw him down.

But Lenny's outward appearance was deceptive, and hid a deep sense of grief and remorse. With little sign of his inner turmoil, he took his own life. It was a horrible blow, a terrible day. Everyone was so shocked. We found out he'd left a note and took a drug overdose. People who shoot police don't get out, and he knew it. It must've become just too much, the bars, the locks, the regimes. He wanted no more of it. He wanted some peace.

SIX

Suicides happened so many times down the years to people I knew. I lost a lot of friends. Some people think you go in and it is a cushy life, but no one takes their own life unless things are bad – and the fact that prison creates such conditions well, I've never understood why that's acceptable, and how it's seen as collateral damage that can't be avoided. It's genuinely scandalous that someone who is held in the care of the state might be driven to end their own life and find a means to do so.

Such blows took a toll and I reacted. I tried to make trouble. I tried to wage war. Soon after Lenny died, I was moved from Albany for a short period to Liverpool as a form of punishment when I was suspected of organising extensive damage to one of the wings. It was bullshit – I was just doing what I'd been told to do.

It went like this. They'd changed the doors – they were 2cwt metal doors that swung both ways. The screws would shout at night for us to bang our doors closed.

I got fed up, so I organised for the whole corridor to bang their doors at the same time. I called it the Jericho Club because the walls came tumbling down. Huge cracks appeared in the ceilings and the spy holes fell out of the doors. They thought I was the ringleader – and I was. It caused some right old damage when these door smashed against the frames. I suppose it was a sign of my growing restlessness.

'I am in a bit of a rut,' I admitted in a letter home to Jane:

I think my brain is being slowly killed. When I get a bad day these days it usually lasts weeks or months. I can't even work up the motivation to write to Marilyn and Sarah.

I see everything slowly crumbling, slowly dying as time goes by. To stop this decay, one needs inspiration. I don't have any at the moment. Maybe if I didn't see so clearly, I could laugh my way through these stages. I do 'see'. The picture is bleak and pretty hopeless. To exist without aim or target is like being nailed to a wall.

All my letters from Albany continued in the same vein: seven years' confinement were beginning to tell. The stress was also lying heavily on Marilyn, and in turn affecting our daughter.

I recognised it. 'I wish there was something I could do to ease their misery. She is obviously feeling the hopelessness of the situation, same as me,' I wrote home:

It is plain and clear that 'they' are not going to give us any respite to the torment. Seven years count for nothing. I do love Mal and Sarah completely but I feel it is not enough to combat the years of loneliness ahead for them. I don't feel any unkindness or bitterness towards Marilyn in these hard times. She is very courageous and loyal person. If she could find some happiness elsewhere I would let her go. That's what love is, isn't it? I can't live again or offer anyone anything of value until I am free. I will get through it, you bet. The bastards aren't going to break me down to a mumbling zombie, not even if they keep me thirty years. I have seen it happen to so many blokes over the years. Big names, little names. Hard men, weak men. They've all cracked. Some of them have deteriorated so badly that they no longer recognise familiar faces. It is very sad to see this happen to good blokes. It makes me very angry and more determined to beat the bastards. They think they can take twenty years of my life, plus degrade me and humiliate me without a fucking row? No way. The bitterness helps me survive.

I missed the warmth of women and children. Have you ever thought of the yearnings of a man for the softness of cuddling his daughter? It's such a small thing, but I would have served another year just to be with Sarah for a whole day.

Another death at Albany shook me further. A man called Rocky Harty had become a good friend – he was a nice kid and someone without a violent bone in him.

I don't know what he was in for and I didn't ask. The people I mixed with weren't nonces, I knew that much. I never enquired into people's crimes. It was up to them to tell me if they wanted to – unless they were serving longer than me, and then that would pique my interest. I didn't want to pry into people's business. God knows you lose all your privacy when you go in, and so you have to respect that one of the few choices an individual is left with is what they want to talk about. I didn't have to tell anybody anything about me and why I was there. My story was well known anyway.

Rocky was in his 20s and came from Camden, so we were from the same neighbourhood and would talk about the homes we'd left behind. He got a job in the kitchens, which was a good number to have. We were chuffed to have someone in our circle there. It could lead to certain benefits, having a mate on food.

Then one day, we got the shocking news that there had been a row and Rocky had got stabbed with a fucking big carving knife – just like that – killed in prison, no doubt over a nothing argument. Mad. A stupid row and that was that, no more Rocky. Awful.

We couldn't believe it – it was a hammer blow.

I can't remember much about the bloke who killed him except he was tall, thin, white and an arsehole. The culprit was taken away immediately. They couldn't have kept him in the same prison. He wouldn't have lasted five minutes. We were the powerhouse in there and we would have seen to him. He would have to watch himself for the rest of his time inside. Someone would always be looking for a brief moment to make him pay for what he did.

Many years later, I received a text message from an unknown number. It was a random bloke, and I had no idea where he'd got my number from.

It said, 'Hi John, I was wondering on your travels to the Isle of Wight, did you ever come across a guy called Rocky Harty?'

I said, 'He was a nice kid, a good bloke but he got killed in the kitchen. We were all broken by it.'

I got a reply back and it said, 'Yeah, that was my dad.' I was so sad they'd had to lose him in such a horrible way.

◆ ◆ ◆

The never-ending air of violence, caused by institutionalised oppression and the prisoners' individual reactions to their circumstances, seeped into everyday routines and put everyone on guard. It was exhausting.

It meant sticking together was important – supporting each other and making sure no liberties could be taken. Everyone goes in and thinks they'll keep their heads down, do their time, that somehow they'll be strong enough to get through it alone. But you soon know that's never going to be the case.

And it wasn't just moral support for the psychological effects of being locked up, and the need for mutual trust to ensure the black-market, tobacco-based economy worked. It was to ensure no one took physical liberties with you.

During one of my spells in Frankland prison, County Durham, I joined forces with a number of other bank robbers and assorted stick-up merchants to create a behind-bars brotherhood. The notorious prisoner Charles Bronson – originally called Micky Peterson – was serving a sentence for armed robbery and was held in Frankland. It was before he had earned his reputation as 'Britain's Hardest Prisoner' and had become a tabloid-created bogeyman. After a short spell outside in 1987, which saw him earn money bare-knuckle boxing, Bronson was back in after being arrested for planning another hold-up.

My friends and I knew Bronson had been done for armed raids, and he qualified as potentially part of the bank robbers' network. We took him under our wing and he was on the fringes of our company.

But then the next thing we knew, he had a row with a friend of ours, a good kid, name of Callaghan. He was a straight-up boy, and you could tell he was suffering, so I'd chat to him, try to keep his spirits up, look out for him, and we hoped we could help him get through his sentence without too much bother.

Bronson spotted Callaghan's frailty and found a dodgy pretence to take issue with him. Bronson attacked him, just like that, out of the blue. He was being a typical bully, throwing himself about, thinking he could pick on someone if he felt like it. He might've thought that, but we didn't. He wasn't going to be allowed to behave that way.

After Callaghan had been badly beaten up, my crew reacted. We went after him. Someone stabbed him in the neck, and from that day on, Bronson never came back to prison wings. He put it about that it was because he was a hard man and mental, but it was for his own protection. Everyone thought he was a fucking prick. He wasn't liked, and that went for the screws as well as the prisoners.

What really got me is that poor Callaghan ended up taking his own life. He had it hard inside – and he didn't deserve a bully like that trying it on for nothing more than his sadistic gratification.

◆ ◆ ◆

The regime at Albany didn't allow prisoners to have cash, which caused us all further discomfort. I was earning 90p a week sewing mailbags. It wasn't enough to buy the all-important stamps, tea and tobacco we all needed to survive. I needed help from my family to get by.

'Half an ounce of Old Holborn costs 67p, Letters 15 and half pence,' I wrote to Jane. 'It is impossible. In Long Lartin we were paid in cash and it created plenty of opportunities to get a living. Here no money ever changes hands – it is all done by pen.'

I had just completed two days in 'Chokey' for refusing to wear prison-issue shoes. 'Chokey' is prison slang for the punishment block, usually a Seg unit where the prisoner is banged up on their own without any privileges and in extremely austere conditions. 'I've worn me own shoes for six and half years. Their shoes cripple me. Got to look after your trotters, ain'tcha?' I told my sister.

Then I asked her to do me a favour – to go and see a friend of mine called VP. 'He said he would get me some smoke,' I added:

> With a bit of that I can get my bits and pieces and live a little more comfortable. A block, he said. I doubt he means the same as I interpret a 'block' but anything helps. A couple of ounces would be nice if it were possible. I could make a little regular income each week then to buy my tea, tobacco, letters etc.
>
> Trouble is it's £90 an ounce! I should be able to keep the money turning over in order to buy more so with luck it won't turn out to be expensive. Black is best ok? In emergency anything will do except 'formula' (crap!).

The ways and means of smuggling contraband into prison have changed down the years as X-ray scanners and detectors have improved. Tricks include 'over' scams – tennis balls packed with drugs smashed over walls by friends with a racquet on the perimeter. A car pulls up, someone jumps out, launches what they can and then gets away. Another way is to use a drone, often carrying a dead pigeon full of contraband that can be dropped when over the right spot. The Prison Service has got better at countering such ways and means, but the genius of the incarcerated can never be underestimated, and when one avenue closes, another opens.

At Albany, items were smuggled in on visits with a little bit of risk taken. Searches were cursory, and a bit of dope tucked into a bra could be exchanged. Visitors would wear new shoes in the size of their incarcerated host, and when the screws' backs were turned, the trainers would be kicked off under the table and find their way on to the feet of the person opposite. Anything sent in from the outside – books, board games, instruments – was supposed to be thoroughly checked, a chore the screws were lackadaisical about, at best.

I remember how the Albany regime often seemed too busy trying to hold a crumbling prison together to police the petty crimes committed by those inside. It was a shithole and it didn't take much to spark things off. There was a constant hum of trouble.

One riot kicked off because they stopped us having plots to grow our own things. We'd had them for years, then one day they said, 'Nope, that's it.' No explanation. They dug up our strawberry patches and rhubarb and the like. Oh, we didn't like that. I was out in the exercise yard and suddenly one of the prison walls started bulging outwards. Literally, the bricks started wobbling and it looked like the whole building was breathing, taking deep belly gulps.

It was the IRA boys – they were handy in a riot, very good at it and didn't give a fucking shit about anything. They'd managed to take off a cell door and were using it as a battering ram. They literally smashed a hole in the wall – it just burst outwards, and then the cell door followed, flying through the window. The IRA boys scrambled their way up to the roofs and punctured all the water tanks. Water flooded everywhere. It was chaos, it was satisfying – taking some anger out on that dump. There was mayhem and the governor had his arse dragged over the coals. You had to love the way the IRA boys took no shit. They were against the regime, they were always with you, always on your side. There were the Paddies who were innocent inside too – the Guildford Four. I knew Gerry Conlan, Paul Hill and Paddy Hill.

Not many people believed you were innocent inside. At the end of the day, no one gave a shit what you'd done. If you were all right, you were all right – and they were, the Irish. I liked them a lot; I looked out for them and they looked out for me. They were anti-establishment and they showed us solidarity when we wanted it and we did to them, too.

And the IRA inmates were always coming up with escape plans, which were a great boon to us prisoners who would endlessly daydream about breaking out. They inspired others not to take what was given to them. As political prisoners, they believed it was their duty to escape. One group of IRA I knew nicked the keys to a dustcart parked in a yard in Brixton prison and rammed the prison gates, smashing them open. Hearing the exploits the Irish spoke about seeped into my mind. I was bitten by the escape bug, and would spend hours fantasising.

I decided at Albany I would exercise solely on the rowing machine. I'd do 10,000m a day. I thought, 'If I get over the wall, I can't catch a ferry, and I probably wouldn't find a boat to nick with a motor – so I'd best get good at rowing.' I reckoned I could do the Solent in 10,000m.

◆ ◆ ◆

Before such dreams could be fleshed out, I was on the move again. In May 1983, I was back at the Scrubs. It was the Prison Service's tactic to keep me from settling, hindering the build-up of contacts and stopping me from getting used to a regime and rhythm, finding a semblance of normality – or finding a way out. With these frequent transfers, I was unable to look for those weak points every prison and every regime has – places I could exploit for my comfort, benefit and potentially freedom.

A side-effect of the transfers was how they limited the possessions I kept. On each transfer, things would go missing or be broken. During the move from Albany to the Scrubs, a guitar I had saved years of prison wages to buy was smashed to pieces in an act of random vindictiveness no one ever took responsibility for. When I asked about my guitar, I was met with shrugs of shoulders and an order to get back in my cell.

The difference between the Scrubs and Long Lartin was pronounced, and illustrated by the screws' reaction to another bird I befriended. I found a baby sparrow, fallen from a nest, in the exercise yard and I gathered him up and took him into my cell.

The poor thing would only feed if I held the food in my mouth. He got bigger and stronger and was perfectly tame. I thought he was smashing.

One day a screw idly came in to find the creature perched on my thumb. 'Massey,' he said to me, 'get rid. Now.'

I took the sparrow out into the yard and watched as it flitted upwards, perched on a wall and then turned tail. Of course, it left me twisted in my guts. I couldn't help but wish that I could swap places with that tiny bird.

On 20 June 1983, four days after my birthday, I thanked the family for a surprise visit they paid, complete with cake. 'I don't know how long I'll be here, Janey,' I said. 'I could get moved at any time. You'd best check before you come. Mind you, at least this time it is only round the corner.'

I was right. My third spell at the Scrubs was over before the summer was out, and I was heading back to the Isle of Wight, this time to high-security Parkhurst.

I was locked into another sweat box, handcuffed to the walls and driven south. There were no windows, so I had no idea how long the journey was taking or where we were. Eventually, we reached Portsmouth harbour and the screw driving the van nudged it onto a public car ferry.

They left me locked up downstairs as the ferry rolled its way across the Solent. The screws went to the bar. I was left in the dark below. It was scary. I kept thinking about what would happen if the ferry got into trouble, if it capsized. I'd be stuck in here and there was no way a screw was getting his feet wet to get me out. I can't ever say I was relieved to be at Parkhurst, but I was bloody relieved when that ferry docked and they drove down the gangplank to dry land.

Parkhurst, where I would spend years on two different occasions, was built in the 1830s for young offenders with the aim of giving them a grounding in Christian values before they were sent off to new lives in Australia. The prison is surrounded by elm trees, and in these trees live thousands of rooks. Anyone who has done time will remember the birds – their calls mark the end of one day and the start of the next.

It had a reputation for housing some of the nation's toughest and some of its nastiest. It was here Reggie Kray would meet and welcome me. Other gangsters in the cells were the Richardson brothers, Charlie and Eddie, heads of the notorious south London gang. Terry Clark, who was the kingpin of an Asian drug syndicate that imported heroin into the UK, Australia and New Zealand in the 1970s, served time at Parkhurst too.

I slotted in. When I got to Parkhurst, Reggie was the first person to greet me, with two carrier bags of goodies. Tea, sugar, milk, tobacco, everything. Reggie was a nice man, very principled, good and respectful. You couldn't fault him. A lot of the bad press he got was down to his brother, not him. His brother was really not well. I last saw Reggie in Maidstone, a few years later. He had been turned into a punchbag and wanted out. He was knackered and out of it, and no doubt death was truly a warm embrace for him. Other inmates included at one time the Moors murderer, Ian Brady, and the Yorkshire Ripper, Peter Sutcliffe.

I was joining a tough regime and monotony was wielded as a form of punishment. A monthly 'dry bath' – or full search – was meant to be conducted randomly for each wing. We could gauge when one was due and generally the contraband found would be just a newspaper or magazine.

The prison was run silently, with the only noise being barked orders and locks being turned, or when a prisoner snapped over a grievance or perceived slight and smashed his cell up: chairs, table, sheets, beds and the tiny window panes – thirty-six in all – all broken in rage. The screws would arrive and the prisoner would be rewarded with a solid beating on their way to a few days' Chokey.

The atmosphere at Parkhurst led to a prolonged period of introspection. 'Sometimes I forget why I am here and I begin to lose comprehension as to why so many people are doomed to suffer turmoil with me,' I said to Mum in a letter sent in September 1983:

> It seems pointless and illogical to wilfully stand by and coldly watch the lives of my loved ones stagger beneath the load.
>
> Then I have to face reality, or go mad trying to reason this puzzle.
>
> Now that Sarah is eight, I feel desperate for time to slow down. To have a daughter virtually born and aged 20 before I can live under the same roof as her is too much hurt to cope with sometimes.

With a reactionary Conservative government in power, my hopes of a softer regime, or at least a properly funded Prison Service to look after the exploding numbers locked up under stiffer sentencing policies, were nothing more than wishful thinking.

We knew the government hated us – considered us scum, a drain on the public purse, and not worthy of being treated as humans. I knew a man called Bobby Maynard at Parkhurst. He served twenty-five years before they annulled his sentence. They gave him £2 million in compensation and then took £100,000 off him for bed and board. They did the same to the Birmingham Six – an absolute liberty.

◆ ◆ ◆

'If I could give up reading newspapers and listening to the news on the radio, things would not be half so bad,' I said to Mum at the time. 'It is the drivel of people like Leon Brittan and Thatcher that keeps pulling the rug from underneath my feet. It is funny but each time I hear the coyotes baying for more this and tougher that, I always think of the *Merchant of Venice*, it's one of the few stories I remember from school … ha!'

I told Mum I'd written similar letters but torn them up, as I didn't want the family to have extra worry. This was a common theme through the decades of letters. I had an urge to share this agony, this frustration – but also to put a brave face on things, so my parents wouldn't suffer too much. I implored them to keep safe and well, so that when my twenty years were up, they were in good shape to enjoy the family life I felt I'd robbed them all of.

'I just want you to know that I love you both very much, no matter what,' I wrote:

I have got a lot of time to make up to a lot of people.

I want to be able to take my mum and dad on a Caribbean cruise, make sure you have nice things and give you a taste of how the other half lives. You have to keep young as much as me. Keep fit and fight back at life and then we'll all make it to the boat, ok?

◆ ◆ ◆

This spell on the Isle of Wight lasted not quite a year. By August 1984, I was back on the mainland, shunted to a cell in the Leicestershire prison Gartree. Parkhurst had been a tough place for the family to visit, requiring a long and expensive journey, and often the need to stay overnight. It meant the move was, for once, welcome.

Visits had increasingly become a crucial point of reference for me. They were limited, and I had to apply for a visiting order. Back in the 1980s, this was a slip of paper to be filled in by those wishing to come. They went through various levels of bureaucracy and were meant to be open and free and in no way rationed. Before they were rubber-stamped, the governor could decide the length of time. Sometimes, for no discernible reason, a mere thirty minutes would be allocated. It meant visits were not only something to look forward to – a moment's respite – but also a source of frustration. I felt constantly angry that it was so difficult to have contact with loved ones – and sometimes felt let down when family members couldn't make it.

'Visits are the only tangible source of relief,' I told Jane:

At least I can speak and touch the outside world that way. I never could understand why everybody stays away so much. It must be a bit of a drag for you all, but not if you all take turns, surely? Nobody pulls together these days. It is the same in here, which is equally depressing. Everyone is only concerned about themselves instead of thinking 'many hands make light work'.

Life in Gartree was a sign of how serving my time was becoming increasingly hard, and the continuing threats by screws added another layer to what I was having to survive.

This sense of persecution was underlined after an incident in September 1985. Among my papers is a statement signed by a fellow inmate, Neville Brown, and dated the 28th. In the statement, Brown outlines how I was being treated from the perspective of another prisoner after a violent altercation that saw Brown rushed to hospital. He was stabbed in the head by a cell-made shank crafted out of a knitting needle.

My name is Neville Douglas Brown, and I make this statement of my own accord, without coercion, threat or promise.

On Monday at about 2 p.m., I was attacked in my cell by an inmate who stabbed me in the head.

Before I was taken to Kettering hospital to have the spike removed, I was questioned about the incident by security officers here. They suggested the man who had attacked me had been John Massey. When I denied this and said I had no reason to believe it was he, they said 'It was Taylor then, but he was put up to it by Massey.' I again said I did not feel it to be so.

On his return from hospital, screws again questioned him – and tried to force him to place the blame squarely on my shoulders: 'Several of the officers who questioned me offered his name – Massey – as being the assailant. They seemed obsessed with the idea he was somehow responsible.'

Mr Brown said he and I got on well, and that rumours regarding a stolen wristwatch that I owned were just that – unsubstantiated rumours:

> My name had been put about as the thief. I had spoken to Massey on the subject prior to the attack and departed on the understanding I was not suspected by him.
>
> The whole atmosphere was amiable. It would be ridiculous to suggest that this amounts to a motive for such a severe action. There are spiteful and malicious rumours spread around by too many weird people who continually try to manipulate internal tensions.

Mr Brown wrote me a character reference and accused officers of harbouring a long-standing grudge:

> I am aware of vindictive allegations against a fellow man of good intent, by a collection of others who appear overtly concerned about bringing harm to another person, that being fuelled by the officers' attitude towards Massey.
>
> They went so far as to suggest he had done similar things in the past and had got away, and saw this as an opportunity to get him 'this time'. To get my help I was offered early release, open prison, and an easy time for my co-operation.
>
> I said again I did not think Massey was my assailant. They appeared agitated and frustrated at what they called my 'uncooperative stance'.

The screws returned to him three times in the prison hospital, giving him a blank sheet of paper and telling him to use it to fix me up. He declined, and instead wrote a spirited defence of me:

> I did consider their proposal as it is my wish to be free as soon as possible, but I couldn't find it in me to condone my freedom at the expense of what is in effect the loss of another man's life when he

don't deserve it. He has done nothing. I am aware of the authorities' attitude towards Massey, it has been seen by me to be petty persecution from them, and he is often taken to the punishment block for trivialities, usually for embarrassing officers. I detected something was not right in the way all involved were pre-occupied with me getting to name Massey as responsible.

While I did not attack Neville, many years later I can reveal the truth of what happened.

I had this Cartier watch. I don't think it was a real one, but it was something I liked and was worth a few bob, especially in the prison economy.

I was in the shower block one day, and I left it on my bed while I was having a shower. I came back and it wasn't there. I went apeshit about it. It boiled down to this bloke Neville Brown. He was a nobody really, just one of the fucking hobbits you meet inside, and had lifted it. I'd had the nod it was him.

I didn't make a great deal of fuss at first – I kept quiet, thought I'd bide my time. I started thinking and put myself in the thief's shoes. I thought, 'What would I do with it?' I wanted it back, badly. I considered the options and thought whoever took it wouldn't be stupid enough to keep it on them, or in their cell. It would be too hot. I started looking about, searching the places I'd hide it if I were the thief. I found it in a toilet cistern, wrapped up in a plastic bag.

I kept cool. Instead of confronting him, I got someone to befriend him, go for a cup of tea with him and tell him how it was going to be. I thought he'd chin him for me and that would be that, but instead my friend stabbed him in the temple with a darning needle, causing some serious damage.

The thing was, Neville knew that I knew and he took it on the chin, took the punishment and learned the lesson. I got swagged in by the screws, taken for questioning because of rumours about this watch. But there was no case to answer. I asked Neville to write a statement and he did. I told him that was that. After my watch went walkies and before Neville got what was coming, I was taken into the Seg unit, but others were looking out for me. There was no way he could get off the hook just because I wasn't around. And in a way it gave me a good alibi. I was neatly tucked up when he got it.

◆ ◆ ◆

Christmas 1985 saw me moved on again, to Frankland prison in County Durham – a long way from family, and a move that I had suspected might happen, as I was making friends and getting used to the system at Gartree. I would have a number of spells at Frankland over the years.

I wrote home to tell the family, 'I have still got a brain damaging headache from the travelling and disruption. I got here in a police van filled with cigar smoke and farting screws.'

I knew some mates at Frankland, but I was kept in an induction unit after I arrived. It was a game – I'd done eleven years inside and the humiliating 'induction' treatment still went on.

I told the family I didn't know how they would manage: 'It's such a ridiculous length to travel, you can get to New York quicker. I know why it's called Brasside now – something to do with nuts falling off in the cold. Brrr.'

That Christmas was spent in a freezing cell. The move disorientated me. Still I managed to raise my spirits with the help of people I knew there. 'I quite enjoyed Christmas though after a while – the boys had bought a turkey and a few trimmings,' I wrote to Jane. 'Stan did the cooking – that is Stan Thompson, a mate of Ted's.'

Frankland had some screws who wanted a quiet life, which gave me and the family a little bit of scope to try to make things more comfortable. Mum, Jane and other visitors would smuggle in bits to help ease the burden.

As we learned the ropes, we realised that we could get away with things at Frankland. Mum once arrived wearing a brand-new pair of trainers that were about five sizes too big. As we sat opposite one another, she slipped the shoes off.

The screw saw what we were up to and he simply came over and said, 'Can you hurry up with that, mate? It's my job on the line.' Mum was a game old bird, and the screw did the decent thing.

Another year, Jane booked a visit to see me on my birthday. They brought a cake in and we met up with two of my friends, Georgie Reilly and Derek Falstead, who were also inside. The screws didn't mind if you mingled with the other visitors. Jane brought in a load of miniatures for us to neck and we went back to the cells pissed as farts.

She used to catch the train up to Durham as it was a horrible drive, and play cards on the way with my mate Ted. She couldn't understand why she lost every game – until she realised that Ted was cheating. He could see her hand in the reflection of the window. I fell off my chair laughing when I heard about it.

Such distractions were important but all too brief. By now, I was talking about getting the 'halfway horrors'. Friends like Vic Pryce, who had stood by me and visited regularly, were trying to help me out. There was a fundraising benefit organised at the Prince of Wales pub in Kentish Town in September 1985, with the proceeds of a £5 ticket going to me. I wrote to the organisers thanking them, but added that I wasn't too interested in the money being placed in 'any investments or possible interest accrued'. I asked Jane if she would be nominated the treasurer of any funds.

Post-Christmas, the stress was really beginning to tell. 'If I could take a pill and sleep for the next ten years, that's exactly what I'd do,' I told my family.

Prison food was often the cause of unrest, and it got so bad that for three days prisoners at Frankland had refused to eat. 'There is a bit of a squabble going on concerning the food,' I wrote to Mum:

Refusing it has left everybody hungry and irritable. Hopefully it will be resolved tomorrow – it is Sunday today and the weekend meals aren't missed that much anyway. A year of repetition of the same inedible garbage has taken its toll on most people. So many have voiced the same opinion yet the kitchen people are disinterested and downright arrogant in their refusal to move their stance ... I'm sick to the gills with this continual policy of confrontation. Every little trifle has to be clawed and fought for. Gain a privilege and lose two is their motto. Thankfully I am at peace in the workshop. The hours fly by and I hardly seem to get anything done before the day is finished.

I did find solace in work. My carpentry and cabinet-making skills were developing and I was still making jewellery boxes, chairs and doll's houses.

The dolls' houses I built were in demand from fellow lags, who would commission me to build them to send out to the confused children of absent fathers. They had another purpose, too. I would make miniature fireplaces, and they were more than just a nice design touch. They contained a secret compartment that could be used to stash cannabis from the prying eyes of the screws.

I was still finding my role as a big brother in demand, despite the lengthening absence, and I tried to settle disputes at home. In a letter to Jane dated April 1986, I broached the subject of an argument between Dad, Carol and her partner Stuart, involving money. I told Jane I could see Dad's point of view about the row, but added:

Stuart was certainly entitled to call in the police. He wasn't brought up in slum conditions and inured to criminal moralistic codes as we were. We have to respect his right to act in accordance with the rules of law as he understands them. Just because he tries at times to mould himself to Kentish Town's way of thinking in order to appease the family of the girl he loves, doesn't mean he is totally integrated with our way of life.

Dad has to be man enough to admit his own mistakes and apologise. Hitting Stuart on the chin only added insult to injury and alienated Carol even further. Carol isn't even interested in the bloody money

– money has sod all to do with it, even though it was Stuart's total payment of his army career. It is a matter of betrayal and humiliation.

I was tired of mediating between family members, and I said to Jane that 'it is possible to love and criticise – breaking through that brick wall of pride and obstinacy is quite another matter'.

But for all my words of wisdom, I was struggling badly inside. A doctor spoke impolitely to me when I had the flu and called on the screws to force me to go to work. It started a row that ended up with me stripped naked in a Seg cell, covered in bruises – and facing three assault charges. 'The doctor is supposed to have had two of his ribs broken and his minder has a detached retina,' I told Jane. 'I'm a bit sore where they mauled me.'

In spring 1986, I was banged up in solitary and I recall hearing about the Challenger Space Shuttle disaster. I wrote home: 'A tragic shock ... I didn't get to see the pictures thankfully. That is heavy duty grief. I suppose the only merciful thing was that they were probably quite unaware of their end. I think I would like to go like that.'

From my letters, my frustrations are obvious: petty rules, like putting a towel round my shoulders in the gym, meant I was getting sent to punishment blocks regularly. A deteriorating relationship with Marilyn added to my woes; Sarah began to develop a phobia about visiting.

The distance was a constant source of annoyance. Not only did family have to apply for a visiting order, which could be refused on spurious grounds, but it was expensive to come from London. I offered to pay the fare, but pointed out that 'at £45 a round trip I can only do it once – they were advertising two weeks in Majorca for £30 the other week'.

The family wrote to the Home Office in March 1986, requesting I be moved closer to home – but got knocked back. 'At present there are only eight prisons in which Category A can be held on a permanent basis,' replied a civil servant. 'It is not our policy to disclose the reasons for a prisoner's transfer but you may be assured Mr Massey's transfer was necessary.'

We faced other petty issues: Jane was told that Home Office regulations meant anyone visiting a Category A prisoner had to provide up-to-date photographs every five years; the family's had run out and they weren't told, so they were turned away at the gates. On the next visit, they were made to bring two new pictures with them, for which they would be reimbursed at 75p per picture.

I was growing more aware of the passage of time: 'I have found four more grey hairs on my chest today. My tiredness is symptomatic of the shock of discovering my age – there is me thinking I am still 27,' I told Jane.

At Frankland, I began painting and creating picture frames. 'I saw a magazine last week that pictured several paintings with astronomical price tags,' I told Jane. 'Honestly I think Michelle or Henry [my niece and nephew] could paint better. A right rip off.'

My talent for tennis and badminton kept me going: I won competitions and was named the Frankland tennis champion in 1986. 'Anyone would think it was Wimbledon,' I reported home. 'They are calling me John Massenroe – ha ha, the crook John Massenroe … I wish I had his bleedin' money. Wouldn't mind having a go at his woman, either, ha.'

I spent some nights sitting up and reading *The Brotherhood of the Rose* – and then caused arguments when I was woken by screws whistling outside my cell first thing in the morning. It caused me no end of stress. It resulted in more trips to the Seg unit.

'I've got myself a suspended sentence for something or other,' I told Mum:

Well, how would you like a whistling screw outside your bedroom door, keys a jangling first thing in the morning … the Chokey is looking like Alcatraz lately, can't even leave the daylight alone … They've put thick Perspex over the inside with two sides frosted. Beds and furniture removed. Raised concrete slab is now the bed. Airless solitary …

Sometimes, I would enjoy spirit-raising moments: a friend of mine was released suddenly when an appeal brought victory, someone would earn parole, someone would simply do their time and disappear. But apart from these brief bits of happiness, there were so many things designed to make a fucking shitty situation worse.

Looking back at Frankland, there was constant, though undeclared, war between prisoners and wardens and it led to frequent, exhausting showdowns. But whatever security measures they put in place, sooner or later a prisoner will find a way of circumventing them.

It's a continuing process, I discovered, and one you think will carry on and on until it reaches a logical conclusion: until you are in a vacuum, a sealed container, and nothing can ever get in or out. This is one of the reasons ventilation is so bad in prisons nowadays. They replaced windows with fixed units and you have to use a dial to open up pinholes. The air coming in is negligible. In the old days you could open a window. It's all done for security – it means the lags can't swing lines to other cells or have drones coming in.

Swinging a line was a classic trick I mastered in the early days. If you were out of something, and you had mates next along the landing, here's what you could do. Let's say you needed a tea bag, letter, pens, whatever. Getting it from a screw was impossible, so you'd use your noggin. You'd get something to form a weight – a bar of soap, a cup, a battery – and attach a line to it. You'd get that by unravelling your blanket or whatever, even a woolly sock, till you had a decent length of string.

Then you'd reach your arm out the window and launch your weighted line as far as you could. Your pal would put his mirror out the window so he could see it, and then reach out with a stick and pull it in.

We had an ingenious system in the Seg unit. They had steel cages attached to the outside of the windows to prevent this sort of thing, but there was nothing we couldn't find a way round. You would get a plastic bag, very light and fine, from the canteen. You'd attach the line to the bag, squeeze it through a tiny gap into the cage and let the wind blow it.

The Seg unit looked out over a courtyard and the wind would swirl about and take the bags up like kites. The guy you were trying to reach would roll up a paper and poke it through the cage bend at the end. He'd catch the bag and pull it in. When you're banged up twenty-three hours a day, you have nothing to do but think up ways to circumvent the system.

In some places, we'd drain the loo and speak down the toilets to each other, or tap on pipes. With some, where they went through the wall into the next cell, you could chisel out the mortar. You could do it from both sides until you could get something fine through the gap. Another trick to help out someone opposite you was to make a cone, attach the line and slide it under the door. You could kick it as hard as possible, or bat it, and sometimes you only needed one shot and it would fly across the corridor, under the door opposite. You could then use it to pass drugs and tobacco across to each other.

It was winning battles like this that made life bearable and helped us get through the day. The needs of the prisoner seem so simple to those who have never served time, but the littlest acts become giant when you're locked up and have four walls to stare at.

After twelve years inside, I requested the family send me a dictionary and thesaurus – 'boredom and crosswords is what this is all about' – but such small mercies were breaks in a long, dark cloud. By 1987, I was severely depressed. I wrote home:

> I can't even manage to write to Sarah or Marilyn these days, yet I love them and miss them so much. I suppose that is why. When I get to thinking about this hopeless situation, it hurts too much to write knowing I can never be truthful in giving them hope.
>
> I can't take that sort of pain too often. It leaves me defenceless and dispirited enough to want to die. It is as if I am an alien living all alone on the moon, nowhere to run to or hide or call for help.

This current bout of depression has got its teeth into me. I would give anything to see Mal and Sarah right now.

At last, in September 1987, I had some good news. Jane had arranged for me to get a new guitar, but it was held back in the governor's office for reasons unknown. Finally, it was handed over, only it didn't work – something that for someone of my practical skills was not so much a problem, more a challenge.

I stripped it down, took the strings off, put my hand inside and felt along the wires – battery terminals, switches, nothing! I can't recall, looking back, whether I was hoping to find some contraband. Was that why the guitar had been held back, and why, when it arrived at my cell, it wasn't in working order?

If I suspected so, I didn't let on when I wrote home about it. I told Jane:

The wire for the transducer just disappeared into the wood as if it were built in. I put everything back together and sat there with the hump for about half an hour until I couldn't stand it any longer and stripped it all down again ... This time I used my magnifying sheet and spotted a tiny pin hole in the bridge. I got a pin and wiggled it about, and lo and behold, the bridge saddle popped up and lying underneath was a long silver strip.

I'd found the elusive transducer! The wire that disappeared into the woodwork was connected to it. I whittled it down, squeezed it, removed some Sellotape attached to the underside of the bridge saddle, put it all back together and hey presto, it worked beautifully. I gave it a good going over and it looks a treat, great sound, well made, the best guitar I've had ... I must make a solid case for it. It is too good a guitar to trust a soft case.

◆ ◆ ◆

This spell at Frankland was to come to an end – without any explanation, as was the usual way – in the autumn of 1987. I was taken back to London and into the crumbling Victorian cells of the Scrubs, the consolation being that it was a couple of bus rides away from the family. I was there in March the following year, trying to persuade the authorities, after thirteen years behind bars, I should no longer be considered a Category A prisoner.

'I got the official notice regarding the Cat. A status yesterday,' I wrote to Jane. 'I am not feeling great about it. I feel haunted by anonymous cowards. They won't show rhyme or reason for their spite and hypocrisy. They inflict their sadism from deep shadows. The light of the day would shrivel their maggoty flesh and syphilitic brains.'

The Scrubs was not going to be my forever home, and I knew that. I spent a hot and uncomfortable summer there before the autumn brought yet another move. This time it was back to Frankland. I wrote to Jane so the family would know where I was and thanked her for her support, telling her how much I appreciated her continuing loyalty:

> I think about it all the time and make wonderful plans of how to pay you back in kind once this never ending nightmare is over.
>
> You'll probably get me fitting kitchen units in tropical hardwoods, scrubbing out the bathroom, digging a swimming pool in the back garden and sending me shopping at fucking Tesco's – but I won't complain!

Around this time, I'd got involved in playing cards. There were games going on and you couldn't help but get drawn in. I had been playing Kalooki – a version of thirteen-card rummy – but I began to get pissed off. I wrote to Jane and told her I couldn't play again until someone had sent a rule book in, as it was becoming a source of confrontation.

'I've stopped playing because of too many arguments concerning the correct rules,' I told her. 'I want them in black and white before

I play again. Meantime, it's costing me money by not participating. A Victoria Sporting Club one or Ladbrokes Casino that can't be questioned ...'

I would eventually quit cards because of the aggravation caused as prisoners lost sums of money they couldn't afford. It meant another way to pass time was blocked off. But I still had badminton and tennis – times of serenity that gave me some purpose. I would be champion in both sports at every prison I went to.

◆ ◆ ◆

In January 1990, I heard news that my co-defendant, Terry Harper, had been released. I felt a mixture of relief for my good friend but it hammered home how long I had left to serve. I asked Jane if she could visit Terry:

> If you have time can you pop over to Enfield? It's Terry, my mate. He is home for good. He is going to do me some photographs so I can see what shape he is in and then it will give me a guide as to how the years will affect me.

Later that year, with Marilyn remaining loyal, I asked her to marry me and she said yes.

I had been given the welcome news that I was no longer going to be classed as a Cat. A – twenty years of it and there it was, I wasn't the dangerous nutter they wanted me to be any more. It was a step in the right direction and it made me more open to getting married.

I had to speak to the governor, Peter Buxton, who had known me for years and done what he could to help in minor matters. Marilyn wrote to Buxton about wedding arrangements and received a disappointing reply. 'I have reconsidered the position in regard to your forthcoming marriage,' Buxton wrote:

In coming to the conclusion set out in this letter I have tried to bear in mind a number of issues, including how recently he was in Security Category A and what bearing that might have on the conditions that might apply if the wedding took place in a registry office outside the prison, and what is practical and reasonable within the establishment.

You may feel at the end of the day that your marriage to John might better wait until a little longer has elapsed since he was Category A. That is however a matter for you and John and not something upon which I can advise.

You can imagine that being advised to delay by a prison governor didn't go down well with me or Marilyn. Buxton continued:

I recognise the final decision I have made – that the wedding take place inside the establishment – will be a disappointment to you.

I am keen that the wedding be as normal event as possible in the unusual circumstances prevailing. In setting a limit of 12 adults I am seeking only to provide for a reasonable number of family members that can be accommodated, moved though a maximum security establishment and safeguarded once here. A small addition of a number of children could also be accommodated. Perhaps you would let me know if under these circumstances you are happy for the marriage to go ahead here?

Buxton also wrote to my probation officer, Mr Snelgrove, to outline his views on the proposed nuptials:

I have recently written to the future Mrs Massey laying out the options for her marriage to John. I explained I am not prepared to consider parole for John, a matter of weeks after regrading from A to B.

Nor do I consider on balance that escorting John to a registry office is the best option: remaining handcuffed through a ceremony is hardly ideal. In the circumstances I suggested either the ceremony takes place here more or less as outlined or alternatively the couple decide to leave matters for a while until marriage in a registry office is acceptable. I understand how important this occasion is to both parties. I have known John for many years and have hopes his progress can be maintained. I obviously see his marriage as a crucial part of the process. For the time being however I am not prepared to change my view.

I remember how we decided to make the commitment – a big thing for us, considering the circumstances – but the wedding never happened. It was the only time in my life I'd contemplated marriage. I proposed to her and I asked Jane to be best man. But then everyone wanted to get involved and there was all this aggro with people starting to get annoyed about who was coming and not, and you should do this and that. It wasn't about the location, about being made to tie the knot in prison, it just became way too much grief, so we dropped the idea.

From Frankland, it was another move, this time to Gartree prison. It was here that I was implicated in a bit of wanton vandalism on my wing. I was put into a Seg unit, yet again, and yet again I suffered the harsher conditions – a limited diet with meals in the cell, no proper exercise, a thin foam mattress to lie back on and gaze at the cracked grey paint on the ceiling, and the constant burning naked lightbulb positioned too high to disable. If being moved to Cat. B was meant to offer a glimmer of hope, it didn't seem that way to me. It was another ingredient poured into my growing sense that, whatever I did, I was marked and it wasn't going to be a case of serving my time and being given a cheery wave off at the gates.

◆ ◆ ◆

After the incident at Gartree, where I was implicated in some satisfying aggression against the prison fabric, I was bumped back up to Cat. A. I remember feeling so worn out and lackadaisical about it all at the time that it almost felt more comfortable: I was back to what I knew and knew where I stood in the eyes of the authorities. No half measures – Cat. A.

A few months after the wedding was cancelled, I was moved south to Winson Green in Birmingham. Instead of settling, for once, I immediately became desperate to move again. Winson Green was a tough experience. I was forced to share a cell with two others on very short sentences. Both would be out in a matter of weeks and couldn't relate to what I was going through. Their behaviour and conversation would wind me up no end. The only chance of a cell to myself was on a punishment block – but it would mean the loss of all minor privileges.

'I've done 17 years and I have to queue up to piss in a smelly bucket? It is a meat factory here, overloaded to chaos point,' I wrote of Winson Green:

> Screws are ignorant robots churning over a mass of motley prisoners – debtors, remands, vagrants and scumbag rapists – all of the shifty eyed and without a moral or principle between them. I am having to resurrect all my old street cunning to keep in front of the bastards. Turn your back for a second and they'll nick your boot laces. Still, it is good training. I was getting stale. It gives me something to focus on. I'm like a spider waiting for some scumbag fly to land on my web. Whoever it is will carry a message to all the other vermin … this is not the way I like to live. It is just survival. I want to do more than just survive – I want to live! A life with friends and people I love. A life without violence and bitterness, hatred and grief.

I saw one possible way to speed things up. I'd heard about a new prison, HMP Whitemoor, which had opened in 1992 and it appealed. Based in the Cambridgeshire countryside, it was one of eight Category A prisons. It was known for its offender behaviour programmes – something that would look good on a record when it came to fronting up to a Parole Board. It also included a Dangerous and Severe Personality

Disorder Unit, and a Close Supervision Centre – meaning there would be people in there who were looking at far longer stretches than I was down for, and with many more problems. I could become a model prisoner in such surroundings and earn parole status.

I put in for transfer, but heard nothing for weeks. 'It seems Whitemoor is being choosy over who they accept,' I wrote.

While firing off letters to Whitemoor and trying to keep my head down as I could see the end of my tariff approaching, there was another chink of light – a hope that I scarcely could bring myself to harbour.

Always keeping an eye out in the newspapers for stories relating to justice, prison and the law, I noted there was talk of John Major's government signing up to the European Convention on Human Rights. If they did, it could be good news for lifers. Such wishful thinking kept me going, but at the same time, part of me didn't believe it. I wrote home:

Apparently under European law it is illegal to detain a life sentence prisoner for more than 17 years. If this is true then presumably I have to be released immediately? There is a large doubt hanging over me. If this is all true, then 'they' obviously know I will be a free man come September, right? So how come they won't have me in Gartree or Whitemoor? Why be so choosy about it if I'm almost free anyway? ...

What provisos will there be, what dirty little loopholes are there for these devious bastards to implement at the final hour? Check out what chances there are for a 'gate' arrest for Sine Die charges left on the file ... I think they are marked 'not to be proceeded with' but does that mean anything in reality? I'm not really worried. I can't see them spending thousands trying to prosecute what amounts to a 20 year old charge. I pleaded not guilty then ... no, it has got to be some other little trick up their sleeve.

Rough treatment was regular at Winson Green. Staff didn't wear the legally required name badges, so if things got hairy, they couldn't be easily identified. I had to make numerous formal complaints about how I was being harassed and bullied, but I was warned that staff felt I was making false and malicious allegations, which would lead me to a long spell in solitary.

And it was around this time that I finally split with Marilyn, and another link to happier days outside was lost.

Above and below: Jackie, Terry, me and Carol.

Me, aged 7.

Me with Dad at Lyndhurst Hall, Kentish Town, moments before my first escape.

Swimming pool – Marbella, mid-1990s.

Marbella with my friend Dave's Rolls-Royce – he always had the hump, so we got him that registration plate.

With my sister Jane in Marbella.

The Los Altos apartments in La Campana, where I first laid low after reaching the Costa del Sol.

On the run in Paris.

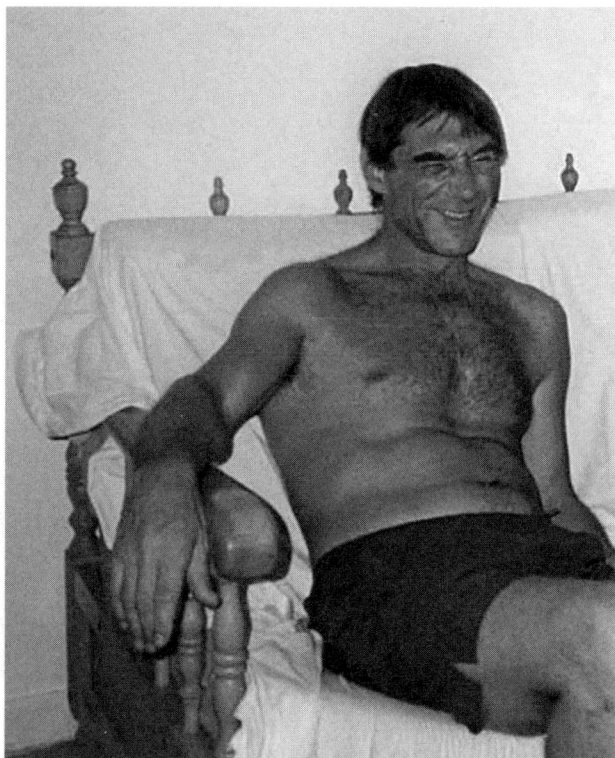

Relaxing in the Los
Altos apartments,
happy to be free.

With Dad in La Campana, enjoying a meal.

Christmas with family – my great-nephews Luke, Harry and Max, niece Michelle and sister Jane – in Pentonville.

Carol, Mum and me at my smugglers' hide out on the Costa del Sol.

A rare release to visit Dad at his nursing home in Hampstead, accompanied by Mum.

Badminton champion, Frankland Prison, 1980s.

Gym orderly at Pentonville, 2011.

Above and below: Building Mum's summer house in 2008 – while still on the run!

The summer house project continues ...

Michelle and I with my nephew, 2001.

Jane and I in the 1990s.

Parkhurst day release with Jane, 2001.

Me and Dan, Warren Hill, 2018.

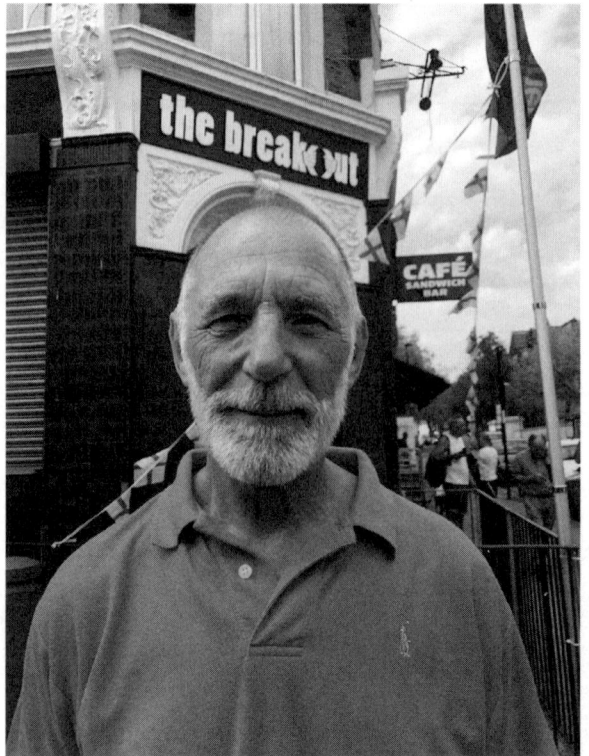

After my release, outside Pentonville.

Me with Jane and Michelle, 2018.

Where I came over the wall, outside Pentonville.

Friends meet up outside Pentonville.

Me outside Pentonville, where I came over the wall.

At Warren Hill prison – a group of boxing promoters and gym trainers came in to speak to prisoners. Some were old mates I had served time with!

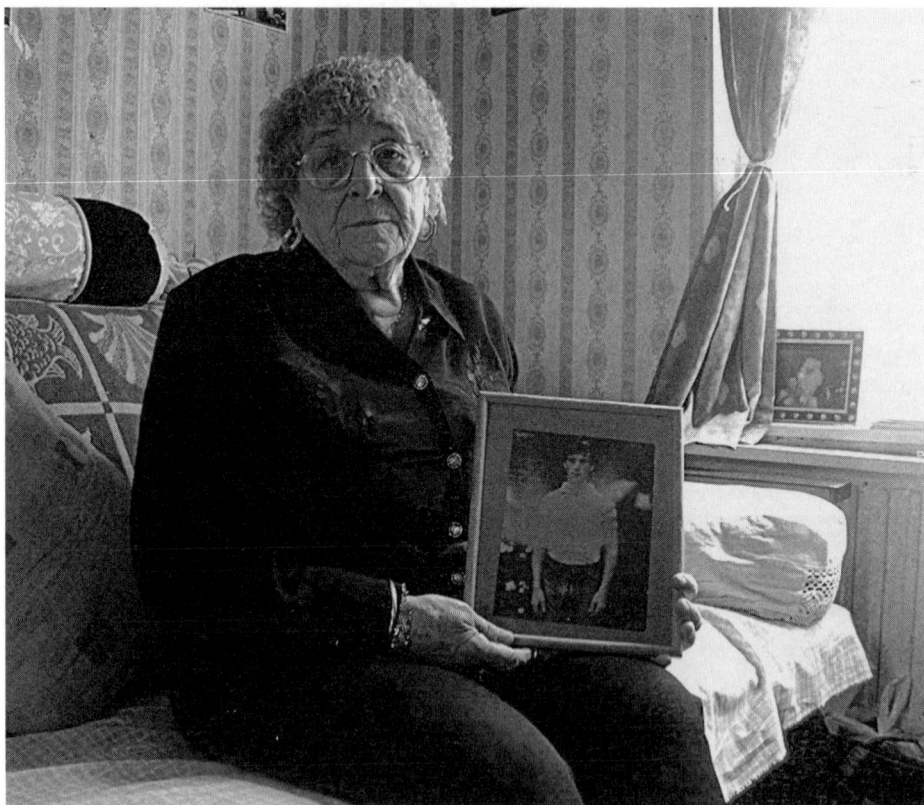

Mum with my picture, 2000.

SEVEN

The constant moving between prisons was meant to stop me making contacts, but it expanded who I was in touch with. There wasn't a jail in the country I could go to without someone who knew me by at least word of mouth. The prisons have a grapevine and you are afforded respect. You get lots of the old bank robbers dotted about the place and they were good people – they had principles and codes of behaviour. I could go to a prison 500 miles away and there would be someone to meet me with that welcome gift of what every lag needs, the sugar, tea, tobacco and stuff to get me settled in.

Not so today. Nowadays, the prisons are full of ratbag gangsters, people looking for status, looking for respect without earning it.

Getting a welcome pack was nice and I did it for others. I remember talking to those in authority about it, and they begrudgingly admitted that back then there was a better class of prisoner. There's no respect or understanding about boundaries you don't cross among younger convicts, and it causes problems – violence, unruliness, tenseness, a bad atmosphere. It's in no one's interests to have a prison run like that, but for at least twenty-five years it hasn't been sorted out.

The overcrowding, the drugs, the private firms cutting all the corners they can – it's so counterproductive. They don't try to solve the issues, they just handle them as they come. In the old days, inmates and screws knew what needed to be done to keep things calm. That went out the window some time ago, along with the idea of personal pride and respect. Respect: a hard thing to comprehend for someone who has never experienced living in a uniquely alien set of circumstances – a place where your freedom and self-determination have been taken away.

Winson Green – what a shitty dump. My spell there was particularly unhappy. I was held there for longer than I was meant to be, a place being found at Full Sutton but taking time to sort. I was told I had only been held in Birmingham because of a lack of cells designated for lifers elsewhere – another grating issue.

Over the years, I came to know some truly awful holes. Some of the places you'd get banged up in were fucking rotten – and this was one of them. You'd get shoved in a Seg unit and there'd be phlegm and shit all over the walls. In those punishment blocks, you'd be frightened to touch anything. They were so dark and dismal. The only way to tell the time was when the door opened and a meal was shoved in. The punishment cells were always bare, fuck all in them. To spend twenty-four hours in one felt like an eternity. I would walk round and round and see what in the cell I could pick loose or unscrew, simply as something to do.

I eventually made it to Full Sutton in May 1991 and received the welcome news that my case would be up for review in October 1992. But my stay in Full Sutton, meant to be more or less permanent until I reached the golden year that meant I'd served my tariff, was cut short with no explanation given only a few weeks after I arrived. Instead, I was shipped off again in the back of a rickety prison van, returning to HMP Gartree in Leicestershire.

Here I became friends with a prisoner called Phil – and I had to watch as Phil was slowly driven mad by the length of his sentence. 'I have come to the conclusion that my mate Phil is stark raving nuts,' I wrote home:

It is a bloody shame, as he is a good bloke in all other respects. I guess it is just another case of the long term destructiveness of such prison sentences. The mind is a delicate mechanism, and reacts in strange ways to overcome excessive stress. Some kill themselves, some go to religion, others lose their memories and some just go crazy. He is surviving by fantasising. It is a good way to stay alive, but what the end result is in terms of irreparable damage is, I do not know. I guess my way of surviving is to fight and challenge the system. What that is doing to me, I do not know. I am alive but in constant anguish and pain. No one is getting freed from tariff dates, no matter how they cope. I am still writing furiously to MPs but I don't have any real hope or faith in all this.

Gartree was to be another short stay, as if the approaching end of my tariff made me a hot potato. A sense of tension was rising. It manifested itself in March 1992 when I was placed in the Seg unit for what records describe as 'a concerted campaign to damage the fabric of the building'.

After these run-ins, they couldn't get rid of me quick enough, and in May 1992 I was on the move again, this time taken to Full Sutton in Yorkshire – geographically a long way from home and psychologically another challenge. I knew soon I would have to present myself in front of a Parole Board and I wanted no fresh blemishes.

Things between me and Marilyn were continuing to cause anguish, and it meant there was a gulf between me and my daughter. Marilyn had married a man she met after we split. I decided to write to him. I told him if he came between me and Sarah, it wouldn't be pleasant. 'Strangely enough it all cleared the air between us. We had a long talk on the telephone and I even like the guy,' I wrote.

Then came my first chance to persuade a Parole Board that I'd paid for my crimes and I was a changed man. I went in front of a panel of three. On the one hand, I felt extremely nervous. I wanted parole so much I barely dared dream it might be a success. But I couldn't help but be wary. I'd had years of constant persecution.

The board heard I'd channelled my aggression into physical education and writing. They noted, 'John is showing signs of maturity and change but is still not suitable for release or open conditions. A further review is recommended for two years' time.'

So that was that. It was a no: I was staying put, sitting it out.

I was sent to Maidstone prison in February 1993 and then the following year transferred to Coldingley in Surrey. I'd been keeping my head down, and officers noted how I'd built a 'blossoming relationship' with my daughter, who was now visiting regularly.

And it was from this prison, with eyes diverted by my seemingly patient demeanour following my Parole Board failure, that I decided I should take my fate into my own hands.

◆ ◆ ◆

Coldingley prison, near Woking, was opened in 1969 and originally had four wings with around ninety individual cells on each. Within its walls were workshops and classrooms, offering a chance to head towards life outside. Known as a resettlement prison, it offered a tantalising sense of near freedom to those who came through the multiple doors and gates and into the prison machine. This was not the end, but it felt like a step towards it.

Such hopes can go two ways – either keep an important spark alive, keep you thinking of that first taste of air on the other side of the wall, or lead to such disappointment and depression that you're changed beyond repair and maybe don't come home at all.

The Coldingley regime didn't want prisoners banged up all day. There was a greater sense of rehabilitation rather than punishment and it gave the corridors and workshops a sense of purpose. But as with so many interactions, the terms offered were designed to exploit and oppress.

For most prisoners, the chance to work was welcome. It provided pocket money and, while dreary and monotonous, it was surely better than staring at the grey and light-blue walls of your cell. But the work was demeaning, paid terrible wages, and was a system exploiting those in its care.

I was compelled to do shifts in the laundry, sign shop, print shop or engineering unit. For me, the payback was the occasional window for light-fingered behaviour – there were items that could be used or traded. It also looked good in front of a Parole Board to talk about the supposed 'skills and trades' I'd picked up.

What was not such a cushy number, and drove me to distraction, were the Offending Behaviour Courses I was compelled to do. Without completing them, I wouldn't get parole. These awkward chair circles in strip-lit classrooms might have been a necessary step to getting out, but they raised my fury.

If you ain't fully involved in it, it's pointless – and there was no way I was going to fall in line. It was meant to work like low-grade brainwashing, all these circles and chit-chat – but it was so badly done and so badly presented, it was a joke. The only way to get through was to keep nodding your head and answering politely. It was just part of the obstacle course you had to do to get further up the road. It was full of nonsense, stuff none of us could relate to.

They'd make us take part in role plays. They wanted you to get up and act it out.

I'd say, 'I'm not doing that. If I'd wanted to be an actor I'd have signed up for *EastEnders*.'

The tutor would say something like, 'If you're sitting in a pub and someone takes offence to something you've said, how would you get out of it?'

I was tempted to say, 'Probably chin the cunt and be done with it.'

I wasn't impressed by the people earning a living running such courses either. They were robots and the host was always an earnest bastard. Using role plays to retrain criminally minded types to react in new ways is pointless. Unless you make up your mind, they're a type of brainwashing, coercion, and not really helping someone truly reform.

I mean, you're not going to get a hairy-arsed criminal to sit down at some offending course and come out the other end as an upright citizen, like magic, inspired by pretending he's shaken the hand of a stranger in a pub who spilt his drink, eyed up his girl or called him a name. It just ain't going to happen, it's not reality.

Such hand wringing in a circle with nine out of ten struggling to keep a straight face was worse than useless. There were skills that I and other inmates needed. The courses used up time that could have been better spent.

As I discovered once I did finally get out, they should teach you all the things you need to sustain yourself once you're free – life skills for the world outside, a world that has changed since you were first banged up. Cooking your own meals, learning about budgeting, handling money, getting benefits, finding work … the list of what they could do to help you find your feet and show you're ready to re-enter society is pretty big. But they offered nothing like that.

They could also teach you about the extortion you'll face when you come out: those money grabs that follow you everywhere today – parking fines, congestion charges. People inside for the long term come out and feel very ignorant. Not knowing your way round the modern world can get you into deep shit. There was a brief programme that warned us off going to loan sharks, I think, but nothing at all on the obstacles of everyday life you soon forgot about after years inside.

This bubbling resentment built up, nibbling away each day as the hours passed and there was no prospect of release. I frequently turned my thoughts towards taking the matter into my hands, scanning each prison I was in for possible chinks and gaps. Due to its relative modernity, Coldingley hadn't yet been knocked about by builders, extensions added, wings demolished, as many of the older prisons have. It meant there were few unintentional quirks to exploit for a breakout. Instead, my mind turned to the prospect of finding a legitimate reason for being on the other side – and once there, I'd find the moment I needed to give me the best chance of getting away and never coming back.

◆ ◆ ◆

As I entered my nineteenth year in captivity, I'd truly done enough. I'd been through the 'halfway horrors' and had slipped into a 'dead' phase that long-term prisoners know, a time when it's a fact they've spent the majority of their adult life inside and that was that – days of their lives chalked off and not reclaimable. Like a marathon runner who's numb for the last 5 miles, having been through the wall and come out limping on the other side, I was on rubbery legs.

My tariff was nearly up. It was only natural I should begin to wonder what a different future held. But the people who held that landscape in their hands wouldn't commit to any definite plans.

Despite it being nearly twenty years since that fateful night when I took another person's life, there was no end in sight, no date to aim for. The phrase used by the hated Judge Mais sounded reassuringly vague to those with the keys to the gates: 'he must serve a minimum of twenty years'.

To me, it meant something altogether very different: 'I will serve a minimum of twenty years, and that's that. After that, we're quits, no matter – you lot will be dictatorial cunts to me for twenty years, punish the shit out of me, and I, being a free and independent human being, will give you back as much as I can with my limited resources, because we are sworn enemies.'

And that's fair: 'You've done everything to your advantage, so instead of punishing me further, admire my spirit. I've done the time and I've done it my way.'

As the day marking my twentieth anniversary in prison approached, no one was suggesting 'that was that'. No one was suggesting anyone was 'quits'.

And then I was told, out of the blue, that my case had been reviewed. It had been done without anyone speaking to me, without any opportunity for me to put forward how I'd reflected on my crime, how I'd changed as a person. In the eyes of the Ministry of Justice, it was simple

– no decision on a date for parole could yet be reached. It meant, said a template letter handed to me one day, any chance of release would be deferred for another three years.

In terms of due process and making sure everything is enacted by public authorities according to the law of the land, three years isn't actually that long a period: imagine if someone with a life sentence was just let go without a series of checks, without weekends out to acclimatise, without some training, some courses? Imagine one day they simply said, 'Right, we've had enough of you, off you go, son …' I would need to start normalising myself to the new world that waited for me. I would need to be able to prove I could do it – go out and stay straight, show I'd learned from my past, become a law-abiding citizen. It wouldn't be right otherwise.

But I needed them to fire the starting pistol for this new phase of my relationship with the prison authorities, once the minimum tariff had been served. To decline to do so for another three years at least seemed churlish, petty, yet another punishment. I was told through this decision that there was no end in sight, so my thoughts naturally began to turn to other solutions. I began to believe that perhaps it was time to take matters into my own hands.

Though Coldingley was a modern institution and a fairly easy place to do your time compared to some of the holes I'd found myself in, I had the horrors, no doubt about it. I could see myself getting older and older. I was heading towards 50 but still felt like that 27-year-old they'd banged up. I saw life slipping away.

I had to do something, anything, to break the monotony and the decline. I decided I would apply for a home visit. I hadn't had one and I thought, 'What have I got to lose?' My dad had just had a stroke and I wanted to see him. I thought it would break the monotony up a bit – I could have an afternoon with the old man.

Maybe the request would work, maybe it wouldn't. But there it was, a little chink of light. If I did get on the other side of the walls with a nod from the wardens, then … well, perhaps a horizon of extraction opportunities would come together. Perhaps I could have a little think about whether I could make that afternoon out last a bit longer than a few hours. Perhaps this was a chance to grab freedom on my own terms.

◆ ◆ ◆

Using a series of coded messages sent out to friends and family, and hushed discussions during visits, I alerted others there was a possibility I'd be calling on them for help. It set arrangements in motion. Friends visited so I could get messages out, see the lie of the land. I had people I could rely on, and that made the decision easier.

And then there it was: the opportunity presented itself when I went out to see Dad. What should I do? Walk away – but in which direction? Some might say it was a bit cold blooded but Dad was old school. He knew the score. He knew there was nothing I could do for him, nothing I could do for the family, if I was inside. He'd had a stroke and was recovering and I knew my family could come to me once I was safely away.

My parents were living in their Castle Road flat in Kentish Town by this point. It's a quiet little estate put up by the council in the 1970s, red-brick terraced homes, three to a block, with a communal staircase and little landings. You can drive in under a railway viaduct complete with arches of grease-monkey mechanics, storage spaces, past a wood yard on your left, and into one of the parking bays outside the flats.

But there's another way into the estate. A pathway between two blocks, an alley where cyclists are discouraged by gates set at an angle. It leads out to the Prince of Wales Road, a busy street with a park called Talacre Gardens, opposite my parents' block. I wondered if this alley had possibilities for an escape route, but nothing was decided. It would be a case of seeing when an opportunity presented itself.

With the date for the visit set, plans had been laid. I was taken by two guards in a van to Castle Road.

◆ ◆ ◆

A friend was circling the park in his car, waiting. He knew I was coming that day and things could fall nicely into place. I knew I had one shot – I knew I had to get the timing right and I had to be patient, but it's easy to tell yourself that and another thing altogether to stay calm and cool.

During the visit, I'd hoped to find a moment to slip out the flat unnoticed, leg it through the alleyway, get in my mate's car, but it hadn't happened. There was no way I could squeeze out of the flat without having the pair of the screws on my arse as soon as the front door was closed.

Then I had a little bit of luck. The screws I was with were lulled into a false sense of security, and one of them was partial to a beer. They said, 'Tell you what, John. This is going all right. Let's pop out for a pint. Treat you. It's been twenty years, hasn't it, after all?'

Dad had worked for many years in a place called Lyndhurst Hall, a red-brick working men's club, built in Victorian times and home to a local trade union branch. He was mates with the caretaker, a bloke called Alex, who I'd known as well. It was near their home and after Dad had come out of hospital, he liked to wheel down to see his mates and have a beer.

So it was suggested we all might like to go for a pint at the club. They took off my cuffs so I could push Dad in his wheelchair across the park to the hall. One screw was a well-known gambler and drinker inside and I thought, 'Hello, this is a bit of luck. I'll take my time and maybe something will offer itself.'

I saw my mate circling the park in his car and I thought, 'Right, take it easy and make sure it fucking works, whatever you do.' It was like being back on a bit of work, the same type of feeling.

So, we strolled into the bar. My family was there and lots of people my dad knew. It was lovely, a really nice atmosphere. My first thoughts were I'd go to the toilet and slip out the window. It would be my friend's job to work out what happened next. I would be in their hands.

Dad didn't know anything about the plan. He had absolutely no inkling. I wanted it that way – didn't want him to worry, and I didn't want to risk anyone giving the game away. I sat down and had a pint and suggested to the screws they played pool with each other while I caught up with my family. I relaxed with them, waiting for the right moment to go to the loo and then make the slip.

There were some kids there, so for a joke, I took off my watch and gave it to one of them. I said to him, 'Pretend to run off with it, go on. Let's play a game where you run away with my watch.'

He did, and with mock surprise, I said, 'Oi, come back here and give me my watch back!' He ran off through the door and I leapt up and went after him – it just seemed playful, like we were mucking around with each other.

I ran out the door after the kid and kept on going. I had a rocket up my arse. 'This is it,' I thought. 'This is it. I'm out now and I have to give it some welly.'

I didn't stop. My feet hardly touched the pavement beneath them. I found a power coursing through me, the adrenaline so strong that each stride was explosive, throwing me further away from captivity and closer to freedom. I had to leap over a hole in the ground some workmen were digging. I jumped across it instead of going round it – and they looked up in surprise at me, looked up as this bloke leapt right over their heads.

I thought, 'The screws must be on my tail now', but I wasn't in the mood to have a look and see. I got up to the road where the car had been circling and I couldn't see my mate anywhere. Fuck. Where was he? I thought he must have turned off and I didn't want to wait for him to reappear.

'Fuck this,' I thought. I had a contingency plan in place, so I didn't fancy hanging round. If I missed the meet, I was to make my way to

Mile End station and there would be someone there waiting. I didn't pause for half a second – no car, so it was plan B, all the way.

The nearest Tube station was Chalk Farm, so I ran in that direction. I thought by then a good five minutes or so must have gone by, maybe ten. I didn't rightly know, but enough time had gone by for the alarm to be raised, so I'd better get myself off the street sharpish. I ducked into a front garden and crouched behind a hedge to see if anyone was following me.

But there was no hue and cry; it was just an ordinary, calm afternoon – surreal how calm it all was, I suppose. My heart was banging away and I expected the entire world to feel it too.

I stepped back out on to the pavement and went on to the Tube station. I got a nasty surprise: where I thought I remembered the entrance there was this solid brick wall. It had been closed up. It just wasn't there. I thought, 'Fucking hell, they've closed the Tube down.'

I was out of breath, freaked out and I kept moving. As I came round the corner, I realised the entrance had moved, and there it was – it was open! I had cash on me, so I got in the queue and waited to buy a ticket. There was an old lady in front taking ages. I was panicking and wanted to be underground as quickly as I could.

I finally got to the window and tried to be nonchalant. 'I'll have a ticket, please, to Mile End,' I said. I got what I needed and took the stairs rather than the lift down to the platform. For some reason, I didn't like the look of the lift. It felt too confined. I walked up to one end and tried to slip behind a chocolate-vending machine. I waited and waited and the train seemed to be taking forever to arrive.

In fact my family had bought me a bit of time by telling the wardens I'd gone to the toilet, but I didn't know that. I assumed as soon as I'd legged it, they'd have ditched their pints and dropped their cues and been up and off after me.

It was quite a journey to Mile End from Chalk Farm – loads of stops and a change at King's Cross. As I sat there, listening to the train swinging back and forth down those tracks, trying not to look at anyone, catch anyone's eyes, I started wondering, 'What if they've discovered my contingency plan? What if I'm walking straight into the arms of the law?'

I decided I'd take another precaution. I'd get off at Bethnal Green, the station before, and walk the rest of the way. I was wearing jeans and a grey sweatshirt. I decided to take the sweatshirt off so I would look a little different. I rolled it up and left it on the seat.

Then a little tinny voice came across the Tannoy saying, 'Please make sure you take your belongings with you.'

I thought, 'Fuck it, they've seen me', but of course it was just an automated message. I relaxed for a moment, until I looked down at the T-shirt I was wearing and realised it was exactly the same colour and exactly the same make as the sweatshirt I'd taken off.

By now, the wardens knew I wasn't in the toilet and wasn't coming back of my own accord. They knew that they were in for it, and the longer I was at large, the worst it looked. There was a fair amount of effing and blinding at Lyndhurst as the wardens panicked. Looking around them at my friends' and family's nonplussed faces, looking at their half-finished pints of beer and quickly abandoned game of pool, they knew they were in trouble. The alarm had sounded and across all points a description was being circulated.

Meanwhile, I was putting distance between myself and those who wanted me back under lock and key. I got out at Bethnal Green and walked into the street. There was this market selling crap and I found a stall that sold T-shirts and bought a black one. I popped round the corner and stuck it on, and then walked to Mile End.

I felt like I had a lightbulb on my head and everyone was looking at me. I knew there was a plan that included me having a lay down at a safe house for a while and then getting out the country, but I didn't know much. I was in the hands of others and that made me feel pretty helpless.

I got to Mile End station and, to my panic, there was no one there. Something had gone wrong. Later, I found out no one had come to meet me at Mile End because they thought I was still up at Lyndhurst Hall.

Anyway, I thought, 'Get yourself together. Calm down. Go to a café and have a sit-down and think it through.' But as I turned a corner, something quite extraordinary happened, something by chance that, looking back, seems hardly fathomable.

I saw a mate walking towards me. His eyes lit up like saucers. His name was Bernie Kahn and I'd met him when we'd both served time in Parkhurst. It was just pure fluke and the gods were with me. I said, 'Bloody hell, Bernie. You have to get me off the street now, mate. I've just had it away!'

Meeting Bernie Kahn was a stroke of pure luck. It meant the well-laid plans, which had gone awry almost immediately when I'd missed the lift and then missed a meet at Mile End, didn't have to end in disaster.

Bernie turned to me and said, 'Johnny, I am sorry, but I've just been slung out the house by my old woman – we can't go back there.' So instead, he got out a little diary and flicked through it. He came up with a name of a pub down in Old Ford owned by a man called Knight – he was a contact of ours and we knew we could rely on him if we needed help.

We walked from Mile End to Old Ford, trying to look like we were two mates out for a stroll. Knight was there and didn't blink an eye when we walked in. He was used to this sort of stuff – he was part of an old bank robber brigade and wasn't fazed.

'All right, Johnny. Good to see you,' he said. 'Fancy a brew then?' He took me upstairs, gave me a meal and a cup of tea and then put me back in contact with my friends.

Bernie and Knight got back in touch with my mate – his name was Jimmy – who was circling the park, wondering where the fuck I'd got to, and he drove down east to get me. He was in a Mercedes saloon, a four-door, a nice car. I got in, easy as you like, and everything was back on track.

It could have been very tricky for me, but I would have worked out something else if I'd had to. Of course, there are millions of people in London and I reckon I would have managed to stay safe for a bit while I sorted out my next move.

As it panned out, I went round Jimmy's mum's house in east London and stayed there. First, Jimmy took me to a clothes shop down the Commercial Road and bought me a set of new clothes. I went into a cubicle and was trying a suit on when I heard the radio: there was a news flash and it was about me. I was scared to come out of the cubicle. I wondered if they had a security camera. What would happen if I drew that curtain and stepped out ... what would be waiting? I took a deep breath and – well, there was nothing to worry about. I got over the shock, bought the new suit and some other clothes and went on to his mum's.

His mum was in and she knew all about me. I had a nice meal with them and then got my head down for the night in a proper bed, in a proper room. I remember looking at the curtains and thinking how something so simple meant so much – a room with curtains. How about that?

I couldn't stay put for long. I didn't want to outstay my welcome and put the goodwill of my friends under strain. They were harbouring an escapee. After a wash and shave, a hearty breakfast and getting into my new threads, it was time to say a profound thank you and goodbye. The next day, they took me to a gym in Canning Town.

Some friends owned it and were expecting me. They took me upstairs to the board room. They'd organised a little reunion and slipped me a few quid. There were some other friends of mine there who had come to see me, people I'd worked with back in the day. It was a safe place, and we had a bit of a celebration. There was champagne and whisky dished up, but I only had a cup of tea. I didn't want to drink – I wanted to have all my faculties.

I was full of excitement and adventure. It had been three days and I allowed myself to think, 'Perhaps I am free.' I could hardly bring myself to believe it. Twenty years is a long time to be inside, but when I was in the gym, seeing my mates toasting my escape, I allowed myself to dream that it was a reality.

◆ ◆ ◆

My family were being carefully watched. They'd been questioned, as had known associates. Across London I would be the subject of morning briefings at police stations, with my name and description handed out.

I became a priority, but I also knew that, after the initial hue and cry, the press would lose interest and the average Joe wouldn't remember anything about me within twenty-four hours.

I couldn't stay in London for any length of time. To do so would be to remain as much a prisoner as I had been behind bars. I had to get abroad.

I started planning, borrowing a flat from a friend in the Elephant and Castle. I lay low on this big old estate. I would go out occasionally. I dyed my hair, but that was about as much as I needed to do, in those days before CCTV and facial recognition technology.

Plans were being laid on my behalf and I knew it was in hand, but the urge to travel was compelling. I decided to clear my head with a trip westwards – I wanted to get out of London and the urge for a bit of company swung it.

I went first to Swansea. Marilyn's brother was living there. I'd given him cars, money and all sorts in the past, so I thought he'd help me out. But when I showed up on his doorstep he shit himself, so I had to leave. Then I went to a little hotel in Cardiff and kept my head down. I was going under the name of Peter Farquharson. I thought it would not be suspicious because hardly anyone knows how to spell it. I remembered it by saying to myself, 'Fuck You Harson'. And you didn't need to have too much identification on you in those days. You'd have a paper driving licence and that was about it.

Then came the message from my contact that things were about to be put in motion. I'd been told by the friend that he could fix things if there were any problems, and he was true to his word. Without him, I would have had a great deal of trouble staying at large.

He was wealthy and he was sorting all this, basically out of the goodness of his heart. We'd known each other for years and he thought the sentence I'd been handed was unjust and knew about what I'd had to deal with inside. He knew I was planning to make a break for it and he knew he could help me. He was generous and a good friend. I'd done some work for him before and he wanted to see me all right. He arranged for a safe house in Woodford Green, so they took me there and I laid low for about a month.

My friend found a pair of pilots who needed cash, and were not averse to earning it any which way, to fly me to Belgium. They were willing and waiting – but I had to wait in the safe house while they organised a passport. It was pretty easy to do. I had a couple of pictures done. One went on the passport, the other went in the post to Petty France where they issued the documents. You then went to the Post Office and asked for a temporary passport. My mate knew someone who worked in the Post Office and it was all squared off for him. Simple, and it meant the passport you had in your hands was completely kosher.

I then had to get to Blackheath to meet these two blokes with a plane. It was after a few weeks, so the whole thing had died down a bit and I was more confident. But I knew the next step was make or break. It was getting out of England where the odds would stack up, where chance would come into it.

My friend drove me south across the city. I sat in the passenger seat, eager to soak up the sights, thinking this could be the last I saw of London for a very long time.

Heading over the river felt good. I was out of the manor and it felt like already another barrier had been crossed. I met my two couriers in a pub in Blackheath. In Belgium, another contact would be waiting with another passport, luggage and more money. Then Europe would be open for me and I could head south.

I spent a restless night at the pilots' home and the following morning they took me to Dover airport, a straight run with no problems down the A2, to a small air field with one strip, and it was here they had a little Cessna aeroplane waiting.

We got to the field and we had to check in with flight control. It was all natural, no questions, and it was obvious these blokes knew what they were doing. I was feeling good. But then the flight control bloke came out to see us on the tarmac and said, 'Sorry, boys, you can't go out today. The weather over the Channel is pretty bad – it would rip your wings off if you went up in that.'

I couldn't decide if I was disappointed or delighted when I saw their little aeroplane. It didn't exactly look airworthy. The controller was adamant – there was no way he was allowing anything to take off and the weather wasn't due to clear any time soon.

We looked at each other and the pilots said they'd been told, if anything went wrong, they had to deliver me back safe and sound to the house in London. I thought, 'That's a long way to go, and what if we get a pull on the way back?' I said to the pilots, 'There must be another way. Let's go to the ferry port and have a look about and get the feel of it. Maybe we jump on a boat?'

They were as good as gold. They knew the situation. They knew the guy who had employed them to do this and they knew they couldn't pull out. They had to get me across that Channel, one way or another. They had already been paid £5,000 each for their work. It was a lot of money. They made a suggestion. They said, 'It's OK, we'll just put you in the car boot and get on the ferry.'

I said, 'No way. That's the first place they'll look, and if they do, it's not an easy thing to talk your way out of now, is it?'

They said, 'Don't worry, we've done this loads of times. It'll be fine' – but I wasn't convinced. My pilots told me that they too were running a risk and to trust them – if I was caught hiding in the back of the car, they'd have some explaining to do.

I thought, 'Well, OK then. We're not flying out and I'm not going all the way back up to Blackheath or Woodford. We're doing this, one way or another.' I said to them, 'OK, but drive somewhere so no one can see me getting in.' They had this blue Ford Escort and the boot didn't look very comfortable, but I was running out of options. Then – as they were about to pull away – more alarm bells rang in my head and when I got those bells I trusted my instinct. I thought, 'No. Get in the fucking boot? No chance. I'd rather take my chances in the back seat.'

The three of us headed down the country lanes of south Kent, away from the aerodrome and into the port town of Dover. It was busy with traffic coming on and off the ferries and I felt a little more secure. Surely we'd be able to blend in?

I got out our passports – they were the temporary type, all the same – and I sat in the back staring down at them. I had all three on my knee, trying to work out if mine stood out. I couldn't see any reason why it might ring an alarm, so I said, 'Right. Let's go and buy three tickets to Calais and get on with it.'

We drove down to the port, bought the tickets and drove up to customs control. There was a weather-beaten shack. A woman in a customs uniform came out and she looked in the car and then peered in at all three of us. We showed her our passports. She took them through the open window and into her little cabin, and came back out again.

Her next question was, 'What have you got in the boot?'

I looked at the other two and thought, 'You pair of cunts!'

'Nothing,' said the driver.

She said, 'Right, flip it open. Let's have a look at nothing then.'

There were three suitcases in there and she opened them up. Thankfully, she didn't spot a bundle of cash – more than £3,000 – that I'd tucked into my shoes. She said, 'OK, fellas, have a nice trip. Take care and remember, when you're off the boat, they drive on the wrong side of the road.' With that, she waved us on to the ferry and I was another step away from capture.

I was supposed to have landed in Belgium and been passed on to another contact, but the change of plan had scuppered that leg of the journey. Instead, a message was sent via London and a new rendezvous in Paris was arranged.

As these boys had already been paid, they had to drive me there. It was a long crossing and the old tug didn't seem to want to make much headway. It was a big boat, and I had this horrible urge to find somewhere to hide. Instead, we stood at the bar for a while and then found a table to sit at. I never felt safe. I was sure something would happen, something would come up.

But it was also a lovely feeling, seeing the boat's bow leave the White Cliffs behind, seeing the coast fade out of view, England disappearing into the distance. I thought, 'I'm on my way – a new life awaits.'

With just a cursory check of our passports at the other end, we sailed through French customs. My couriers nosed their Escort out onto the motorway and we headed south. The pair wanted to stop and get some food but I was insistent – we go straight to Paris, no fucking about.

I was impressed with the French roads. They were like billiard tables, and every kilometre clocked widened the gap between myself and captivity.

I'd been told to head to a station on the Paris Metro where some old friends would be waiting, but timing was tricky. I had no idea how long my journey there would take and the pilots weren't much help. The pair of cunts tried to sell me the car when we arrived. I declined.

My meet was arranged with a couple: my mate Jimmy – Jimmy the Dodge, as we called him – and his wife. They were pootling around Europe on a long holiday.

It turned out to be a complete balls-up.

I didn't arrive till after dark and I called them up. They said to meet by another Metro station at a certain time and we still had some hours to go. I said goodbye to the pilots, thanked them for all they'd done, and there I was – in Paris, on my own, and as far as anyone around me was concerned, a free man.

I'd been in prison garb for twenty years. All I wanted to do was get changed, get into a restaurant and eat something nice. I wanted to relax a bit.

I waited at the Metro and noticed this police car had gone round the block four times. They kept stopping, slowing down and looking at me. It gave me the heebie-jeebies. Had I been betrayed? How? What the fuck where they doing? The next time it cruised past, I thought, 'Fuck this.' I decided I should front them up.

The car stopped again, so I went up to them and asked them if they spoke English. I asked them for the directions to somewhere. They heard my accent, stared at me and then drove off again.

I phoned Jimmy up again and asked, 'Where are you?'

He said, 'I'm here!'

I said, 'No, you ain't. I am!' I thought he was fucking me about. In the end, I decided to pick a landmark he couldn't miss. I chose the Arc de Triomphe – I mean, why not? I knew it wasn't far. I said, 'I'll see you there.' By now it was about 1 a.m. and I was exhausted. Finally, I met with Jimmy and his better half. They took me to a pension and parked me up for the night.

I asked them where they were going and they told me they had a suite at the George the Fifth hotel. I didn't know what it was and it didn't make much of an impression. I spent a poor, restless night in this hostel and was up first thing when daybreak came.

I got up and had a walk around the town. I changed some sterling into francs and then I did a bit of shopping. I had no idea what I should buy or how much anything cost, but I wanted something to do, something to keep me occupied, and I hadn't gone shopping since 1975. I couldn't speak much French, so I would see something and have to point at it, like a typical ignorant Brit tourist. I bought some sunglasses. They appealed to me, so I thought, 'I'll have that,' and bought them – and it felt good to be able to hide behind those glasses, watch the world go by, a world where I could be a free man.

It was an indescribable feeling. It was lovely, beautiful. It was amazing to be out and doing things under my own steam. I had never been further than Jersey in the Channel Islands before. This felt good.

◆ ◆ ◆

Just as Belgium was only going to be a staging post, the same applied to Paris. This wasn't a city I was going to spend any time in. It was part of my journey, a place where my network could keep me safe.

My final destination was going to be Marbella, Puerto Buenos, on the southern Spanish coast. I had a flat ready there, owned by Mr X's girlfriend. I could live there for a while until I decided what I wanted to do. He said that if I liked it, he'd sell it to me. It was worth about £25,000 and he said he'd give it to me for next to nothing.

Before I left Paris, I met up with Jimmy and his wife again. They took me for lunch at the King George hotel and at this point I got the right hump. I said, 'You fucker. You stayed here last night while I stayed in some poxy piss-hole.'

I'd been inside and on the run and I wanted some of this. We had lunch in the restaurant and sat in the middle of it, round this massive table with all these polished French waiters fussing round us. It was beautiful. They took me up to their room and I had never seen anything like it. It was complete luxury. It must have been pretty expensive, but I resented them for showing me this place when I'd slept my first night out of the UK in a flea pit.

Knowing there was a flat on the Costa del Sol waiting for me, I didn't see much point in hanging round Paris, especially knowing I would be spending limited funds on uncomfortable accommodation. After lunch, I took a walk and had a think. I didn't fancy flying south, so I thought I'd get a train to Madrid, change there and go on south.

I had a photo taken with my arm around a gendarme with the Eiffel Tower in the background. A nice souvenir.

Meanwhile, I gave Jimmy money to buy three tickets. He booked them for that night, an overnight sleeper. It sounded like the safest way to travel.

We got on at about 10 p.m. and guards lowered some bunkbeds in each compartment. I remember thinking it was a bit late to kip. I was used to going to bed earlier in the nick. I settled down for the night in the bunk but again, like the night before, I couldn't sleep. The train sped south, through the dark night, and we began to climb into the Pyrenees. I was wide awake and looked up at the sky and it was totally peppered with stars. I hadn't seen anything like it in all my life. It was a clear night and there were hundreds of them. Hundreds and hundreds – more than I could ever imagine.

I sat there looking at them, and was shaken out of this by the banging of doors and the braking of the train. I thought, 'Oh bollocks, here they come.' I still didn't quite believe I wasn't being followed. I thought of all the different scenarios that might play out, but as I poised and got ready to make a run for it into the hills, I heard a guard saying it was the border crossing. The train started up again, trundled on into Spain, and I could breath a sigh of relief.

As soon as it was light, I got up, and an hour or so later I was in Madrid. It was the longest train journey I'd ever been on. I was pleased to get off, but it was an amazing experience. We got out the other end and Jimmy was talking about getting on another train to Marbella.

I said, 'Jimmy, I just can't stand another train journey after that one.' He went off and bought three flights for us. His wife was still with him, a lovely girl. She was very kind and thoughtful towards me, not overbearing, but sympathetic. It meant a lot to me, and I remember it all these years later.

So I flew to Málaga. Jimmy had the address of the flat and a key for me and we got to the coast. It was pretty smooth – no questions asked, an internal flight, so minimum checks. We got out into the heat and sunshine of southern Spain, got into a cab. The cabs were white Mercedes, and I thought, 'You don't get that in London.' The driver took me to the flat, a nice little place in La Campana, near the bull-ring in Puerto Banús. Jimmy and his wife stayed for a bit, about an hour, and then left – leaving me on my own, and free, with a new life stretching out in front of me.

EIGHT

Once in Málaga, I made a call to a safe house so word could be got to my benefactor that I was safe and well. He would fix up some work, and I was happy to do whatever came my way. I thought I could do some driving while I settled down. In the meantime, I had plenty of money to keep fed and watered.

This really was the first time I'd been properly on my own, with no one to rely on except myself. It felt really great. A bit of solitude was welcome, too. I had no deadlines to meet, no instructions to obey.

I went to the local *mercado*, got myself some provisions, went back to the flat and stayed in. It wasn't a problem to let the family know I was safe. I could send a message via a third party and they would go round and call on my sisters, my parents. We couldn't risk having verbals on the phone, but it meant I could let them know where I was.

I settled into the flat in a nondescript modern block called Los Altos. Some were homes to Spanish workers; others, holiday lets. No one paid any attention to who was coming and going. It was perfect.

I had some money stashed away and time on my hands. Puerto Banús looked fantastic. I'd landed in a rich part of Spain. There were millionaires strolling about, luxury yachts in the harbour, a port with these terrific shops selling all this high-end designer clothing. There were cafés, restaurants, bars and clubs. Can you imagine? It was like a feast to the senses after being inside. The sun was shining. It was unreal.

The area's reputation for providing British criminality with a safe haven was rightfully earned. After an extradition agreement between the British and Spanish governments collapsed in the 1970s, it had attracted its fair share of those who wanted to avoid meeting a copper. There had been the likes of Great Train Robbers Charlie Wilson and Ronnie Knight living in Marbella, others such as Freddie Foreman, an associate of the Krays, and it attracted a number of lesser-known, and therefore successful, bank robbers and the like.

There was a bar on the beach front called Sinatra's and if you sat outside on the terrace long enough, you'd see a load of people come past who you knew from back in the day. I would meet people I knew and they would have heard about my flit and they'd buy me a pint.

Such acquaintances could prove helpful. I was still using the temporary passport I waved at the customs officer in Dover. I needed new identification and work. I couldn't survive for ever on the cash I'd brought with me.

Once again, contacts came in handy. By the 1990s, the heyday of the Costa del Crime was fading – Charlie Wilson, for example, had been killed in 1990, while others had found themselves attracting the attention of Spanish police. British and Spanish authorities were by now cooperating, extradition treaties were in place and Interpol was on a more solid footing as European integration continued. It meant the coast was no longer a place of unmitigated freedom, but there was still a good network that I could call on.

I met a guy I'd known from inside who had come to Spain and established himself in the puff trade. He would bring Moroccan hashish into Spain, sell some locally, but mainly ship it on to the UK, where there was real money to be made. The friend offered me a job as a babysitter for the consignments before they were moved northwards. I had to look after tons of the stuff as it came over.

They took me to a big villa, with six bedrooms and a swimming pool, about half a mile outside of Puerto Banús. It was up a private road, out the way, and it made me feel even more secure. I thought, 'This is it for me. I could stay here for ever.'

It was beautiful. It had a compound surrounded by high walls, big double doors and cameras directed on the entrance. I walked up and thought, 'Wow, you'd need a few quid to stay here.'

My mate said to me, 'This is what we want you to do.'

Trucks would come in with hash from Morocco. They'd drive in through the double gates and I had to unload them. I'd carry the lot into the house and into a room we'd set aside for it. In there, we'd count it, check it all, weigh it up.

Then I'd get various orders for amounts and sizes that I had to wrap up so it was ready to be transported on to England. There was some beautiful stuff coming through – all sorts of Moroccan hash, Moroccan pollen – different types, different grades. You'd get a few kilos of the really good pollen and then a ton of other types of hashish. Sometimes I would be given 60kg bales to wrap for the big-time dealers, but usually they would be around 30kg at a time. I'd wrap it up in the quantities required, sometimes into nine bars, sometimes 5kg.

And as soon as I'd done one load, another would come in. This was once, twice a week, depending on orders.

There was a trick to it. You'd start by putting the hash into cellophane and shrink-wrapping it. Then you'd get 2in electrical tape. They showed me how to do it so it was both airtight and watertight, and once it was wrapped, you'd rub the package in soap which helped disguise the smell and further sealed it. Then we would take the packages into another room which was kept sterile. You weren't allowed to smoke in there – it had to be a completely clean room, the door to it was always shut and it was kept as a totally separate space from the rest of the house.

Cars and lorries would appear with couriers to take the dope onwards. I had the job of helping stash the wrapped parcels so they wouldn't be discovered. We'd create ingenious secret compartments in the lorries. There was one lorry we used that did hundreds of trips back and forth. On the tailgate there was a drop-down metal lift. It had a large piece that could be removed. You'd take this long piece of metal off and behind it were these long trays, which we'd load up with packets of hash. We'd slide the metal section back in, rivet it again so it was welded shut and Bob's your uncle – it was ready to go.

The work gave me a safe haven. I was living in a villa that cost £2,500 a month, so they were obviously doing good business. Eventually, I was asked what I needed to cover my expenses and how much cash I needed over Christmas. I said, '£10,000, please, for a Christmas blow-out.'

Looking back, they ripped me off. They knew I was on the run and I didn't know the trade and what the going rate was. I should've really worked it out, but I didn't.

At Christmas time, I shut down the operation and cleaned up the villa. It was time for a holiday. They came up to see me and handed me £10,000. I got the family over for Christmas to visit – my sister's husband James drove everyone over in a minibus.

I remember seeing this van drive up to the double gates, and I opened them up for my family. It was the most wonderful feeling. I took them out around Puerto Banús – every club, every bar, every restaurant.

The sunshine, the freedom, the stark contrast to doing porridge filled me with happiness. I felt I'd served my time, I'd paid my dues, and if I could keep my head down, I could retire in the sun and put a violent past behind me.

The lifestyle suited me. I got on well with the Spanish – nice, friendly people with no airs and graces. It was affordable. You could go out in Puerto Banús and pay a couple of pesetas for a nice beer and kick back and watch the world go by. I made friends out there and lots of people knew my story.

There was a curry house on the harbour called Mumtaz and it was owned by a Pakistani man with an English wife. He was called Harry and he was proper down to earth, a top bloke. We'd go in and sometimes he'd lock the doors and have a proper drink up. We were his friends before we were his customers. We'd sit at a long table eating lovely food and watching the yachts come and go.

He'd make me laugh: I remember there was this one massive yacht that came in, a huge thing, and walking down the gangplank was Peter Stringfellow, all flash and showing off with that ridiculous haircut. He made a beeline for the curry house. Harry saw him coming and, as he came in, he just said, 'No thanks, Peter – jog on mate, we're closed.' It was like he could sense a show-off, a flash git, a mile off and wasn't dazzled by anyone, wasn't impressed by wealth or fame.

Harry would introduce me to lots of people. He used to call me JM – John the Murderer – and it stuck. He'd tell everyone that was my name and then crack up. No one knew if he was being serious or not.

The one thing he did definitely take seriously was his food. He was brilliant. He made beautiful spreads and it was easily the best curry house there – and as a restaurant, with so much competition, it had to be good to survive.

◆ ◆ ◆

Another link to my London life appeared in Spain in the shape of a new girlfriend, a woman called Mandy. We'd met briefly while I was on the run in London, following the flit from Lyndhurst Hall.

The circumstances were surreal. I was in hiding but I had to go back to the manor to sort a couple of things out. I was in a taxi when it pulled up to let people get over the road.

A family friend, a woman called Jackie, walked across and I couldn't resist saying hello. It had been so long since I'd seen her and I thought it would be a bit of a laugh, a bit of a surprise. I quickly got out the cab and she took me up to her flat and made me a cup of tea. Jackie was Mandy's mother-in-law. I knew her daughter, Esme. She lived nearby and had twins.

They were a good family. Jackie's son, a bloke called Monty Beeks, was a friend of mine. He ended up getting stabbed to death in the Napier pub up the road, by a man called Johnny Lomax. Lomax was a bit of a fruitcake. Monty and Johnny had an argument. Johnny had come over to him and said, 'Why are you with those white cunts?' He was a Black Power merchant. Monty stood up for us and he got stabbed in the leg and it severed his artery. He bled to death, there and then. It was terrible. He was a good bloke and a very good boxer. He was really promising.

Anyway, we went to Jackie's for a cuppa and a catch-up, and then Mandy came in. I had a flat to go to, a safe house, but it was in Blackheath. Mandy said she would drive me over. She gave me a lift and then, to my surprise, she called in a few days later with her daughter in tow, Chelsea, a lovely kid. I asked them in and we formed a relationship from there.

I said to her, 'I have to go to Spain, I have to fuck off', and she said in a few weeks she'd come and see me, and that's how it started. She moved into my flat and she loved the lifestyle. There wasn't much for Mandy in London. A fortnight's holiday turned into a month, then two, then three. She and Chelsea decided to stay for good.

As things settled, we had the good news that Mandy was pregnant. It seemed that things were truly changing. I was going to spend the rest of my life in Spain, find permanent work and my old life, the clanking of the cell doors, the nightly terrors and nightmares, would be but a memory. I was using my brother-in-law's name when I needed to deal with the authorities and no questions were asked.

As far as I was concerned, John Massey had disappeared, gone for good – and I didn't believe the British police were too bothered about finding him again. After all, I'd completed my tariff. They surely weren't going to be fussed about what I was up to if I kept my head down, stayed abroad and gave them no reason to seek me out.

Baby Terry, named after my brother, was born in 1995, and seemed to signify another chapter in my life. Things were looking good.

◆ ◆ ◆

The joyful occasion, however, went tragically wrong very soon after.

We had our baby son and he was the most beautiful thing I've ever seen, the most gorgeous little boy. I thought I had it made: my own family, my own boy for me to look after and care for, to nurture, to help grow up. I was a dad again.

We lost him when he was just 4 months old. Cot death. We put him down one evening and that was that – he passed in his sleep. No one knew why. It was the worst thing I'd ever experienced.

It knocked us both flat out. I lapsed into a deep, deep depression and Mandy fell completely apart. Our happy dream on the Costa del Sol turned into a nightmare. We slipped into daily, heavy drinking sessions to numb our grief.

One night, we entered a bar in the resort of Fuengirola. It's a town further down the coast from Puerto Banús, sandwiched between Málaga and Marbella. It has a centre that was once a fishing village and conjures up images of the old, Moorish Spain, and then became a satellite town for the bigger settlements either side of it. The tourist boom meant a few hotel and apartment complexes sprang up – and, along with them, sawdust pubs and bars to service the package-holiday crowd.

We were in a place called The Cottage Bar. The bar had been owned by an Irishman who'd left Dublin with a few quid in his pocket and wanted to see out his days in the sunshine. It was managed by locals and, being right on the seafront with a pool behind it, the place was popular with both Spanish and expats. It was slightly unusual in that it was known for not having any of the usual attractions – a TV showing sport, fruit machines flashing in corners or set menus and outside tables to entice the holiday maker. It was a simple place, clean and well run. Sparsely decorated in the usual Spanish style, it had terracotta floors and a balcony running round the bar – the manager slept upstairs. It wasn't a large, bustling tourist trap, but a nice place with a nice vibe to it.

We had pulled up outside and gone in to have a few drinks. Everything was still so raw from the death of Terry and we'd been on one, trying to drink away that awful sadness that filled us and overflowed. The place was empty, except for three guys sitting in one corner and the barmaid.

We'd been in bad moods and gone a bit hammer and tongs at each other. It was soon after little Terry had died and we weren't dealing with it. Mandy was very tearful in the bar, so I said to her, 'Go to the toilet, clean yourself up, love, and I'll order us a drink.'

To get to the toilet she had to pass these three blokes. They were being loud and obnoxious, which wasn't the usual thing for The Cottage. They were English, and I heard one say, 'What's the matter, darling? Who's upset you? Is it that cunt over there?'

I thought, 'Hang on, did I hear that?' It was aggressive and so overt. She looked at me and I said, 'Don't worry about them, Mandy. Go to the toilets, sort yourself out, ignore them.'

The next five minutes were to drastically alter my life. I went to the bar to order a drink, and as my back was turned, one of them got up and locked the doors. Another picked up a bar stool and smashed it over my head.

One of them had owned a bar nearby and the barmaid was his girl-friend. They thought they ruled the roost, were kings of the castle, and they were hostile.

But they didn't know what buttons they were pressing. The bar stool was heavy and I took a real blow, but I didn't go down or exhibit any real hurt. I was drunk and charlied up, numb with pain. I spun round and said, 'What the fuck did you do that for?' I hadn't experienced an unprovoked attack for a long time. He had a smile on his face but fear in his eyes – it was a shock I hadn't gone down.

He raised the stool to do me again, so I went to take him on. I had a small penknife in my pocket, a beautiful little thing I used for crafts and stuff. And as we squared up, I felt for it.

I would tell police I had grabbed a knife from the bar, one that had been used to cut lemons and limes, as I didn't want to be accused of going equipped. It was like a Swiss Army knife, so I opened it up in my pocket. I took another blow from the stool and another bloke leapt on me and got me in a choke hold. There was one in front and one behind and another jittering about on the sidelines. He was egging his mates on, thinking they were going to give this mug a good kicking, have a bit of a laugh, three on one, and wander off leaving me in a pool of blood with no comeback. But they didn't know what they were getting into.

I remember thinking, 'I've come all this way to get away from this sort of thing and here I am, having a dust-up with three English guys.' I remember a strong sense of déjà vu, thinking, 'This is how I got a life term in the first place', feeling like I was back there in Hackney. I wasn't having any of it. I wanted out and as quick as I could.

My first thought was, 'I have to get this bloke off my back.' I was taking some real beats, so I got my knife and cut his arm. He had me in a stranglehold. I was conscious about not causing him serious injuries. I thought, 'Right, I'll cut up his arm and get him off me, get it over and then get out of here.' I wasn't going to stab anybody. I needed to get free so we could have it out with a punch-up, one on one.

I managed to cut two of them on their arms and then the third rushed in. I saw them off and squared up, ready for a proper fist-fight. But they'd seen I wasn't a pushover and they started shouting at me, 'Just go! Just go!'

I said, 'You lot have changed your tunes, haven't you?' They were cowards – three on one – and when I'd got loose they decided none of them fancied it after all. Hitting me with a bar stool from behind isn't the way to start a fair fight, and that stool was heavy. I've never understood why it didn't fracture my skull and knock me flat. The girl behind the bar was screaming. In the end, those three guys couldn't get me out on the street quick enough.

I looked over at Mandy, who'd come back in from the toilets, and she was laughing hysterically. It was the shock. She looked at me and said, 'You look just like bloody Rambo.' I was covered in claret, and two of the guys looked like stuck pigs, all covered in blood too.

We knew we had to get away. Mandy made a run for it and didn't look back. I don't know what she did or why. She had the keys to our flat with her, but I had the keys to our car. She disappeared. I had to drive to Puerto Banús on my own, reeling from what had happened, in a state of shock.

I knocked on the door of a friend's place and got a change of clothes. I was bleeding, so I patched myself up a bit and thought I should drive back to Fuengirola. I tried to find Mandy and get back into our flat. She was nowhere to be found, so I stopped at another bar as I couldn't get into our place. I had a drink to calm down and try to work out where Mandy could be.

It was while I was there that the Spanish Old Bill came crashing in with guns drawn. I had no idea how they found me. They must have had my car's number plate and a description, and seen it outside.

I was furious. These guys locked me in a bar and tried to do real damage, and when they'd come unstuck they couldn't call the Old Bill quick enough.

They could've killed me, those dumb-fuck drunks laying in with bar stools. I thought, 'Maybe I should send a few friends round there to oblige me, sort it out,' but I didn't. The final insult was when I heard they got compensation for their injuries. Fucking ridiculous.

I don't know what possessed me to fight back. I'd got away from all this. Should I have gone down and taken the beating, and let that be that? Or taken the punches and then got a crew to work them over at a later date? I'd carried on that night as if nothing had happened, I didn't understand the seriousness of it. I was in shock.

The police were shouting away in Spanish and they gave me a beating when they got me to the Fuengirola police station. I went to court the next morning and was sent to Málaga jail, a place called Alhaurín de la Torre.

I still had a false passport – I had for a time been using my brother-in-law's as a cover – and I was confident this would prevent them from finding out who I really was. But it came unstuck when they took my fingerprints and held me for about ten days. If I'd got bail before the results had come back, I could've skipped, but I didn't. I didn't make bail, and Mandy didn't try to get me out quickly enough. They wanted to hold me, like they knew something was dodge.

They found out my real identity from my prints on file back in the UK and the shit hit the fan. My days on the run were over.

Once the British authorities had identified me, I was taken from Málaga to the Carabanchel prison in Madrid to await trial for attempted murder. It had been a key jail for the Franco regime and housed political prisoners. There were dark reminders of tragedies. It had bullet marks on exercise yard walls from the firing squads that murdered the left-wingers who fought the Fascists, and anyone else Franco didn't like the look of.

I hear it's closed now, and I'm not surprised. It shouldn't have been open when I was there. It was like something out of fucking *Midnight Express* – completely medieval. I had to get used to it as I wasn't going anywhere fast. After I was transferred to that hell-hole in Madrid, I was made to wait for three years for a trial.

◆ ◆ ◆

There was to be an agonising twist as the vagaries of the Spanish legal system played out. I was taken in front of a judge who threw out charges relating to me being an illegal alien and on the run. I was told I could go free, but I first had to be bailed for the charge relating to the bar fight.

The judge also refused to send me back to England because written into the Spanish constitution is a rule that they can't extradite you somewhere if you will face life imprisonment or the death penalty, as neither tariff exists in Spain.

The Madrid court was called the 'Identity National', the highest court in the land. Its verdicts don't get overruled. You meet the judge in very informal surroundings, nothing like in England. You go into the judge's offices and sit down in front of him.

In my case, the judge's name was Eduardo Fungalillio. I had to appear because by then there was an extradition warrant. He was in a wheelchair and I thought, 'Fucking hell, he's been crippled by some-thing. He probably hates the bloody world, doesn't he? I don't have a bloody chance with this bloke, do I?'

After about a minute, my court-appointed lawyer for the extradi-tion business was digging me in the ribs and saying, 'Liberty, liberty', and the judge is smiling at me and gesturing that he considers the twenty years I have done is more than enough. He keeps saying, '*Sufficiente, sufficiente* …'

I thought, 'Fucking hell, is this bloke telling me I'm OK?' The fact was, as soon as I got to Spain, I should've given myself up and by now I could have had residency status and still be out there. They wouldn't have had any chance of extradition if I'd done that, but I didn't know the score.

I kept in touch with this judge down the years and we exchanged letters. He sadly died in a road accident.

I got hold of a lawyer to fight the attempted murder charge and the fact I was wanted for absconding in the UK, but how to pay for his services became a sticking point. My solicitor was a right colourful character, a man called Marcus Montes. He was bloody expensive but he only took high-profile cases and he was a winner. He had a waxed Salvador Dalí-type moustache and gold-rimmed spectacles, and a black cane with a gold tip. He was excellent but I couldn't get him when I was trying to fight the extradition. I couldn't afford to keep him on. He kept sending me letters saying he'd help, make it all OK – if I had the money.

Still, I believed I could fight the charges relating to the brawl and Spanish law was on my side regarding being packed off back home. It was just a question of making sure I was adequately represented.

I returned to Carabanchel jail and expected my name to be called out for bail, but it never was. The problem I faced was that I didn't have any representation to apply for bail for the wounding charge. I relied on Mandy to sort something out. That was a huge mistake. She went round collecting funds from friends to help get a lawyer, but no lawyer ever saw a penny of it. I thought she was helping me out, but she wasn't. She was collecting cash and spending it on booze instead. She was going on drunken binges. She was too out of it to help.

She insisted she was sorting it and that it was arranged for me to be smuggled out of the country as soon as I made bail. But she was in no fit state to organise anything.

The tragedy she'd gone through, having lost her child – she wasn't in control. It was too late when I realised and I couldn't do anything about it. And all the while, I was rotting away in an awful prison, thinking I had help being organised when nothing was being done.

Eventually I got a court-approved lawyer and I could see this was potentially the beginning of a long road leading somewhere I didn't want to go. If I'd got bail, I could have skipped. But they stopped me going free because of this brawl. It was a legal catch-22. I could get freedom from the sentence I'd skipped in the UK because the Spanish courts said I'd completed my sentence under their laws, but I couldn't get freedom from this tuppeny-ha'penny issue of getting in a fight in a bar after I'd been attacked. I was gutted. It made no sense.

The brutal reality of life behind bars hit me, but I was at least prepared for it, having done a twenty-year stretch already. At first, I had the hope that the time inside would be short: the solicitor's words 'liberty, liberty' went round my head, and I was sure the incident in the bar could be sorted out.

Every day they would call out names over the Tannoy, a list of people who had got bail or freedom. I was waiting to hear my name – 'John Massey, liberty' – and I couldn't understand why it wasn't being called. I was expecting my lawyer to get me bail at least, and maybe even the charges dropped completely, but he wasn't getting heard by the right person, or the bureaucracy wasn't moving quickly enough. Something was holding it up, meaning I was stuck – no cavalry coming over the hill, no way of stopping what I knew in my gut was coming.

◆ ◆ ◆

I was in jail for three years. They started out with the most serious charge they could think of and then it went down a peg, and then another. The result was, I went and did another twenty-three years inside.

In the end, I was charged with assault. I didn't even get a proper trial. The judge would make a deal. 'Accept three years, which you've already done, and that's that,' they said. 'We'll have your phone number and address and you can do the last month in an open prison.' It was down to the discretion of the judge I was in front of. I was innocent, but this sounded like a good deal. I thought, 'OK, have a phone number and address. I'll do another month. I'll take that.'

But it wasn't going to be another month. Before I could get out, I got the news I'd been dreading. The UK government had come to an agreement with the Spanish justice department. I was going to be sent back to Britain. By Christmas 1998, I was in a prison back in Málaga, waiting to be flown to London.

Back home I had a network of friends I could turn to and I knew the ropes, but Spanish prisons were a different matter. My letters show the considerable strain I was under. I was forced to fight for everything, every scrap of food, every drop of water, every moment of peace. If I didn't, liberties were going to be taken. I was targeted by a Moroccan gang who'd been banged up for importing hashish.

'It is difficult and painful to write as I have broken my hands again,' I penned that Christmas to Jane. 'The doctor took the plaster off my left hand so at least it is possible now. Fucking Moroccan heads are made of iron.'

Gangs saw I was on my own and would disrespect me, and had to be taught the hard way that I wasn't to be messed with. The Moroccan gangs thought it was fine to spit on the dining room floor. They had no scruples about them whatsoever – they behaved in a way that would lead to confrontation. It wound me up.

You had to queue for your phone calls. You could wait for hours. One day, this Moroccan bloke strode up and said he was in front of me now – that he'd been out in the yard exercising but now he was back and he was ahead of me. I told him to fuck off, he was taking the piss. The only language he understood was violence. The phone call was important. It was my only link to the outside world.

And while I could get by using Spanish, being a foreigner means you stand out, and they thought I was an easy mark. I knew from experience of British jails that you have to nip these things in the bud or they'll be all over you.

They called me the '*Loco Inglese*'. Once that got about, I was left alone. Anyone taking liberties, I pinged them immediately. No arguments, no trial, no questions, just bosh. I'd take them out, no matter what the consequences, no matter what damage they thought they could do to me. It meant people stopped taking the piss. It was dog eat dog. It was like the jungle: there was no humanity, and I was on my own so had to look out for myself.

I felt abandoned. My family were unable to visit or to be sure the letters they wrote would reach me. I had no friends inside and was unknown to other prisoners. I had to prove myself again to keep safe.

Being skint was torture. 'A simple cup of coffee and a cigarette on a cold day sounds easy enough but it isn't easy at all. I can survive no matter what hardships but survival is all it is,' I wrote home:

All the other factors of life like friends and family become distant memories. After a while of living like an animal in here I exist on pure aggression to get what I need. That means I am fighting and hurting people. Being unable to express myself and speak the language, everyone tries to take liberties and steal what little I do have. Now after putting a few of the bullying types in hospital, the other Spaniards give me some respect and life is a little better. They are a bit more polite and do not push in front of me in queues and such like. But everyone here is poor or heroin addicts. I don't want that sort of life ever again so I react with violence when I don't get enough food on my tray or the screws talk to me like shit.

Spaniards are scared of screws and they bow and scrape like the cockroaches they are, but I say to them – I am now in forever and I don't give a shit about sanctions or an extra month on my sentence, I tell them my sentence is forever so fuck off or I will send you to hospital, you cunt. This they find hard to understand because life sentences do not exist in Spain. Anyway, I seem to be making some headway at last … But I have no money at all. Unless I get some money by next week sent in or from somewhere, I will have to sell my last possession – a telly someone left me a year ago.

The regime in the Spanish prisons mimicked the unruly nature of the convicts. Both fed off each other.

In Carabanchel jail, when I came in, I was shown this big, long wing, all dark as there weren't enough lights. I was told go and find my own cell, wherever there was a space. They said, 'There you go', shoved me through these big iron gates and said, 'That's you.' Horrible, a proper shithole. Real dungeons. Filthy.

The screws were very aloof and arrogant. Most of them were 4ft-nothing but you'd think they were Godzilla, the way they treated the prisoners. They were scumbags. Coming from the English system, where I stood no bollocks, I opened their eyes up a bit. I wasn't respectful like most Spanish prisoners. I didn't give a shit about them, especially when they were so little. I didn't feel physically intimidated. They couldn't take me on and they came to know it. They demanded respect, the way all bullies do, but got none.

They couldn't believe it when I stood up to them. And the other prisoners would stand back and think, 'Fucking hell, what is he doing?' They would threaten you with Chokey. They called it '*Chapino*' and it was a hellish fucking dungeon, fucking completely medieval. Damp, cold, water flowing down the walls, rusting metal chains that made you wonder who'd been strung up there.

I used to say, 'Take me to your fucking *Chapino* then' – the opposite of what they expected. 'What you think you've got down there, lions and tigers, you cunts? Take me there, I don't give a shit.'

I once demanded a single cell. 'What do you think this is, a fucking hotel?' they said.

I said, 'Yeah – I've been in worse in your shithole of a fucking country, you fucking mugs ...'

My nihilistic approach to my health, safety and future was partly due to being consumed by grief over the death of my baby, and partly the potential of being shipped back to the UK when freedom had seemed so close and distress about Mandy.

'Losing my little Terry has consumed all the joy in my life and I can't come to terms with it, no matter how I try,' I wrote home. I also tried to understand what Mandy had been through and, on my better days, not blame her too much:

M is a real pain and at times a really horrible person, but there are reasons behind everybody's behaviour that others can never understand.

It is always easier to hate and attack rather than love and support and help those who portray horrible characteristics. The way I see things is she needs help and a lot of friendship from others. And hopefully everything will come all right for her some day in the end.

The days ticked by and I was kept in the dark as to why I was being held and what the future held for me, until early one morning.

At 4 a.m., a group of guards starting banging on my door. There was a rattling of keys. They came into my cell, heavy handed, barking in Spanish. I remember how the Spanish prison wardens wanted nothing to do with me as I was taken away. They turned their backs, tried to avoid my eye. They left the job to the notorious Guardia Civil, an armed police militia known for its brutality. They handcuffed me, marched me out of the prison with no explanation. They threw me in the back of van and drove me under lights to an airport, like I was fucking General Pinochet.

All my protests that I was innocent, that I'd done my time, that I'd only accepted the plea because of the offer they'd made – after all, you don't get three years for attempted murder, you'd get a fifteen-year stretch for that – all my arguing was futile. No one was paying me the blindest bit of notice. They wanted to shove their batons in me, twist the cuffs tighter, throw me out the country like an old bone.

And then I saw we were at the airport and there were two cozzers from Scotland Yard waiting on the tarmac.

'Hello, John,' they said. 'We've been looking forward to seeing you again, mate.' They took me on to the plane and I was handcuffed to one on each side. Trying to eat a plate of dinner double-handcuffed was fairly ridiculous. I tried saying that to them and pointing out I was hardly going anywhere, but they said there was nothing they could do. I think the other passengers enjoyed it – it was a bit of a spectacle. But these Scotland Yard detectives were also all right. They chatted politely, asked me questions, helped me out. They were good – they were just doing their job.

These detectives, I learned, had enjoyed a couple of days away at the taxpayers' expense. They'd wangled it so that they got to the city forty-eight hours earlier than needed. They'd spent a pleasant time having a drink and dining out, a welcome break. It meant they were in holiday mood and as pleasant as you could want, considering.

I thought, 'OK, off we go. I'll face the music and I'll be out soon enough.' After all, I'd nearly done my tariff back home. Little did I know what was in store.

I didn't feel quite as down as I might have done for another reason. The Spanish cells were making me ill: I had a prisoner's pallor, and the poor food, lack of exercise and my solitary existence were sapping my mental and physical health to a point where recovery would never be complete – it would become a question of what degree. At least the wait was over. I'd get those months owed paid down and begin again.

NINE

I was first taken from Heathrow to Wandsworth prison, where I spent a couple of nights in a cell, which was spartan but a couple of Michelin stars up from the hole in Spain I'd been in. I was then moved to the high security of Belmarsh. I was classed as a serious escape risk: as well as the fact that I'd done a bunk and stayed at large for so long, it was a matter of dented pride for the authorities. I'd mugged them off, and now it was their turn to give me back what I had coming.

It wasn't going to be the last time I saw the inside of Britain's most notorious Category A institute, but this time my days there were cut short by a quick trial at Blackfriars Crown Court.

I was brought before a judge and decided to plead not guilty to escaping, pointing out that when I left the two screws playing pool, I'd completed the recommended tariff. The explanation fell on deaf ears and I was given a six-month sentence to run on top of the time the system claimed I had to sit out for my murder conviction.

I thought, 'Six months. OK, I can do this', but there was a catch. There is always a catch. You don't get any remission automatically after six months, and the time out counted heavily against me when it came to parole. What was meant to be a few months back inside turned into more than ten years. 'Six months,' I thought. 'Six months. Not too long.' I couldn't have guessed it was going to be many more years.

◆ ◆ ◆

Getting used to the system in England again took a bit of time, but I was helped by friends. Prisoners knew my story; they admired that I had done what they dreamed of, making that break, the feeling of running away from your captors, carving out that window of opportunity and grabbing it. Being somewhere I could speak the language, have family close to hand and not wonder each day what was being served for lunch, or whether I'd have to single-handedly take on another gang wanting to rough up the *Loco Inglese*, meant there were silver linings.

I settled back into the routines, getting a job as a cleaner which gave me time out of the cell, concentrating on carpentry, playing the guitar, playing badminton, defending my titles as a prison tennis champion and writing letters to my solicitor, friends, anyone who would listen, asking for help to get a favourable parole hearing.

I went to the prisons I'd seen as a young man; a summary of where I had been incarcerated can be found among the piles of paperwork amassed on me by the state, by solicitors, by my family. My whereabouts are thoroughly documented. When on the outside, someone's locations are noted by addresses for council tax or utility bills. This doesn't occur for prisoners. Their lives are documented by the visitor requests, the weekly workshop wage, letters from the Parole Board, the written warnings, the glimmers of hope from solicitors and the knockbacks from almost everywhere else. A travelogue of the British prison network is among my papers, starting on 30 October 1975 at Brixton prison on remand, and then running for the next thirty years until September 2007.

The following roll call of places and years illustrates my travels: Brixton 1975, Wormwood Scrubs 1976, Wakefield 1977, Wandsworth 1978, Wakefield 1978, Long Lartin 1978, Albany 1982, Parkhurst 1983, Gartree 1984, Hull 1985, Frankland 1985, Wormwood Scrubs 1986, Frankland 1988, Long Lartin 1991, Gartree 1992, Birmingham 1992,

Full Sutton 1992, Maidstone 1993, Coldingley 1994, Belmarsh 1999, Long Lartin 2000, Parkhurst 2002, Sudbury 2005, Pentonville 2007. And there were others to come – time spent at Ford, Pentonville, Belmarsh again, Rochester and Warren Hill.

◆ ◆ ◆

My second post-escape Parole Board hearing took place at HMP Long Lartin in February 2002. At the interview, I spoke about the murder all those years ago. The board noted my 'version of events was consistent with previous reports', suggesting I was willing to confront what had happened. However, I'd switched to apparently having 'little remorse' for my victim, speaking about the injuries to John Dove. And then I switched again, remembering with a look of genuine pain the effect my actions had on the victim's family and showing genuine and deep remorse for what I'd done.

When I had moved to Long Lartin in 2000 from my temporary stay at Belmarsh, I'd seen my status as a Category A prisoner downgraded to B. In return, there was a sense of cooperation coming from me. The board heard I hadn't completed any work on offending behaviour and coming to terms with my crime, nor had I been helped to control my temper, or to learn and use strategies to stay out of trouble. A psychologist had recommended me for such courses and the board's report noted, with a hint of surprise, that I was interested.

'Mr Massey had demonstrated a willingness to work with "the system", which had not been thought possible by many report writers earlier on his sentence,' they said. Elsewhere, I was described as having a 'mixed' attitude towards staff and was warned for being abusive and showing a lack of respect.

After weighing up the application, the Parole Board would hit me with a double blow, the sort of catch-22 I'd come across in the monolithic corridors of rules and procedures that my life was at the whim of. The board said they recommended I remain on 'closed conditions', as punishment for the five years I'd had on the outside, but having been told I should do some courses, I was taken away from Long Lartin, a prison I had better memories of than most, and shipped to Parkhurst on the Isle of Wight. The reason given was that I could be assessed better for two possible behaviour management courses.

Back across the Solent, back to Parkhurst. I arrived there on 22 May 2002.

By now Dad was getting progressively more fragile. His breathing was laboured. Suffering from emphysema, he had two small tubes going up his nostrils, pumping oxygen. Travelling to Long Lartin had been a case of being helped into a car and helped out the other end. Parkhurst was a different game. They would have to catch a bus or Tube to Waterloo, get a train down to the Hampshire coast. They'd have to catch either the Portsmouth or Lymington ferry and find a cab at the other end. The cost of the journey was high, with little help available, and they couldn't afford an overnight stay anywhere, so the four or five hours' travel there and the same again back was gruelling.

Mum and Dad wrote to the Ministry of Justice asking if I could be transferred to London. They contacted the Holborn and St Pancras MP Frank Dobson and called the *Camden New Journal*. The newspaper spoke to them about their predicament and went over to see them in their Castle Road flat to get the story. The newspaper took up my case and began to try to help.

In February 2004, I finished two courses: the Reasoning and Rehabilitation programme and another called CALM. I also agreed to join an Alcohol Awareness course – there was a waiting list, but it seemed like things were moving along a little.

'Mr Massey's Risk Factors have been identified as poor emotional control, entrenched criminal lifestyle, failure to anticipate consequences, using violence for revenge and use of weapons,' a prison report noted. But these characteristics were linked to my murder conviction and the report added that there 'had been few signs of such behaviour in recent years and he had shown that he had been able to manage his emotions and deal effectively with conflict'.

I was described as 'polite and respectful towards staff', and did my job as a cleaner to a high standard. The reports from those who were with me daily supported the premise that I was ready, at the least, to become a Cat. C prisoner. The Parole Board weren't sure and instead recommended I be transferred to open conditions. This was noted in Whitehall – and then rejected by the Home Secretary, David Blunkett. I was told that because of my violent past I should complete another course. They added that an immediate move from Cat. B to Cat. D, after many years in a high-security environment, wasn't a good idea. They said my progression had to be slowly-slowly.

I reacted with exasperation to this ruling. I was offered a transfer to a Cat. C prison, suggested by the Home Secretary as a compromise and another step towards freedom, but I refused to go. I remained on the Isle of Wight, locked up in Parkhurst. Denying me a transfer to a Cat. D regime was just another example of the malicious vindictiveness I was purposely subjected to.

But the sense of injustice didn't send me off to war. Experienced wardens and other prisoners recognised where I was and people were willing to listen. I recognised it was time for everyone to try to muck in, to get through this and out the other side.

When the door half-opened, it happened quickly. Another year had passed, another summer of badminton in the sun, another winter of dark Channel skies and storms out at sea. Things had been going well, better than I'd hoped. I had the run of the old building, trusted by prisoners and wardens, and I was enjoying the peace of mind of knowing I didn't have to prove anything to anyone, didn't have to get involved with anything and could sit this one out.

I had become an Enhanced Prisoner in 2002, and had been reported as 'handling his knockback really well', in terms of my last meeting with the Parole Board. That had led to me being given some extra freedom on the wing, which I 'had not abused', and being handed the trusted position of wing cleaner.

It gave me the time to slowly make my way back and forth, up and down the balconies and stairs. I was diligent. My skills as a carpenter and guitar player come from my need to make sure I do a thorough job. My diligence as a cleaner was remarked upon. The place was kept spotless. It gave me the time and space to think, to consider what had happened and where I was now. Time could disappear productively by sketching out what I would like the future to look like and thinking how plausible my visions were.

The Parole Board heard that I'd spoken at length with a psychologist about my crimes. I'd begun to move from questioning what good could come of going over old ground to finding a 'deeper level of insight into his actions and its consequences. He had reviewed his previously held beliefs and attitudes and expressed regret for his actions and remorse for his victim,' my prison record notes.

Soon after this report, I was on the move again. I don't know why they eventually took me from Parkhurst – perhaps the pressure my parents had brought to bear paid off. The *New Journal* had been writing pieces about me and Frank Dobson had been lobbying. Maybe they realised it was ridiculous keeping me where I was, a waste of resources. They must've needed my bed for some other sorry bugger. I went from the high walls and constant sense that something could kick off at Parkhurst to an open prison in the Black Country.

◆ ◆ ◆

Sudbury was built as a US Air Force hospital for the D-Day landings, and parts of it hadn't seen a lick of paint since. It was mucked about with to make it a prison, but you're still housed in the same building as those pilots and bombers recuperated in.

I got there in 2005 and the place had been under the microscope. A report a couple of years before I arrived found that 350 prisoners had walked out in five years. The governor said it was because the place was overcrowded, but the advantage of this for me was they started putting a little bit of money into the place, and they were under pressure to improve the low standards. It was where Harry Roberts, who shot up three coppers, spent his last days inside, as did Ben Gunn, the Welsh bloke convicted of murder when he was just 14, who served thirty-two years. He was well known among inmates for his constant complaining to management, like he was a guest in a five-star hotel. We liked that approach. He never let anything go past him.

I'd been in Sudbury before and I knew they held courses in construction, something I knew my way round, and I hoped to get some work passing on trade I knew.

My journey from Parkhurst was, as ever, in a tiny sweat-box van. Again, I was handcuffed and left inside the vehicle as we crossed the Solent, filling me with a terrifying hour where I thought every swell meant I was heading to Davy Jones' Locker.

But the trip to the Black Country was well worth it. It was a vast change from Parkhurst. I liked it. I had a bit of trouble as soon as I landed there because they wanted to put me in a double cell – with three of us squeezed in – and I wouldn't fucking have it. I didn't like the look of the two blokes I was asked to share the cell with.

I told them, 'No, I ain't having that.' I said, 'Get the van out and take me back to Parkhurst, fuck this.' I was going to sit it out until they came up with something.

A quarter of an hour later, they said, 'No, we've found a single cell.'

I thought, 'That's not too hard, is it?' And they gave me a cleaning job as well.

I didn't want a job in the shops, the conveyor belt-style work they love prisoners to do. Too many cunts bossing you about, thinking it makes them something. But as a cleaner, you do a job and the rest of your time is your own. The screws could see if they left me in peace, they'd get no grief off me.

I got an outside job in an old people's home. I got a bike and cycled there and back each day on my own. I did maintenance and odd jobs, and it was lovely. I would run errands for them, get chocolate and newspapers. I went at 6.30 a.m. and got back at 7 p.m. each night.

◆ ◆ ◆

Being an old air force hospital may have made Sudbury barely fit for purpose, but it also meant it was a good place to explore. As I walked through the grounds, finding my feet, getting to know the layout, I noticed a run-down building standing on its own by the main gate. I thought, 'What's in there? Why is it standing locked up, untouched for years?' I couldn't help thinking about it.

One day I thought, 'Fuck it, I'm going to have a look.' I forced open a side door and crept into a dark and musty corridor. I followed it a few yards, my eyes becoming accustomed to the gloom. There, in front of me, was a good-sized hall. At one end there was a stage, and a load of seats were stacked up all over the place. It looked like it had once been the officers' mess, or the air force entertainment area, but for the last sixty-odd years it had been used as a dumping ground for crap.

Hanging either side of the stage was a big set of velvet curtains. They were ripped, so I took them down and, using skills I'd mastered from sewing endless mailbags, I stitched them back up.

I explored, climbing back stage and poking about. I uncovered a sound system and big speakers. 'Hello,' I thought, 'this could be ideal. This could be a nice little project.' I didn't ask for permission to start with – why give them the chance to find a reason to say no?

I cleaned everything from top to bottom, and I got it looking like a theatre again. I did the electrics for the lights, fixed up the gantry and it was great to see the stage bathed in light.

I turned my attention to the pulleys back stage and I worked out what did what and what went where. I took down the blocks and tackle, cleaned them up, re-threaded all the ropes. I checked out the stage, testing for weak points and rotten floorboards, and fixed that up as well.

I swept and dusted, cleaned and polished. It filled days that needed filling. I wasn't doing this for anyone else but myself and it allowed me to escape the reality of my world.

I had to tell the screws what I was up to eventually, and when I'd made headway I let a couple of them, who had treated me with respect, see the place. They were pleased with what I'd done, admired my handiwork.

With the screws onside, the next step was to ask if we could use the theatre. I'd met a few others who were musicians, so we formed a band with a drummer, bass, rhythm guitar and lead. I managed to get us permission to rehearse after 9 p.m. roll call. They let us go into the theatre and stay there till midnight. As the place was on its own, near the gate, we wouldn't disturb anyone. I loved cranking up the volume.

We played bluesy rock and we called ourselves Grounded. After a few rehearsals, it seemed natural we'd put on a gig, especially as I'd fixed the theatre up so well.

I had a load of posters made and put them up round the prison. We worked getting our set right and we did a gig to the whole place. It was a lovely feeling. I was as nervous as fuck. My sister Jane came. It was a nice buzz afterwards and it was well received.

But my hard graft getting that theatre in use didn't go unnoticed by less charitable and less well-meaning members of the prison hierarchy. At Sudbury, there was this vicar, a fat little egg on legs. Sometimes you get vicars in prison who are all right, but you often get these little Hitlers who think they have the calling and are special, that God has told them to come into prison and help save the evil convicts. They could be proper pious cunts, annoying wankers with their holy airs and graces – not what a prisoner on a life stretch needs to hear.

Now I had the theatre all shipshape, the vicar, the twerp, starting demanding use, saying she wanted access when we'd arranged to rehearse and that she should have priority. I said 'Oi, what part have you exactly played in getting it shipshape? You want to use it? Get in line, sunshine, we have first call on it, and you need to understand you can't just come in here and push us out.'

She went crying behind my back to the governor. She didn't have the manners to ask me directly. Instead, she went straight to the governor and demanded time at our expense. It had been lying empty, but now I'd put the graft in, she wanted us out. It reminded me of that tale about the chicken who bakes the bread and can't get any of her mates to help grind the corn and all that. This poseur didn't seem to have a Christian bone in her body.

◆ ◆ ◆

My disillusion at Sudbury, having had a good spell there at first, was profound. Thankfully, I wasn't going to be there long. In 2006, more than thirty years after my original crime, the unthinkable happened. The bomb I'd been waiting for dropped and I wasn't ready for the explosion.

I went before a Parole Board. I didn't hold out any hope, and the hearing seemed like it had gone the same as previous ones. A fortnight later, I was told I would be released under strict rules. I would be placed in a hostel run by the parole system, and if I could keep my nose clean I would be allowed a widening set of rights, a more relaxed curfew and some return to normality.

But things went wrong almost immediately. My parole officer got me through the hearing and we discussed how we could make sure this worked. We asked very clearly – my solicitor, parole officer, letters from family – that if I was released to a hostel, could I please be sent to a halfway house somewhere near the family, so they could look after me.

I requested, if there wasn't a room available near my family, please could they delay my release until something came up in Camden. It may sound strange, after waiting all these years for my freedom, to ask for a few more weeks inside. But it was important. I was facing a new life, a new world to get used to, and I wanted to be near to my sister and parents to ensure, when I needed that extra support, they were close. I didn't want to take no chances. If that wasn't possible, I asked if I could wait until it was.

It was a common way to be released: you'd get parole and be held until a suitable space came up. You'd see blokes who had been told they were free six months previously, but a room had yet to come up. I thought it wouldn't be a problem, but it was.

Maybe in their keenness to get rid, I'd been told a room in Camden Town was ready for me, and I said my goodbyes, handed out the items in my cell I wasn't taking, packed a bag and got ready for the next step in my so-called rehabilitation.

But it went wrong. At the last minute they reneged on what they'd said about where they would send me. I got out, met the probation officer at the gates, full of excitement and nerves, and he said, 'You're going to Streatham.' I asked why and was met with a blank refusal to discuss it.

It was a wind-up. I'd waited for so long to get on the outside and had a place arranged in my mind's eye. I'd been told I was going somewhere that wouldn't play havoc with my nerves, that would make me feel at home. Suddenly I was headed to south London where I knew no one, placed in a small room in a hostel crowded with younger offenders, all of whom had serious drug addictions and mental health problems.

I found it very hard. It was a combination of things, ranging from the noise of the streets at night and a filthy room – I'd always prided myself on keeping my cell immaculate, and the bedbugs and years of dirt made me feel deeply uncomfortable – to the air of menace, as well-built young gangsters stalked the corridors. They didn't know me, and bullies were looking for victims. It meant I had to make it clear I wasn't to be messed with. It made for an inauspicious start to my days as a free man.

Then there was the fact I was on the other side of London to my family. I had to leave at 6 a.m. each day to travel to north London to pick my mum up. I'd head to her house, get showered there and changed, and we'd go up to see my dad. He was in a care home in Cricklewood. We'd spend the day with him.

The Streatham experience signified that the nightmare wasn't yet over. Being so far away from home after being promised somewhere in Camden was always on my mind. It was a hell of a place to commute to during rush hour, and then getting back again in the evening – it would be tail-to-tail traffic and you would be stressed all the time about being late. Coming out into this after such a long stretch was mental.

The time I could spend with my pa was going to be cut tragically short and have ramifications for my future. Dad went downhill quite quickly after I came out. His health had been bad for a while. He'd had the stroke and emphysema caused by his work. It was awful to see. I was out of prison, hoping to spend good-quality time with him, but then – bang – he started getting really sick, as if he'd been holding on all this time for me.

A few weeks after I was released, he was transferred to the Royal Free Hospital in Hampstead. He had blood poisoning. He'd been fitted with a colostomy bag and caught an infection from it. He got septicaemia. It was bad news.

We gathered at the Free. We hoped a course of antibiotics might do the trick, but the diagnosis was more serious. The doctor at the hospital got us all together, the whole family – it was about teatime – in this room on the ward. It was lit by a strip light, had horrible faded yellow walls and cracked lino. It was a place that would send a chill up your spine, a room where you just knew bad news was given. The doctor said, 'We're really sorry, but your dad will not last another twenty-four hours.'

I had to be back in Streatham in time for lockdown: my curfew was from the early evening. I did the dutiful thing: I called my hostel and told them what was going on. I said the family didn't want to leave

Dad's bedside. I told them it was my duty as a son, after all these years, to be there for Dad, like he had always been there for me.

The hostel replied, 'No, Mr Massey, you must come back and observe your curfew.'

We'd been told to expect Dad to die that day. I got the doctor on the phone to explain to the probation team, but they just wouldn't listen. I'd missed so much of his life and I wasn't going to leave.

They said to me, 'Come back to Streatham and if we get a phone call in the middle of the night we'll call you a taxi.'

I thought, 'That's not how it works.' I'd get a phone call to tell me Dad had died. I wanted to be there for his last moments.

I spoke with the rest of the family and decided I would face the consequences. I couldn't desert now. The hostel had my phone number, they had the number of the hospital, they knew where I was, they knew the ward, the room, everything, and they had heard what was happening directly from the doctors. There were policemen downstairs they could have sent up to get me if they'd wanted to. They could see the logic – but they stuck to this ridiculous, rigid decision.

Spending those precious hours with Dad was to have consequences.

◆ ◆ ◆

I was the last person he spoke to before he died. In that last night, he slipped into a coma. The rest of the family had nodded off and I watched over him. It was the early hours of the morning. I had to wake them all up and say, 'He's gone.'

Despite the trauma and grief, I thought, 'At least I'm able to spend time with Dad, and I'll be able to grieve with my family.' But this wasn't the reality. At this point I was supposedly a free man, but I was still not free.

A hostel is more rigid than an open prison. If I'd still been in the open prison, they would have been more amenable. They'd let you go on home leave five days at a time, whereas the hostel wouldn't let you have any home leave at all. At an open prison, they're trying to train you to live at home, but when you're released you're no longer good enough to do that. It didn't make any sense.

And the anxiety I felt – a lifetime in prison had clearly affected me – was made even worse by the surroundings I was dumped in. I was made to reside with people I really didn't want to mix with. You had people kicking off day and night. You were shoved out on to the front line, into a danger zone, a place where violence and drugs are rife, where there are people with some serious problems and no help.

Here you are, trying to work out what's happened, what the new world is like, and instead you're hoping no idiot is going to try something on, smash into your room, find a reason to start a fight. All of this instead of a loving environment at home, where things are relaxed and you can be reintegrated back into the real world.

Before Dad died, I had found that the rules were hard to follow. They seemed designed to set ex-prisoners up to fail, and make their lives as uncomfortable as possible. I ended up getting a written warning.

Each night, a probation officer came round and banged on the door at 11.30 p.m. They got you up to sign a piece of paper to confirm you were there. It was a roll call. I would be fast asleep as I needed to get up early so I could get up north across the river for the day, get out of this slum, but they wouldn't let you get an early night. They'd wake you and insist you sign this book.

Malicious behaviour showed who was in charge. After the 11.30 roll call, I'd get back into bed, turn the light out, get my head down. At 11.45, they'd knock on the door again and say, 'Right, get up. You're on cleaning duty.'

I refused. Fucking cleaning duty in the middle of the night? For who? I wouldn't have it. I didn't use their facilities, nothing. I ate and washed elsewhere. The only thing I used was my bedroom and I kept that spotless. I wasn't going to get up in the middle of the night to mop the kitchen floors and the living rooms for some sloppy, dirty bastards when I hadn't been anywhere near them.

They said, 'No, Mr Massey, you have to show you are community spirited.' But at 11.45 at night? I kept saying, 'No way' to their silly diktats. They responded by saying they'd evict me, and that was tantamount to being recalled to prison.

That's what happened and my records were marked that I was No Fixed Abode. It was nonsense. I was living with my family, keeping my head down, somewhere I could get my life together, not a grotty hostel full of criminals.

They said that if I didn't go back, it meant I'd become 'unmanageable'. I didn't understand how they could say that. I was still visiting my probation officer twice a week. They could easily keep tabs on what I was up to. I was under their control.

In the end, a lot of people in this situation blow up. You're set up to fail. It was like, 'Fuck it, you want out. Here you go. Have some of this and see how you like it.'

After Dad's death, I felt that now I'd broken the curfew rules, there was little to be gained by heading back to a place where staff and residents were acting aggressively towards me. If I returned south, I would likely be arrested and sent back to prison. Instead, I decided to live with family and wait to see what was in store.

The trouble is, unless it's a sensational incident that recalls you, they have to get someone to issue a warrant. That takes a few days, or even weeks. I settled down at a relative's house and began to think maybe I'd been forgotten, or that the police wanted to turn a blind eye. Maybe they'd had enough of me as I'd had enough of them. Maybe that was it – we're even.

I found some work through an old friend. Honest, paid work as a Marks and Spencer's shopfitter and I enjoyed it. If I'd been in the hostel, they wouldn't have let me get a job. It's another way the system is stacked. You have no money or dignity and are more likely to get up to no good with time on your hands and no cash in your pockets.

I got into it. They were a good bunch. We'd get a twelve-hour shift to do the fitting out. We'd start at 9 p.m. when the stores closed and we were a well-oiled machine. We were so good at it, we managed to shave several hours off each shift, but we'd get paid full whack. We went all over the country, which was nice for me, having only seen it from the inside of a prison van. I did it seven days a week and the cash I earned paid for Dad's funeral.

As the days turned into weeks, I began to feel my case was so unimportant I must be lost in the system. Bringing in money, keeping busy, seeing family. It was what I hoped being released would be like. It meant I felt more secure and happy than I had for years.

But of course the criminal justice system hadn't forgotten. It was just moving with its customary, agonising slowness. Things came to a head when Mum fell ill.

Mum had been understandably hit by Dad's passing, but she'd always been strong, so it was worrying to see her listless and under the weather, tired. She was taken up to the Free for some tests and treatment, and was given a bed there.

I went to see my mum and she said she wanted some things from her flat in Castle Road, down in Kentish Town. I walked down from the Royal Free and I decided I'd stop off at the Fiddler's Elbow to see a mate. He wanted me to say hello and tell him what was going on, as he'd been a good friend of Mum's too.

I'd been in there for a few minutes when two plain-clothes police officers walked in. I clocked them, and was sure they clocked me, but nothing was said and nothing happened. Having arranged to meet my sister at Mum's place, I drank up and left.

After getting Mum some bits and pieces, Jane and I set off to return to hospital. It was then that things began to turn surreal.

We left Mum's flat and walked past Buttles Woodyard and up Castlehaven, where I'd done a bunk to Spain that time. As we were going, a helicopter came up over the top of us. There was frenetic activity around one of the houses, and I saw they had marksmen pointing guns over the road and armed police aiming at the door. We walked right into it.

I said to Jane, 'That's for me, you know.' I was convinced, because I'd seen the two plain-clothes coppers earlier.

She said, 'Don't be so paranoid. They wouldn't waste all their time and all these people on you – who do you think you are, Al fucking Capone or something?'

I said loudly, 'They must be filming a scene for some programme or something', and then the inspector in charge started getting uppity as we approached, asked us where we were headed and ushered us through the cordon. We carried on walking, over towards the swimming baths on the opposite corner.

I couldn't believe it when I looked back at the house on the other side of the road they were about to raid – it was number 117. Our number in Castle Road was 117, but this was Castlehaven Road, round the corner. It dawned on me they must have fucked up and got the wrong bloody road. We'd got through their cordon, strolled past right under their noses. It must have terrified the people inside 117 Castlehaven Road. I've thought since then of knocking on the door and asking what happened.

With this, I knew my time was up and I didn't want anyone to be put in danger. I knew they were coming, sooner or later, and when they did, I didn't make a fuss. They found me at a relative's place and they knocked on the door.

'John Massey?' they asked.

I said, 'Yes, that's me. I'd been wondering when you were going to get round to this.' They took me to Holmes Road nick and I spent the night there, and was sent to Pentonville the next day.

◆ ◆ ◆

At Pentonville, they locked the doors and let me get on with it. They have to give you a review after twenty-eight days, so I thought it would be a case of twenty-eight days inside and they'd look at my notes and I'd be out again. I hadn't committed what is classed as a crime. I'd broken parole under extreme circumstances.

But nothing happened, there was no review, no word, no nothing. I was left for six months in the Ville. A solicitor managed to get it taken to a judicial review and the judge decided to order the Parole Board to look again at my case. I got that, after waiting six long months, and got a knockback. I wasn't going anywhere: I couldn't be trusted, I was clearly a danger – all the usual bollocks. I was told I would have to wait another year before I had any chance of this being reviewed.

And it was a total madhouse, Pentonville. The conditions are extremely rough. It's riddled with vermin, rats, cockroaches. Everyone there is in different circumstances and that makes things tense. It's a holding pen.

There are very few lifers there. For me, the difference between myself and the others in there was this: most of the prisoners have an idea of where they stand, how long they have, what they need to do, but when you are a lifer on recall, you know absolutely nothing. You're completely reliant on receiving something from a Parole Board. There's no end date to work towards and the system is so clogged up and under-resourced, there are inevitable delays.

All this puts an extra burden on you and means your review is continuously postponed. Because of this underfunding, and the turnover of parole officers because they are paid shit and treated worse, the system is in meltdown. You're a piece of meat. The only thing that gets you to a decision is the lapse of time. I kept thinking, 'Why's it taking so long to remedy a situation that's a non-indictable offence?' They wouldn't give someone five years because they'd missed an appointment.

Being in a shithole like Pentonville was hardly good for my mood. At first I was banged up twenty-three hours a day. How much time you spent in the cell all depended on staffing levels. If they were short staffed or overcrowded – and they always were both those things – there would be trouble, and there really was trouble at the Ville. The alarm bells would be going every two minutes.

Added to this, the little but important comforts that long-term prisoners build up were missing. It drove me fucking mad. I couldn't get a pillow, a cup, a knife, toothpaste or a bit of soap. It's difficult to describe how that feels. Left to your own devices, left to stare at the walls and ponder your fate, unwashed and stinking. You have no control over what's going to happen next. If you rang on the bell to ask for something, the screws would come in and say, 'You can't use that bell unless it's an emergency – why are you ringing that bell?' and then they'd give your cell a going-over.

You'd have to piss in a pot or shit in a bucket, and then have nothing but the same bowl to wash in. It's Dickensian, but at least the Victorians might have had a sense of humanity. They built the cells we were in for one person, and that was 150 years ago. Now they were being used for two or three people. When you got a hot day, with three people there, it was intolerable. Freezing in the winter, boiling in the summer. There was never any time you felt comfortable.

◆ ◆ ◆

I spent another three years at the Ville, waiting for a Parole Board to hear my case. Despite having proved to one board that I should be released – despite having only broken the terms of my release to be with Dad when he died – it was decided I wouldn't be let out.

They listened to what I had to say, listened to my solicitor, and ignored us. They decided to send me from the Ville to a Category D prison rather than release me.

One day, I was scooped up without any notice and driven to Ford open prison in west Sussex. It should have been a good sign, something to raise the spirits, and let's be honest, anything would be better than that dump full of poor cunts having their sanity spun in ten different directions. However, even this caused me frustrations. First, I only got there five months after being told I was going to be moved. That's how long they'd planned it, and how long it took to fill out a poxy form, find a sweat box and a driver, and embark on that colossal hour-and-a-half drive south. That it should take five fucking months to arrange one transfer of an old-aged pensioner shows how fucked the system is.

When I arrived, they said, 'Unfortunately, Mr Massey, you're two weeks too late for a course you have to do. You've missed the start of the "short" programme of rehabilitation you need to complete. The only other one we have is a "long" programme.'

I said, 'Hang on, how come? How can you argue the toss over a couple of weeks?' It wasn't like I was dawdling, taking my time to sign up or fucking anything. It made a big difference – the long programme meant I wouldn't eligible to leave for over a year, but the short programme would have been finished after four months.

Despite coming up against yet another kink in the system, I realised there was little I could do and I tried hard to keep my nose clean and my head down, and fulfil all the things they required. I got on with it and was there for four months. I began to earn trust. I was taken out on two escorted visits to a nearby town, and I knuckled down and waited for the time to pass.

As the days slipped by, I hardly dared hope this time that when freedom beckoned it would be for good, but I knew I had to be seen to be doing my part. I was told I had at least two years to serve for a civil recall, as it's called. That's the equivalent of a four-year sentence, all for staying by my dad's bedside.

But despite this extra time, Ford was all right. Anywhere was better than the Ville, and Ford had things I could get into to help see off these extra days. It's in the countryside, near Arundel, which I really liked – made a change from some of the shitholes I'd been in. There are rows and rows of Nissen huts and one big brick building. It was another former air force base, used by the Fleet Air Arm during the war and then turned into a prison in the 1960s.

The cabins had double cells. I wasn't having that, and told them so, said I'd prefer to be on a Cat. A if I had a cell to myself, rather than this place with someone else in with me. Thankfully, somewhere someone listened and I was given my own 2m by 4m cell in the main block. It was OK, with newish shared shower units.

I got used to how things worked. With an open prison regime, you have to do three roll calls a day when you have to be in what they euphemistically call your 'room'. You have your own key, to let yourself in and out – the first time I'd had a set of keys in my hand for four decades. It was a nice feeling, something as simple as having to remember your key.

My mate Peter Jenkins was at Ford with me. I met him there and we had a mutual friend called Eastwood. He was always on the ear-hole for teabags and coffee; he was always pleading poverty, so he was dubbed Skint Eastwood. The relationships you form inside are often intense. You either get on with someone or you fucking hate them. I was never really interested in what people were in for unless they were nonces or something. Some people would ask you before they asked your name, deciding if you were their type of wrong 'un. It was a personal choice.

Personally, I didn't want to hear people's life stories, see all their paperwork and have them bore the fucking life out of me about how fucking innocent they really are. It's like when you go round someone's house and they bring out the family photos and the holiday photos. You'd ask someone what they were in for and never hear the end of it. There's nothing more boring to me. It would go on and on for ever, so I got to the point where I wouldn't enquire.

Ford was a mixed place, with some good blokes in there and some proper wrong 'uns. The regime was good, too – really lax, which meant the screws and governor were under the cosh a bit. In 2006, two years before I showed up, seventy prisoners in one year alone had done a bunk, including three murderers coming to the end of their sentences. They were always short of staff – something that was to directly impact me later – and, incredibly, because of the lack of man-power, Ford was a target for thieves from the outside. People would break into the workshops and nick stuff – pretty funny. It was helped by a moody CCTV system that never seemed to work properly, which was all right for us inside.

Some inmates would slip out at night and go to buy booze, and it was easy for puff, phones and all sorts of contraband to be smuggled in by your nearest and dearest. Being drastically understaffed – something the Independent Monitoring Board highlighted – meant you had the run of the place and made for a good enough atmosphere. But it also had bad effects, as I was about to find out.

I'd been in there for a few months when disaster struck. I got a message that my darling sister Carol was in intensive care, in that same hospital where Dad had died, and she was asking for me.

Carol and I had always been very close. We had that rapport. She was a great sister, someone I truly loved, and we never let each other down, never.

She was well educated, bright, kind, caring. We could talk about all sorts of things. She never asked for anything – and the fact was, she had asked to see me, and I knew deep down that made it even more urgent. She was in a really bad way and wanted me there. I was beside myself with worry.

I approached the governor for compassionate leave to visit her in hospital. I explained where she was, got a doctor to confirm her condition. She had late-stage cancer and the prognosis wasn't good.

But they said, 'No, Massey, you don't meet the criteria.'

I said I was Category D and should be allowed to go. But I stood there and listened politely, got the knockback, and left the governor's office all meek and mild. I was strangely calm, when I should have been angry. They should have said, 'Yes, off you go. Have forty-eight hours and best of luck, mate', but instead they said, 'You're not going anywhere.'

Rather than argue the toss, I thought, 'Fuck this, I need to go and see my sister.' 'Can you arrange an escorted visit?' I asked. 'No big deal,' I thought. 'I need to see my sister, she's dying, and nothing can surely get in the way of this.'

They said, 'We're sorry, but we don't have the staff available to do escorted visits.' I walked out of that office with their decision ringing in my ears and couldn't understand how what seemed like a matter of compassion could be so callously thrown back at me.

So I made some arrangements and slipped out with a work party one day. I carried on walking and got out through a hole in the fence. I jumped on a train to Victoria and went straight to see Carol. She was conscious and happy to see me. Her liver had gone. She'd been a drinker and when they took her in she declined very quickly. She went into a coma and died two weeks later.

The justice system was playing with the last two weeks of my sister's life. She was close to me, so close – just two years older than me. I couldn't have lived with not seeing her when she called for me. I had no regrets making that decision. Afterwards, when I'd left Ford, the criminal system and the screws said my thinking skills were twisted, and they said I had to go on a course to make me more obedient. But if they asked me the same questions a thousand times, I'd give them the same answers. Would I walk out again to see Carol, knowing what was in store? Yes. Yes, every time.

I knew there would be consequences, even though I didn't understand the extent of the vengeance they would go to. But I'd still make the same decision. I can now live with her passing.

◆ ◆ ◆

After Carol died, I decided not to return to Ford, and not to hand myself in.

By now my mum had moved up to Barnet to live with her granddaughter Michelle, so I went up there for a bit. I built her a summer house in the garden, so she could sit outside but not get cold. It seemed the police had decided to leave me in peace, but I was always aware this burst of freedom could end any day.

I've been asked by lots of people why I didn't give myself up after my sister died, but I thought, 'Why should I?' It meant even more to be around for Mum after the death of Carol, for support and that. Above all, I knew the penalty for one day was the same as for one year. It wouldn't make a blind bit of difference if they decided to pick me up again and throw me back inside.

The end of a ten-month stint on the outside came in unexpected circumstances. They called up my niece, Michelle, and said it was Sussex Police. They said, 'Tell your uncle to give himself up.'

I don't know why they called her. They didn't send anyone round: it was just phone call. I thought, 'A phone call? I may as well make the most of the time I have.' I didn't bother hiding any more and I wasn't hard to find. I knew the knock would come one day and it did, but I'd had long enough to build my mum her summer house.

Eventually, two officers were despatched to pick me up. The police were very reasonable. We had a good chat before they took me away and they said, 'Sorry, John, if we'd been aware of all the facts, we might have given you ten minutes to slip off.' It was a job they didn't want to be doing. They wanted to be out catching proper criminals. They were apologetic when they arrested me – I'll never forget that. But they had to take me back, and the revolving door at Pentonville spun again after another night spent in the cells at Holmes Road nick.

Once back in those hellish surroundings at the Ville, I tried to explain to anyone who would listen why I had behaved as I had. I kept on at the screws, governors, visitors, the *New Journal*, anyone who would stand there and get their ear bashed for a couple of minutes.

I once asked this assistant governor what he would do if someone he loved was in a car crash.

'I'd drop everything I was doing and go to them,' he replied.

'And what if the governor stopped you, and said he couldn't spare you from your shift?' I asked.

'That would be ridiculous – I'd just walk off,' replied the AG.

I asked them what the fuck they were having a go at me for then. I did what anyone sane would do. My sister was dying. I had to see her. That was it. But they couldn't see it that way. They saw it completely differently if it was their own circumstances. They just couldn't put themselves in my shoes and admit what I'd done was reasonable. They acted like robots.

So I was once again back behind bars, and again, having to wait for a Parole Board to meet to see if I was going to be released any time soon.

TEN

My brief time out and about after Carol's death proved to me I could happily live again on the right side of a prison wall. It seemed a straightforward path. I'd been given parole before, I'd be in an open prison, and both of the times there had been an issue that had exonerating circumstances, namely the death of a family member, which has to be about as exonerating as you can get.

I was sure I'd be returned to where I'd been – Ford or Sudbury or wherever – and serve out a little bit more time before being told that was me done. But I should have known better. The vindictiveness of the system is never going to let you come out even. And the stupidness of how the system works, or doesn't work, and the fact it's run by brainless box-tickers should have made me wary. But no – I thought I'd go back inside, be sent to a low-security place, stay there a few months and then be shoved out through the gates.

From the Holmes Road nick – a nick I knew so well – the sweat box didn't head south to Sussex or north to the Black Country. Instead, the van drove a couple of miles east and the doors opened and revealed where I was. I was far from happy – they'd taken me to the Ville again, and this dump was going to be my home for some time.

After two more years of rotting away in the Ville, I wrote to Terry Waite, the vicar who'd been held hostage in the Lebanon in the 1980s. I'd written to him before, thinking he would understand my position, and he always replied.

His letter this time was the usual morale booster, but with no answers except the hardest one of all – that I should be patient, and that was all I had in my armoury to keep me sane. Terry wrote:

Dear John,

This will be a very quick note as I am about to depart on my travels but I wanted simply to say that I have been in touch with Jane again and I very much hope you will get permission to visit your mother on an escorted visit.

I am quite sure you will behave responsibly but I do understand well the frustration you experience in this extraordinarily difficult situation. Please do keep in touch and I will certainly keep in touch with Jane and she knows that she can contact me at any time.

These little notes, little gestures, helped enormously. Getting a letter was always welcome and anything that helped me be sure I was rightfully aggrieved helped me, made me think I wasn't going mad, that this was wrong.

As Mum's condition got worse, I became increasingly desperate to see her. I asked the governors over and again if I could get a trip out, but was met with a firm no. Mum was finding it harder and harder to visit me, and it was reaching a point where she wasn't even able to make it easily in a wheelchair. It was painful, cruel and deeply unfair to make her go through this.

The crap conditions at the Ville didn't help me settle, and I wanted out, one way or another. As my latest parole was knocked back, and as Mum's health slipped away, I thought, 'Fuck it, I'm going over that wall, whether they want me to or not' – so I did.

You put any living creature in a cage, what is the first thing they do? Circle about, go round and round, trying to find a way out. That is the most natural thing to do. It's instinct. It's like a salmon swimming upstream. Get a plant, put it in a dark corner and it grows towards the light. You can't legislate against nature. It goes against the grain.

As soon as I was back in Pentonville, I thought about getting out, and when I found out Mum was too ill to come and see me, that was that. They weren't letting me go to her, so I'd just have to sort it. I snooped about, used my head, weighed up my options and found the false ceiling and skylight I told you about.

The day I went through the Ville roof and over the wall, Jane got a call from her neighbour who said, 'You've got a fucking TV crew outside your yard', and the police were there too. The Old Bill paid her a visit and told her if she didn't get in touch within twenty-four hours they were coming round and kicking her door in.

I called her from near Pentonville, from a phone box on the Cally Road. She was in my neighbour's having a cup of tea and when she answered she thought it was the prison phone number. She just said, 'Hi, John. I'm round Maria's having a cup of tea.'

I said, 'OK, Jane. By the way, I'm out.'

Jane, bless her, didn't fuck about. She was straight down to get me. I'd got the suitcase that had been left for me and made my way to Kentish Town where I met Jane and we travelled together to see Mum in Kent.

Jane got her collar felt. Old Bill said they had found her fingerprints on the suitcase I had with me, but she just said, 'No comment, no comment, no comment' to all their questions, and I told them I'd got it out of her loft without her knowing and they had no way of proving otherwise.

I look back and I think I was quite green in terms of keeping myself on the outside after that breakout. For example, the house I was finally nicked in – the guy had been on my contact list at prison, so it was hardly any wonder they thought they should check him out. It didn't take them long. As I say, I was a little bit green about that.

Thinking back, I reckon that someone must have grassed me up. They didn't arrive like they were looking for a bloke to have a chat about whether he owned his wife's runabout or not. They had a tooled-up team coming in through the front door. I went straight to the back door and they were already coming in over the garden fence. They had me surrounded.

They took me first to hospital, to UCH. I had broken my foot as I went over the wall, and the doctors strapped it up and gave me some painkillers. They were OK. They knew the story. I had a bit of toothache, too, and joked with them about seeing a dentist. In fifty years, I never saw a dentist. The dentists inside are bloody butchers and just rip everything out. They had to be avoided. The two coppers I was with sympathised but said they couldn't help. A bit of toothache was going to be the least of my worries, I was soon to discover.

◆ ◆ ◆

The atmosphere changed very quickly once I was away from the hospital. The sweat box was taking me back to prison, and not just any prison. I was going to be held at Belmarsh, the most notorious high-security prison in the UK.

Opened in 1991, it's in Thamesmead, where the old Woolwich Arsenal stood. It's a fucking horrible place, full of fucking horrible people. The prisoners are dubbed threats to national security, so you can imagine who they throw in there. They hold people on indeterminate sentences. And it may be full of unsavoury prisoners, but the fucking screws are the worst in a crowded field of total cunts. It wasn't called the UK's Guantánamo Bay for nothing. The screws there didn't give a fuck.

Even Her Majesty's Prison Inspectors, useless bunch that they are, found Belmarsh to be to keen on violent methods of prison control. A report from the inspector, not long before I arrived, criticised what they called an 'extremely high level' of force to control the prisoners, and said that an 'unusually high' number of prisoners were victimised and intimidated.

After a night in a police station – I don't remember which, since they all look the same inside – I was questioned by a couple of detectives and they wanted me to implicate the people whose house I was in. I kept shtum and refused to speak. I didn't like the tone of the questioning. They were aggressive, threatening me. It was bluff tactics the police use. They switched the interview tape machine on but they didn't say a dickie bird. The whole process being futile, they lost patience and I was shoved in a sweat box and driven to Belmarsh.

I was cuffed behind my back – done to cause maximum discomfort – and went under a blue light all the way. It felt excessive and I hit every bump in the road; I was knocked about. It didn't surprise me, though. It seemed like the usual overreaction.

I was taken into the reception at Belmarsh, where my property bag had come from Pentonville. They opened it up and this foul stench came out. The screws had tipped effluent into it. Everything was ruined. The shit must have hit the fan. They were totally enraged about it. They'd poured shit and piss into my bag and given it a good shake about. It was disgusting and should have warned me what was in store.

After the strip-search and questions to confirm some details, it was through the next set of doors and into the room where they turn you into a number. They put me in 'patches' to signify that I was a security risk, then took me straight to the Seg unit. I couldn't believe how excessive it was, and hoped this was a short, sharp shock to tell me who the boss was.

But it was just the beginning. All the spiteful tactics came out as they were trying to decide where to put me, in the top-security unit or Seg. I was in there for seven weeks.

They told me I was being held for 'escaping from lawful custody'. That meant I was banged up twenty-four hours a day. If I wanted exercise or to make as phone call, I had to make an application in writing each morning. No one told me this was the way things worked. I was unaware. If you don't make an application, you don't get the two key things that break the hell of solitary.

I was exhausted by this constant battle, but I kept telling myself, 'Prison is prison.' Being in isolation meant I didn't get to see or speak to anyone for seven weeks. The screws said fuck all, not that I wanted to make chit-chat with those cunts. I had to walk around an enclosed yard, but I got the hang of it. I was on my own, and I did an hour's exercise each day, once I'd realised how to get that sorted. No solicitor came to see me and it felt like I was disappearing.

Eventually, I managed to get a visit arranged and on the day my sisters and Mum were due, the screws got me from my cell, using the usual aggro, as if they needed to warn me off from trying anything. They took me into a visiting area but kept me away from anyone else while we waited for our visitors to arrive.

Slowly, numbers were called out and inmates were escorted to cubicles. Everyone was called in – except me. I couldn't understand why. I knew my visitors where waiting a short distance away. Behind a few walls and bars, there was my darling Mum and my sisters. I waited and waited – and then after thirty minutes a screw came in and said, 'Your visit has been terminated. Back to the cell with you, Massey.'

They said there was a problem with my mum's ID. Jane and Kim had brought Mum with them in an ambulance, only to be told this frail old lady in a wheelchair, come to see her son possibly for the last time, didn't have the right identification. It was something to do with the fact she didn't live at her old address any longer because she was in an old people's home. They told her she wasn't coming in. How fucking rotten and stupid is that?

There was no point arguing, as I discovered after being told to shut the fuck up and get back in line. It was driving me mad. I thought, 'What the hell is going on?' Even when I managed to get myself a phone call, I had to fill out an application laying out who I was ringing. When I finally got a call, I put Jane's name on the list as she was caring for Mum.

I got to the phone booth, dialled the number, and there was my sister's voice. You don't know how good it felt to hear that, after being held in silence for so long. Jane answered and said, 'Hang on a minute,

I'll put Mum on.' Guess what happened next? The cunts listening in immediately cut me off.

I asked why, and they said because I'd spoken to the wrong person. 'Your mum's not on the list, just your sister Jane. So you broke the rules, Massey.'

It was evil. I couldn't get any messages out, let anyone know how I was getting on, or speak to a solicitor to try to get things moving along. I was in a hellish limbo.

◆ ◆ ◆

As it always is, I got a surprise one day. The door was opened, four screws were standing there, and they told me I was off to Blackfriars Crown Court – or at least, I was going to attend via a video link. I saw a solicitor and we had a chat. I sat in this shabby room with a dodgy screen that kept freezing, with no chance to speak privately with a brief.

At Blackfriars, my solicitor, Alison Morgan, had prepared a case that on the face of it seemed indefensible. I was charged with escape. I'd been behind bars at Pentonville on 17 June 2012, and then, two days later, 19 June, had been found in Kent. There could be no doubt, surely, that I had escaped, broken out unlawfully from custody. Surely it was cut and dried, open and shut?

Fuck it, I was pleading not guilty anyway. I saw my family on a TV screen, and watched as my sisters waved, tried their best in the limited time they had to comfort me, let me know they were doing all they could. But what could they do? They had found a sympathetic solicitor in Alison. They had written to MPs, raising questions about why I was being held in Belmarsh. The *New Journal* had written about it and been to see the Howard League for Penal Reform to seek advice.

But being in patches at the other end of a dodgy video feed did nothing but make me feel more helpless. I had been swallowed up and was slowly being digested by a system designed to work in as frustratingly slow a manner as possible.

The judge sat at his bench, an elevated position in a court decked out in a cheap pine veneer. In court were the usual clerks, stenographers, the counsel for the Crown and my solicitor. Up on the wall was the screen where I would peer out from, like something from *Nineteen Eighty-Four*.

There was a delay as neither party could hear the other properly, leading to tinkering with microphones. The judge, in an exasperated and condescending way, had asked his clerks why the accused wasn't there in person; a mumbled response about there being a lack of staff to accompany me set the tone.

I was already at a disadvantage in being denied the chance to appear in person. It fucked me right off, and was down to the staffing arrangements of a private company who had won a contract to take prisoners to and from the courts. Not only did it rob me of a fundamental human right to defend myself in the flesh, it psychologically made me look dangerously guilty. Here was a man who needed four guards and a special van to take me across London, and there wasn't the manpower.

It took away the important chance to have my day in court, a day out, a break from the soul-destroying monotony, a chance to have different surroundings, for my eyes look upon something other than four grey walls scratched with desperado graffiti.

I got to wave at my family and a friend, which was nice, but it made me feel how far away I was. The judge remanded me in custody because I wanted to plead not guilty to escaping. I said to the judge, 'You left me with no choice, so I'm pleading not guilty to what you're accusing me of.'

Let me give you an example. You get cases where you owe somebody money for drugs. If you do a certain thing for them, you're doing it under duress, therefore you're not guilty. I said it was the same with the escape.

'I was under duress,' I said. 'I had to do it.' Like Steve McQueen giving the Nazis the run-around. It was my duty, and they should respect that. I wasn't harming anyone – the system had set out its stall and I said it wasn't right, so I tried to fix it in my own way. Fair enough, they'd nicked me, used their resources to get me back inside, so also fair enough, I'd used my own ways and means to get out. I just had to do it. I had to get out. If I hadn't, I'd have been a danger to myself.

While my solicitor was sympathetic and understanding, and seemed to agree that pleading not guilty would be a good way to highlight what I felt was the absurdity of my situation, she got the wobbles and before the hearing she decided she didn't want to go with it. Neither would the judge. They said I'd end up with a heftier sentence if I pleaded not guilty, that I didn't have a leg to stand on. But as it turned out, I got the maximum anyway.

After this, I got sent briefly to Frankland prison in County Durham, and then, when they got round to it, they shipped me back south to Belmarsh.

The governor at Frankland was a decent fellow. When I was there before, he'd been a welfare officer. He was a decent guy, and he'd been promoted to number one. He seemed pleased and a bit surprised to see me – and his reaction was a morale boost.

It didn't last long. After a month and a half at Frankland, I was woken at 4.30 one morning and given twenty minutes to wash and pack. I was told I was going back to London, as I'd be sentenced in a few days' time.

I got transferred back to Belmarsh and spent a couple of nights in one of their Seg cells. Then I was driven to Blackfriars court and told I was sentenced to two more years, which, on top of a life sentence with an indeterminate release date, meant nothing. They had the power to extend it as much as they liked, and it was as pointless as telling me I might have jelly and cake on my birthday.

It was nonsensical: they read the sentence out and then in the same breath said it was to run with my life sentence, with a release date to be determined by the Parole Board. In other words, I was back to where I was in 1994. I had served it, done the time they'd given me in 1975, done it over and over, and then over once more – and still didn't have any daylight in sight.

◆ ◆ ◆

Now I had to try to negotiate my way through the regime at Belmarsh. When you've been put in a maximum security prison, what's the point of being put into patches? You're being watched twenty-four hours a day. No one gets out of a place like Belmarsh. They put all sorts in there, terrorists and mass murderers. It was a challenge, in a way. I would have loved to escape from there and the thought constantly crossed my mind.

Escaping would have been a great way to stick two fingers up. It's part of the prisoner's daydream, a way to pass the time. Every possible way of getting out is considered, brief moments of respite earned by imagining overcoming the guards, a helicopter landing in the yard, a riot, the walls being broken down by a JCB, a disguise and switch at visiting times. They all crossed the mind.

I can't understand the mentality the Prison Service have towards people who do a runner. It's natural and normal for anyone incarcerated that they want to be free. And how they run the prisons makes it at the forefront of everyone's minds. It's the fear, the brutalising, the way they strip you of your humanity and try to make you feel subordinate. The outcry over my escape was over the top and engineered to be that way. They wanted to create a culture of fear, make an example of me, show there was a comeback.

After hearing my fate, I wondered where I'd do these two years. Would I be allowed to go back to my previous status, the old boy whose luck was such that the quirks of the system meant I was still paying for firing off a pistol at a copper, or would I serve this new sentence as if I was a fresh-faced danger to all and sundry?

The answer came soon after the verdict. I'd been in Belmarsh for a bit, trying to work out if this was a brief sojourn in Cat. A, trying to work out how settled I should try to be, wondering what they had in store for me, when I heard a key in the lock and the heavy cell door swung open.

There stood a high-ranking prison officer I had got to know through stretches at other jails. I was surprised to see her, and even more surprised by what she said. I knew her from times past and she'd always been an evil cow, a real witch, a play-it-by-the-book, nasty piece of work. I looked at her, wondering what was coming, wondering why she'd come down to my landing.

She said to me, 'A lot of people want to kill you, Massey.'

I said, 'That's a bit strong …'

'You've ruined a lot of lives. You've caused this situation, you've brought this down on yourself, and you're going to see exactly what you've reaped and sown, mark my words.'

I was in a dark place already. This surprise visit with a chilling message – was it a warning? – didn't help.

Everywhere I turned, there were screws trying to put the fear into me. They were trying to terrorise me. I had felt it as a kid at that children's home when they tied me down. The brutalising, to make you feel subordinate – and you begin to think, 'This ain't right: we're equals when it comes to Judgement Day. I know what put me inside was wrong, and I know there's a payment, a column of in-goings and out-goings. But if I understand why the representatives of the society I've been born into say one thing, they must have the nous to also hear me out on equal terms.'

I was kept in limbo: I wasn't told how long I was going to be Cat. A or what I would have to go through before I would be transferred. I had no idea when I could apply for parole after I'd completed the two years I was serving.

Because of the creaking infrastructure, because Belmarsh was full of those convicted of serious violent crimes, I was shoved anywhere they had space. I didn't get returned to the Seg unit. I was put out on the wings in patches, to show all and sundry that I was on special measures, and couldn't carve out some sense of normality.

One morning, after about three months, I went out into the exercise yard and I'd done about two laps when a load of screws came out. They were in paramilitary uniforms – they don't wear those scratchy trousers, starched white shirts and blazers that look like a cheap school uniform. They look like militia: combat pants and tight-fitting vests with pockets for God knows what. Ammunition? Tear gas? Pepper sprays? Tasers? Cuffs? Truncheons? They looked like a bunch of grouse shooters out on a weekend's hunting. Their faces gave it away. They were up for trouble and I was their focus.

I knew I was going to get a strip-search, but I wasn't aware of the whys and wherefores. I'd done nothing since the gates had closed to warrant a proper spin. There was nothing they could pin on me.

They took me to my cell and inside there were eight of them waiting. They had a dog.

Security audits mean if you're stripped they are obliged to film it – but they can always find a way around this rule. So they took me into my cell and closed the door; it was very stiff, formal and threatening. They ran through a list of things and asked me the usual questions. 'Do you have anything on you that may cause harm? Needles, blades …' They told me to strip. As I was taking my top off, I got punched from the side. It was the signal for the others to crash in. I got a kicking for the next twelve minutes. They smacked me in the jaw. It was a hefty blow. They were weight trainers on steroids and cowardly shits. It was young men beating up an old-age pensioner.

It was the usual trick – pretend they thought I was kicking off – but it would have been completely suicidal for me to have done that. Me against eight? I can look after myself, but I'm not stark, raving mad.

It was orchestrated. I put it down to the senior officer who had come into my cell and made threatening noises at me previously. She put them on to me. They got all hyped up beforehand, they were hysterical, like football hooligans. The wing was locked down, but prisoners were watching through their doors. They handcuffed my hands behind my back and they kept on punching and kicking me.

If it wasn't for my experience in taking beats and my fitness, I wouldn't have survived that thrashing. They tried to break my arms and legs. They twisted my fingers, trying to dislocate them. It was spiteful. I had to weather the storm, try to soak it up, but I was on my last bit of strength. I had someone kneeling on my neck, I was getting kicks in the ribs, they were bending my legs back, trying to break my kneecaps. I ended up with a dozen different injuries.

I know the screw who threw the first punch, but I won't give him the satisfaction of naming him. Instead, I'll call him Two Bit.

Two Bit was in charge and after they'd kicked the shit out of me, they had to somehow get me, groggy and bleeding, from the cell to the Seg unit. It seemed like 10 miles away, even though it was a few hundred yards. Being outside the cell didn't help me avoid more punishment.

They'd carry you in a way that looked like you were struggling and give them justification for a few blows. I was on my last legs. I'd had my clothes ripped off, my arms pulled about, and I was still handcuffed. A member of the healthcare team is meant to come when the alarm bell goes. They are there to be monitors, but it never happens. The bell had gone but they were nowhere to be seen.

The screws dragged me into a strip cell, and finally a healthcare worker appeared and asked me if I was OK.

I said, 'No, I am not fucking OK. What do you bloody think? Look at me.'

He said 'OK' and then he left. He was laughing with the search team.

They said, 'He's all right. You aren't needed here', and he didn't say fuck all but smiled and left them to it. I was bleeding from the face, the back, the nose, the mouth. My shoulder was dislocated. It took me two years to get movement back. My fingers were bruised from being twisted. I had terrible cuts across my back, my knees were scratched and there was bruising on my chest and stomach. But that cunt said there was nothing wrong with me and fucked off.

What normally happens after a violent incident is you get put into a Seg cell, and you don't come out. They put me into a holding cell, then after an hour they took me back to the wing. That's unheard of. If you're charged with assault, which is what they wanted to pin on me, you never get out of the Seg unit until you're dealt with.

It felt strange. I didn't know what they were up to. It was a mistake on their part because that afternoon I had a solicitor's visit booked. I walked in as I was, still bloodied and bruised, and there was Alison Morgan.

She said, 'What happened to you?' There were cameras everywhere and she couldn't understand how I'd got into such a state. She got a notebook out and wrote down all the injuries I could show her. When she left, she phoned Jane and went to a police station and filed a complaint.

I didn't get to see a doctor for two weeks, but even then I still had a lot of the injuries. He recorded them.

Jane was given a crime number, and I had requested a complaint form that alerted the governor I was alleging assault. I was immediately given a sheet charging me with assault, flipping the tables.

So again, I was taken down to the Seg wing for adjudication. During the proceedings the screw who led the beating showed up as a prosecuting officer. He was the one who filed the complaint. He sat with his elbows on the table and his fist up against his chin, chewing gum and showing off to the governor, with his biceps bulging and mean eyes staring me down.

The governor started by asking the screw if he'd made out an incident report. They're meant to be respectful and talk like they are in the army.

'Yes, of course I have,' he replied.

'Where is it?'

'It's upstairs.'

'Well, then, go and get it!'

The governor sent him off and he never came back. The charges were dismissed. That fucking screw was lying through his teeth and I was fucked off that I didn't get the opportunity to tell the governor what had happened.

◆ ◆ ◆

I was shoved back into a cell and I was subjected to more security spins. That horrible bastard was still on the team. They were very wary of their actions but they'd already done their damage.

I put in my complaint, saying who had kicked the crap out of me, which the governor answered. He told me he wasn't proceeding with any investigation because the police were now involved, so the matter had been taken out of his hands. I put a complaint in to the Independent Police Complaints Commission as well. This also got nowhere. It was ABH, they told me, so they wouldn't get involved – they said it had to be GBH. No one came and took a statement or examined me. I had the governor and the police playing off each other. My case wasn't being investigated.

I tried the Board of Visitors, too, who are meant to be able to help with these types of things. No one from the board came to see me. A week later, I got a brown envelope slid under the door from the board, stating that they had gone to the governor and he'd said there was no case for his screws to answer, so that was that. They just accepted the governor's word.

◆ ◆ ◆

I found out there had been a bit of fallout – not because of me, but because one of them did something else that wasn't ignored. I'd been moved to Rochester prison, down on the Medway in Kent, when I heard on the grapevine that the ringleader had been sacked.

I had got a job as the equalities rep. I met these two women who mentioned they were ex-Belmarsh prison officers. They said they knew him. They said he was an extremely violent man. They suggested the screw had been on steroids, which didn't help his mood. They told me how pleased other staff were when he'd been giving his marching orders.

'Right then,' I thought, 'Fuck it, I'm going after this cunt.' I got in touch with a solicitor and we went to the parliamentary ombudsman, hoping to get an investigation started. I still couldn't understand how an old man could get the crap kicked out of him in Britain's most secure prison and there not be one single film still of it. It was bollocks.

I went to the parliamentary ombudsman with a solicitor – a no win, no fee. They were completely disinterested. It felt like there was a concerted campaign of cover-up. It's rare you can get a successful prosecution of these people. I thought they should be in a cell next to me. It fucked up my rationality. I have to believe the good guys are the good guys or the system doesn't work. You get branded as being anti-authoritarian, but if the authority is a rogue authority, how can you have respect for that? I'm not an anarchist. I believe there should be police, prison officers – they're all part of protecting civil society. I don't want to disrespect that at all, but this lot are criminals.

◆ ◆ ◆

My time at Belmarsh came to an end after twelve months of torture. I was moved to Rochester, a place I knew from my youth. It was the first borstal – and gave those hated institutions their name. The village of Borstal, a place just outside Rochester, saw a prison built there in 1870. In 1902, they turned it into a young offenders' institute, giving the world the name.

I didn't know what to expect. It had been changed into a prison for adults serving four years or less and had a bit of an angle on rehabilitation. I was too long in the tooth to get my hopes up, but anything was better than fucking Belmarsh.

I stepped out of the van and noticed how fresh the Kent air felt. It's up on a hill, with the Thames estuary below, and you could taste the ozone. It was big, and a welcome change from the grottiness of Thamesmead.

I had another surprise. I did the usual strip-search, form filling, induction for the millionth time and was escorted to a cell. I'd only been in for a few minutes when the door opened and a screw came in.

'Mr Massey, welcome to Rochester,' he said.

And I thought, 'Well, this is a bit different.'

If someone is polite to you, it's the hardest thing in the world to be anything but polite back, so I said, 'Thank you very much. I can't say I'm overjoyed to be here, or this is my chosen and preferred placed of residence, but it's a step up from my last home.'

The screw smiled and asked me if I wanted to work as a mentor. It was a touch and I said yes immediately. It meant you got to wear this special band that gave you some freedom. You were free to leave or enter any wing, go anywhere on your own. I always tried to get as much freedom within prison as I could, hence the cleaning jobs. It meant you were your own boss – you could do the job at your pace.

Mentoring meant meeting first-time offenders as they came in, making sure they settled and got through their sentences with as little hassle as possible, and hopefully decided never to risk a spell again. I managed to score another job on top of it, too. The guy in the cell next to me was leaving and he said, 'There's a job going, it's a doddle.' He put my name up and I went for an interview. It was decent pay too – £20 a week, the best I'd ever had inside.

There were three people in this office called the Safer Custody Suite, and they took me on. My job was to go round the wings and put up leaflets on noticeboards about courses and jobs, opportunities.

I would come across guys who were having problems coping. They would send me along to deal with someone because, the fact was, anyone going through hard times could turn to me. Anything they were experiencing, chances were I had too.

Because of the length of time I'd served, people listened to me. When they heard I'd done a forty-year sentence, their three-year stretch didn't sound so bad. In many cases, where they'd lost the will to live and were contemplating suicide, I used to relate some of the stories of hardships I'd been through, and they'd compare it to their lives and realise that they would come alive again. They would say, 'If you can do all that time and be standing here in front of me, well, I can fucking do it too.'

It was tough – I would meet a lot of young men who were suicidal. The older guys were more experienced and knew how to cope. But the young guys didn't. They were lost souls and they became reliant on the system to feed and clothe them. When you're in a crowded prison environment, it's dog eat dog and they didn't know how to handle it.

Rochester, like every prison, had a large number of inmates dealing with addictions. There were people battling demons and plenty of drug counsellors making a living off them. It's no good talking to them unless they have a genuine desire to stop taking drugs. I thought you had to find that first with them or it was pointless. That's where the strength and willpower comes from.

I was never soft. I never gave anyone the kid-glove approach the system sometimes does. When an official was talking to prisoners about drug use, I thought they tended to mother these youngsters a bit too much. From my experience, it was the wrong approach. I would be stone cold and stark about the situation, tell them how it was in reality. 'At the end of the day,' I'd say, 'it's up to you – you can sink or swim. After this point, when you're banged up, there are no more lifelines being thrown.'

You have to tell them the hard facts of life inside, explain that nobody gives a shit about you, so you have to pull yourself up, put one foot in front of the other and sooner or later you'll get to where you're going. You have to do that – not lie on your bed, become withdrawn and slowly disintegrate. It was about giving them something to fight for.

But I soon realised the listener's job they'd given me had problems. Lots of people applied for the job as it looked good on the parole, but you could be pulled out of your cell at any time of night or day. You could be woken up at 3 a.m. and called to a wing to listen to someone, and then you'd get there and all they would want was a cigarette paper. It was used and abused.

But the work in Rochester was good for me after the hell of Belmarsh. It got me out and about, and it meant I could use the gym every day. I could stop here or there to get a cup of tea, speak to people, and do it in an official capacity.

Sometimes prisoners used to ask me to be a courier for contraband across the wings. I used to stop them dead and say, 'No fucking way. Go about your own business.' One of the things I did in jail was I slammed the door immediately when something came up like that. Don't get involved, at all. Keep well clear. You say yes once, and that's that. They'd come to your door and ask for something, and if you gave in to them, they'd be back six more times that day. They would have you down as an easy touch. A lot of people didn't have the ability to say no – they'd beat about the bush, make excuses, instead of just saying, 'Fuck off and don't come back.'

People were always wanting to borrow things, asking you for tobacco or what-not, and you'd have them buzzing round you for ever, so I just said, 'No, fuck off out of it.' I'd convince people that once my door was closed, that was it. Don't knock, don't look in – that was my peace-and-quiet world.

I made sure everyone knew it. When any arsehole came knocking or looking through the flap in the door, saying, 'John, John', I'd say, 'Oh, do fuck off.' It worked for me. For others, they could be polite but they would end up in a ten-minute conversation with some cunt they didn't want to know and then the person would be back the following day, and they'd work on you until you'd caved in. I left no room for doubt about what I meant when I told someone to go away.

◆ ◆ ◆

It usually takes a Parole Board a minimum of fourteen days to write up their report and send it to the governor and the Probation Service. You're conditioned for everything to be glacial in terms of processes, systems, steps. There's slow-moving, and then there's prison bureaucracy.

I'd been moved once again, this time to Suffolk, a place called Warren Hill. Rochester hadn't been too bad. It was a dump, it was prison, but people kept themselves to themselves, I had a few pals and I was playing a bit of badminton. But I needed to move on to another prison with something like open conditions before I could be let out, but an open prison wasn't about to be offered, considering my track record.

So I was sent instead to Warren Hill, a place for young offenders, a prison that made a thing about how it offered education, training, rehabilitation. They made a big song and dance about day release and looking after owls, hawks and eagles or something at a nearby bird sanctuary. That wasn't for me – apart from anything else, I was about fifty years too old – but the regime suited me. It was unsaid but in the air that maybe Warren Hill could be my last stop.

I settled in and then had another parole hearing. I thought, 'Fuck it, let's have a real go at this one.' I grew a beard. All the other hearings in the past, I was clean shaven, and they had a young picture of me on the folder, so they looked at it and thought, 'He looks young. Fuck it, he can do another ten-stretch.'

I thought, 'I'll go in looking old, walk in slowly, take my time to sit down, all that.' I answered the same old questions the same old way, and felt resigned to the inevitable knockback.

My solicitor thought it had gone well. They always said that, but this time, it felt like it was said without optimism and instead was a statement of fact. That was on the Tuesday. On the Friday, my welfare officer had clocked off for an early weekend. Apparently, a letter had come for them telling them that I'd made it, I'd been given parole – but no one could find them to pass on the news. I was left in the dark.

On the officer's return on Monday, they found me in the gym. I was working out, and they said, 'Mr Massey, we have some news.'

I stopped, and my first thought was that something awful had happened. The Parole Board take their time and not a week had yet passed.

'You've got parole.'

I could hardly believe it, but I knew this didn't mean I could head back to my cell, pack up what I was keeping and give away the rest – say, 'Thanks for the bed, I'm off.' It could take months for a hostel to be found, for everything to be put in place. Still, they hadn't said I wasn't fit to be on the outside.

The following day, I got a visit from the governor. 'Mr Massey, I hear you're leaving us?'

'Yes, indeed, I am, and as soon as I can.'

'Well, Mr Massey – do you have someone who could be here for you tomorrow, say at 8 a.m.?'

I got the news about parole on the Monday, I had the answer on the Tuesday and I was kicked out on the Wednesday. Even after a seemingly set-in-stone two-week wait for any parole verdict to be announced, you normally have to wait to be set up with the hostel by the Probation Service and all that shit.

I actually got one of the fastest releases known to a lifer. I never knew anyone to get released so quick – it was like they wanted one last spin.

They had found me a room in a hostel in Camden Town where I'd have to spend a few weeks. The paperwork had been done, and basically, after all this time and just like that, they wanted rid of me.

They put £43 in my pocket, a quid for every year inside, and told me to clear out my cell.

I called Jane. 'I'm coming home,' I said.

'Oh,' she said. 'I'll put the kettle on.'

EPILOGUE

by Dan Carrier

I first heard the name John Massey one early summer's day in 2001.

I was sitting at my desk in the newsroom of the *Camden New Journal* and I absent-mindedly answered the phone: 'Hello, news desk.'

The woman on the line asked to speak to a reporter.

I introduced myself. She told me her name was May Massey and asked if I could help.

She said her son was serving a life sentence in Parkhurst on the Isle of Wight. She had asked – pleaded – numerous times for John to be transferred to a prison closer to London. Her husband Jack, John's father, had become too frail to travel to the Isle of Wight, but for reasons unknown they were being soundly ignored when they requested a transfer. May and Jack had been visiting John in prison since 1975. I had no idea that this chance phone call would eventually lead to me greeting John Massey at the gates of HMP Warren Hill as he walked away from forty-five years of incarceration.

I went round to visit May a few days later. She lived with Jack in a flat in a red-brick council estate in Kentish Town, which has a railway viaduct snaking through it, with a few businesses under the arches. It's quiet, tucked away, with a homely feel that suggests you might move in and, all things being even, never leave. I was buzzed in downstairs, made my way along a corridor and up to a landing, then knocked on the door.

As Jack and May told me John's story for the first time, I looked about their little home. There was a series of intricately decorated boxes on display – John, who had learnt cabinet making, had made them for his parents. There were family photographs in frames, glimpses of happier moments.

May and Jack explained John had been inside a high-security prison since his mid-20s and that, as they got older, it was getting harder to visit. Jack had emphysema and travelling once a month on a train and a ferry, lugging a bottle of oxygen with him, was a huge strain. They insisted their boy was no danger to the public and had done his time. There was no good reason he should be kept on the Isle of Wight.

They picked up the pictures of John and placed them in my hands, explaining where and when each shot had been taken – framed memories from times past kept on the sideboard. They brought out the ornate jewellery boxes he had made. They were honest and kind.

I was intrigued. I made a few calls, hassled the Ministry of Justice and the Home Office, asked the Howard League for Penal Reform for a quote, spoke with some respected criminal barristers and wrote a story.

I began a correspondence with the Masseys and, a few weeks after the article was published, I got a letter from Parkhurst. John thanked me politely for my interest and for taking the time to visit his parents. John and I started writing to each other, even having the occasional phone call. As I got to know John, I looked forward to his letters and the unknown number that popped up on my mobile at unpredictable times.

It could be hard to know what to say. The question 'What you been up to then?' sounds hollow when the answer is 'I'm in prison, aren't I? So not a lot.'

And then when they ask how *you* are, you don't feel exactly great turning round and saying, 'Actually John, thanks for asking, I'm terrific. My wife is gorgeous and she loves me to bits, my family are healthy, I love my work and I'm going out raving tomorrow with my best mates.' It doesn't feel very sensitive.

But I soon realised that prisoners aren't resentful when you start chatting about your day. John wanted to know all about my family, my work, what I was up to. He didn't want me to pretend that I hadn't been out for a lovely meal, off to a gig, planning a holiday. 'No way, don't clam up, tell me everything,' he would say. 'Go and make the most out of every day, because I bloody can't.'

I began to visit him once in a while, wondering which prison in which corner of the country I would next find him. After he was finally transferred from Parkhurst, the frequent transfer strategy carried on. His family would keep me informed of his whereabouts, his health and his chances of breathing fresh air on the same side of the wall as the rest of us. Frankland, Parkhurst, the Scrubs, Pentonville, Rochester, Warren Hill – all prisons John and his family knew inside and out.

To see John, I would have to fill in a Visiting Order, provide personal details and identification, then find out where he was doing his bird this time. I'd catch a train out of town, head to, say, Rochester and catch a taxi at the station to the prison. The driver would always give me a certain look when I said I wanted a lift to the nearest prison. I'd be taken into a visitor's reception area, given a locker to leave everything I'd brought with me in, registered, given a number and told to wait to be called. I ignored the bit where they asked me what I did for a living. I wasn't allowed to take a notebook in, so every time I met John, I had to try to memorise what he said if I wanted to write another piece on his continuing incarceration.

I'd be searched and frisked and marched through locked doors and passages, each turn confirming that John had no command of his own destiny. He was most certainly, unquestionably, banged up at

Her Majesty's pleasure. As I walked through to meet him, I would look about and wonder how on earth anyone could do a bunk from one of these places – anyone who says they don't think about this is surely lying. Through each door I felt a little more claustrophobic, a little less in control, and I was consumed by a strange sense of guilt, as if a misdemeanour I wasn't aware I'd committed was about to be raised by one of the pasty-looking guards with the grey bags under their eyes.

Down another corridor, through another gate and I was in the visitor's hall, where John was waiting. I would buy all I could from the canteen and lay it out in front of him – biscuits and chocolates, little tokens of affection – and then go through what could be an interesting or harrowing – or both – two hours of visiting time. I'd do all I could to create conversation, to be that outlet, that window into the world beyond the walls, all the while watching the other prisoners as they saw their loved ones under close supervision.

Prison – the deprival of some one's liberty by a collective of other human beings for breaking the rules we have drawn up. It is such a fundamental power to exert over someone else. Apply it wrong and the consequences are unfathomably difficult to comprehend. A society needs rules for us all to abide by and sanctions when they're not – but when there is a line blurred between justice and the standards for its application, it creates scope for a deeper consideration of the exerting of collective power over an individual.

John Massey did something very, very wrong, and that is not in dispute. But his story of why it happened and how, and what effect it had on a number of people's lives, deserves consideration. I wanted to hear from John what it was like to be inside for so long. I hoped to understand why this had happened. I wanted to write his story for him, casting no judgements as I listened, and I hope I have provided him with an honest voice.

Over the years of visiting John, getting to know his family, hearing the issues over his case – his criminal past, his conviction, life inside and on the run, the reasons he was still locked up – we spoke about how we'd tell his story when he finally stepped outside. This book is the result.

On his last day behind bars, I travelled to Warren Hill with his sister Jane and niece Michelle. We got there just before 8 a.m. but if we expected John to be sitting outside and ready to hit the road, we were misguided. Even when his time was up, there were hoops to leap through – many doors to be unlocked and forms to be checked and his meagre personal items handed over. We told the reception we were here for John and were sent to wait outside in a car park swept by winds coming in mercilessly from the North Sea.

Eventually, the large wooden gates, studded with iron work and set into a windowless, 40-ft-high brick wall, slowly opened. John stood there on the other side, alone. Clutching a plastic bag in one hand and a guitar in the other, he was travelling light. Behind him, we could hear inmates leaning out of cell windows, cheering, clapping, making noise any way they could to mark this momentous occasion.

'What do you want to do right now, John?' we asked. 'Fancy some breakfast?'

'Fancy some breakfast? Not half,' he replied. 'Know anywhere selling lobster thermidor at 8.30 in the morning on the M11?'

His sense of humour was going to be tested in the coming weeks. After checking in with his parole officer, a courtesy visit to say, 'Yes, I really am out,' John headed to the hostel where he would spend his first eight weeks. He had been clear he wanted to stay in Camden and his wish could not have been more fulfilled geographically. He was placed in Arlington Road, which is in the heart of Camden Town. The hostel was directly opposite the famous Good Mixer pub, home to the Brit Pop movement, which had a very late licence, catering for noisy rock-and-roll types. A handy location for family, but a dramatic change to the quiet of the Suffolk countryside.

John was not used to this, and the drunks beneath his bedroom window were only the first cold shock of many. Leaving prison is not a case of stepping out of hell and into utopia; he had been thrust into a world he did not recognise.

He was sent out of prison with £43 in his pocket, a quid for each year he served. He had no bank account, no doctor or surgery to register at, no driving licence, utility bill or passport. He had eight weeks at the hostel and, once his spell was over, it would be up to him – sink or swim.

He began by looking for a council flat, but was told he had almost no chance of earning enough points to get on to the waiting list. A private rental was eye-wateringly expensive.

Luckily, a spell on friends' sofas did not last too long. He got a break: a place came up at the St Pancras Almshouses, a beautiful little Victorian estate in Kentish Town that offered affordable studio flats to over 55s. Not only was John eligible, but his sister Jane was already living there, so it seemed to be the perfect answer.

It was interesting to see how John was adapting. While he got little support from the authorities, the grapevine hummed with news of his release and offers of congratulations came alongside offers of help.

A few days after he got out, he received a call from Turkey. On the other end of the line was a man who had served sixteen years for drug smuggling and had got to know John well when he was inside. He wished John all the best, laughed when John asked how the news of his freedom had reached the Bosporus Strait, and asked if he needed anything. John didn't want to be in debt to anyone, so politely declined the offer. However, his friend was keen to do what he could, so he sent an associate round to John's new place with a van to use and some money to buy a few tools.

John was pleased as punch with the new van, but it soon went sour. John could not get used to the idea that there had been some changes since he last drove; now there were some serious restrictions to what you could do in a vehicle. He'd never been one for the rules of the road in the first place and he couldn't get his head round the fact that he couldn't park here, there or anywhere without a ticket or permit, or that he couldn't drive south of the Euston Road without coughing up more.

John called it organised crime and point-blank refused to pay any tickets for congestion zones; when he got tickets, he just ignored them. It eventually reached the bailiffs and he told them all where to go.

Another issue John faced on release was drugs. Inside, he had been partial to taking whatever was about, but never had a problem. He recalled once being given a stash of smack and, being green, didn't really know how to take it or what to do – but also didn't want to ask.

He went into his cell and snorted a huge line, he recalled. He had the terrible experience of a near overdose, puking up foam, emptying his guts for twenty-four hours non-stop and hallucinating for about the same length of time.

I checked up on John as often as I could but it was hard to know what he wanted and what was an intrusion. It so transpired that John had fallen into using drugs and was being circled by some pretty unsavoury characters. As well as the criminal aspect, and the heap of trouble he could find himself in with the police and his landlord, John was in his 70s – while taking Class A drugs is not a good idea for a young person, for a man of his age, it's very risky. It wasn't too long after John began dabbling in Class As that he suffered a stroke. Having been fairly fit and healthy inside, coming out was not doing him any favours.

He found a rehab centre in Liverpool and signed up for a three-month residential stay. But he was home within the week, annoyed at being told he had to share a room with someone else. As he explained, it wasn't in anyone's interests, least of all the poor sod bunking with him. John's sleep terrors, caused by the trauma of late-night beatings, meant he did not trust himself. 'I don't want to be half-asleep and get the fear and sock the nearest person, do I?' he said. This first attempt to clean up failed, but he later got a residential rehab booked in Hull, where he spent three months cleaning himself up.

John had always tried to keep up to speed with what was happening outside, he said, and he was grateful he did. It made the transition that bit easier. 'It meant I knew which politician I should currently hate,' he said. 'I did not make the mistake a lot of my mates inside had made. I was not content to lie on the bed and smoke puff and forget about the big, wide world. I wanted to know what was going on. I bought a newspaper every day, always turned on Channel Four news, I was like a sponge for information all the time. I never got left behind. A million times the screws and governors said, "Oh you'll find it strange being outside again, John." I tell you what – the only fucking thing I found strange was being in prison, that's the most unnatural place, environment, not out here. Keep up with politics and what's going on in the rest of the world and you do not suffer the culture shock when you get out.'

At first, John found work through mates, doing carpentry, but his attempts to do it above board fell at the first hurdle. After battling to get his pension – a battle in which he enlisted the help of his MP, Keir Starmer – John discovered that doing any paid work meant his pension was cut. He only found this out when his money was stopped for three weeks over his first free Christmas.

'I wanted to do everything legal,' he said. 'I didn't want anyone to pick me up on anything. I spent £400 to get a work card to get on building sites. I had this friend who had a company in Moorgate, who would give me all the work I wanted. But it had to be straight. I did half a day's work for him. Then they stopped my pension for three weeks over Christmas, I wasn't allowed to work. The pension issue was a massive wind up. I had been told I wasn't entitled to a pension as I hadn't paid any stamps for years. But I had been working for the Queen, fucking sewing mailbags, cleaning. Work in prison is compulsory, why isn't that worth a stamp entitling me to a state pension?'

John spoke frequently about wanting to build a new life. Underlining all of it was a need to be treated with decency and respect. He was never ashamed of his past but was very wary of how others would react.

Writing John's story has been a mixture of listening and research. I have taken everything he has told me at face value. It is his truth, his story, though others involved will tell their versions that may differ from how John has seen it. It is as accurate as possible under circumstances that mean some assumptions and guess work were needed.

'One of the things that affects me, now that I am out, and confuses a lot of people, is I have great difficulty remembering dates or times,' John said. 'It's because when I was inside I did not have a calendar. Monday through to Sunday, to Christmas, to Easter, to my birthday – it was just one long stretch of time. No day was special. It meant I didn't get traumatised by anniversaries. I just don't know the dates. Time, for me, was just one big, long streak. If you are going to mark off the days, it becomes an eternity. You are making things hard for yourself.'

It doesn't make it any easier for the biographer, though.

◆ ◆ ◆

Finally, a word about Charlie Higgins.

While I've been writing John's story, I have kept what happened in my mind. I'm not here to make excuses or issue apologies, and in no way do I want to dishonour Mr Higgins' memory. It is about marking what happened and paying respect to that, and remembering at all times that what matters is the tragedy that someone lost their life and the effect it had on others.

When I was reporting on John, I was always conscious of this. After he escaped from Pentonville, I decided to find Mr Higgins's son. I discovered he was running a pub in Essex, so I went to meet him. He was polite and gave me some time. He had heard John had escaped and wondered why he hadn't yet finished his sentence, adding that he didn't want to talk about John and his father on the record because of his mother. I respect that and offer those who suffered from this my understanding.

I have not personally profited from the writing of this book.